A FIELD GUIDE TO THE

BIRD SONGS
& CALLS

OF BRITAIN AND NORTHERN EUROPE

Dave Farrow

CARLTON
BOOKS

THIS IS A CARLTON BOOK

This edition published in 2008 by Carlton Books Ltd
A Division of the Carlton Publishing Group
20 Mortimer Street
London
W1T 3JW

A CIP catalogue for this book is available from the British Library.

ISBN: 978-1-84442-042-1

Project Editor: Gareth Jones
Copy Editor: Liz Dittner
Senior Art Editor: Gülen Shevki-Taylor
Designer: Emma Wickes
Artists: Brin Edwards, Mike Langman
(for full credit listing see page 224)
Sound Recordists: Dave Farrow; Hannu Jannes;
Jan-Erik Bruun; Jean C. Roché Jérôme Chevereau
(for full credit listing see page 222)
Production: Lisa Moore

Printed in Dubai

PREVIOUS PAGE: CHAFFINCH (SEE PAGE 198)
BELOW: LONG-TAILED TITS (SEE PAGE 173)
OPPOSITE: KESTREL (SEE PAGE 50)

CONTENTS

Foreword

An oxymoronic fact of bird watching is that the presence of a bird is often detected by our ears long before our eyes even get a glimpse of a feathered form. More often than not our eyes lose out altogether, rendering the understanding of what's making the songs, calls and twitterings even more crucial.

I once spent the morning with a blind birdwatcher and it really opened my ears to the clues, cues and information that we visually perfect individuals tend to ignore for the most part.

It's not that we *can't* hear these sounds, it's just that many of us do not know *how* to listen – we are, as a species, acoustically lazy. Now an important part of training those flaps of skin on the sides of our heads is to know exactly *what* to listen out for and have something to inspire us to listen in the first place.

This is where Dave Farrow's masterpiece of a book comes into its own. It not only describes the utterances of the birds, phonetically and descriptively, but the clear and high-quality recordings on the CDs that accompany the book allow you to make up for any shortfalls in another person's interpretation.

This is much more than an audio library in the guise of a book – something overlooked by other bird song guides. The recordings and writings both compliment each other and the guide also provides species artworks too, doing the job of a field guide and allowing the reader (or listener) to cross-reference the sounds with descriptions and illustrations of the species in question.

There is nothing more mnemonic than seeing a bird and hearing its call at the same time and a guide like this makes that often challenging skill much more achievable.

Hands up I admit it! Every springtime I struggle to re-learn all my common garden warblers – a skill that is often only possible by sound alone. But with this book those embarrassing moments of self-doubt are banished to the past for ever. Just a quick flick through the CD tracks and my ears are refreshed, and I know what I'm both listening to and looking for.

Nick Baker

GARDEN WARBLER
(SEE PAGE 157)

Introduction

Field Techniques for Birdwatchers

Birdwatching or *birding*, as it should really be known to cover all the various permutations and different disciplines, has exploded in popularity in recent years. Many people coming to birding at a later age lack a background of childhood birding, when one could creep up on birds and learn fieldcraft by trial and error. Modern birding hotspots in western Europe are often in nature reserves, with restricted trails and hides to view from, and it is here that many beginners start their birding. This is all very well, but it doesn't teach you the fundamentals of how to watch birds, especially when the birds in question are being looked at from some range with a telescope. Of course this is partly due to the increased popularity, and the subsequent pressure created by the rise in numbers of birders, but what do you do when you are alone and not led by pretty signs and comfortable viewpoints?

Active birding technique can be divided into two approaches: the peripatetic and the stationary. The first is based on keeping on the move and covering a large area in order to find as many birds as possible; the second involves sitting still in a good place for birds and waiting for them to come to you. The former is usually more productive, as you are covering more ground and therefore more habitat types and different bird territories. You also have the options of moving quickly – when you have more chance of surprising birds – or slowly, which can allow you to sneak up on them. The sitting method also has its advantages, as birds are usually more confiding when not alerted by the movement of the observer. Equally, aerial bird

GREEN
WOODPECKER
(SEE PAGE 111)

activity over a wider area can be seen more readily when you are sitting or standing in one place, as you are not constantly looking down to see where you are walking or continually adjusting your vision to ever-changing surroundings. Hides are an obvious place to sit, but bear in mind that your overall view is restricted in such situations. A good example of the merits of the sitting technique is seawatching, when one sits on an exposed headland or promontory and searches for seabirds passing offshore or resting on the water. An eye on the weather and the season is most important, with onshore winds and squally showers often bringing the birds in close enough for viewing. Migration periods in spring, and particularly in autumn, are usually the most productive times to seawatch.

One of the most important things of all with birding is to get out early. Bird activity is at its busiest in the early hours of the day, from pre-dawn until a point somewhere between mid-morning and lunch. Exactly when this activity dies away depends very much on weather and temperature; on some days there will be just an hour or two of activity before things noticeably go quiet, whereas on others it will remain busy until noon, with a secondary period of activity near the end of the day. When it is hot, bird activity tends to die down sooner. When it is windy, birds will be more active in sheltered areas. In cold weather, sunny aspects will be favoured. However unpleasant it might make conditions, rain can actually be a birder's friend – the period directly after rainfall is a time of much avian activity, and a mixture of sunshine and showers is often a very good time to be out birding. On hot, torpid days one often wishes for rain to "juice things up"!

The main benefit for the early-riser is that there is much more vocal activity in the early morning. Birds will often make use of the improved acoustics in the cool morning air, in the breeding season often starting with a "dawn chorus" well before first light. This is by far the best time to listen and appreciate bird song, even though at higher latitudes it can mean very unsociable hours! Many songbirds are best located by voice, and so this is definitely the best time to find them.

Another important issue is fieldcraft. Using adept fieldcraft will hopefully produce close, prolonged and intimate views of birds, so much more satisfying than staring at them through a telescope at 500m range! Fieldcraft revolves around stealth, and an understanding of what scares birds and what does not. Noise is a very important consideration. Not surprisingly, making bangs and crashes or talking in loud voices is not advisable. I am sure many have been out birding, perhaps for a quiet meditative scan of the marshes or mudflats, only for some

JAY
(SEE PAGE 187)

other birders to come along making a huge amount of noise. Talking loudly, clanking their tripods, slamming hide doors, rustling their waterproofs, blathering on about their latest overseas bird trip, their pagers producing an incessant bleeping… All very infuriating! But with a little thought and preparation it is possible to get away from the busy hotspots and explore less well-known birding places, where you can find your own birds and have a much more rewarding experience.

GOLDCREST
(SEE PAGE 166)

How should we conduct ourselves out in the field if we are to maximize the chances of getting close to birds? One interesting aspect to the noise rule is that whispers and high voices will be more readily heard by birds than a low baritone murmuring, which may either fall outside the hearing range of a bird or at the very least be unlikely to sound like an alarm call. So it is always best to try and speak in as quiet and as deep a voice as you can.

Visual signals are also important. For example, wearing a white shirt in a dark forest is one of the worst things you can do; if you think how white or pale patterned shirts light up in a nightclub when the UV lights are switched on, you will have some idea of the effect. It is likely that many birds can see in the UV spectrum, so dark, non-reflective colours are certainly best. One thing that many people forget is the similar effect created by exposed white skin or even shining white or very blond hair. Every time you raise your binoculars when wearing a short-sleeved shirt, a flash of white appears as your forearms come up, often startling enough to birds to make them flee.

Another important issue is movement. Sudden movements are likely to spook a bird, especially one that is close and perhaps as yet unaware of the observer's presence. So, the trick is to move slowly. If your binoculars are on a short strap, then it is less

far to raise them to your eyes, and keeping your elbows in close to your torso reduces your profile. Pointing at a bird is definite no-no. Many of us are told as children that it is rude to point, and in many Asian cultures this is most definitely the case. Birds don't like it either! If you point at a bird with an outstretched arm, it is very likely to go, but how can you point something out to your birding companion? The answer is to keep your elbow in close and indicate with just the forearm held in front of the body. Equally, the most effective way to find a bird that another birder has already located is to get directly behind them and look along the line of their binoculars or telescope.

Stalking a bird is often the best way to get close views. If you walk directly towards a bird, unless it is a good runner it has no alternative but to fly off. A tactic that can be used to avoid this is to walk in what – to the bird – will appear to be a circle around it, subtly and gradually closing the distance between you and the bird in an elliptical fashion. The use of cover is very important when stalking. For humans the main giveaway is our two legs – most birds will flee at the sight of a biped – and so if you can hide or advance using low cover that hides your legs, so much the better. In open country, try advancing at an angle of 30–45 degrees towards the target, and it should remain, alert and watching you, but still in position. At the end of the day, the bird would far rather remain feeding, or continuing with whatever it is doing, than fly away. To take this to its physical extreme, all you need to have exposed towards the bird are your eyes, so if you can hide or obscure the outline of your body completely, so much the better.

Care must also be taken with the position of the sun. While it is standard procedure in photography, and also in many birding situations, to get the sun behind you, once a bird is aware that you are up-sun of it, it will spook far more readily than if it has the advantage of the sun. For example, when "pishing" (see below) at a flock of small birds, the birds may respond by approaching the source of the noise, reacting to what sounds to them like an anxiety or alarm call. They will therefore be on the alert for danger, and so will try to take the position of advantage with the sun behind them. Therefore, when stalking something, you will probably get a lot closer if you approach towards, or oblique to, the sun – the bird will act more confidently, as it can both see you and have the sun advantage.

"Pishing" is the practice of making "psshh" noises to elicit the attention of a bird that may be hidden out of view in a bush, encouraging its curiosity and thereby attracting it into view. Although highly variable in its effectiveness, it is often worth a try. Squeaking and kissing noises may also produce the desired result. Although not without its critics, tape-luring ("tape" meaning any format of recording) is fairly widespread these days, but it should be handled knowledgeably and with sensitivity in terms of the impact it may have. It is almost never necessary to blast tapes out at high volume, and it has to be said that "trawling", (playing a tape speculatively to elicit a response and therefore a position on the target bird) has limited effectiveness, and that quite often you get no response unless you hear the bird calling first. In that instance, it is only necessary to play

LITTLE OWL
(SEE PAGE 100)

a short sample of the bird's call, and not at a loud volume, and the bird should come in. How quickly it does this and how long it remains in view often depend on how much movement it detects, or how obvious the human interlopers appear to be. Most importantly, do not keep playing the tape once the bird has moved into view. Let it sing and proclaim its dominance over the facsimile!

Armed with all these skills and techniques, any observer should be able to enjoy a more productive birding experience. However, do not expect them to work like magic. Trial and error, and as many hours in the field as you can manage, will teach you eventually how to obtain fantastic views of great birds and thereby give you much pleasure. So, all that is left is to get out there and enjoy yourself!

How to use the Book and CDs

The individual species accounts in this book are divided into three sections:

Identification

The section on identification describes the salient physical features of the bird, both from a general descriptive viewpoint and also in terms of highlighting the main differences between similar species. It is not meant to be an exhaustive identification tool, and certainly some subjects (such as immature gull plumages) are simply beyond the scope of this guide and would require the checking of additional references.

Habitat

The second section covers habitat, and also distribution. While close attention has been paid to describing the habitats favoured by individual species, care should be taken with this, as birds do sometimes occur outside their preferred habitats. The ranges given are rather general, and not supported by range maps which have limited accuracy anyway when produced in a small scale.

Calls/Song

The third section focuses on vocalizations, and the described calls and songs are a summary of the best known of these. Although comprehensive, the text cannot be exhaustive, as many birds have an extensive range of calls used in different situations. I have used a variety of resources in the compilation of this section, ranging from my own recordings to those published by others, and including other texts describing the sounds of particular species (although in many guides these are often minimal). Where possible, I have studied recordings in digital display using editing software, so very complex sequences have been broken down into clearly differentiated notes by stretching the time window while viewing oscillograms of the recordings.

As far as the transcriptions of the calls are concerned, I have tried to convey the sounds using words, but these are my rendered translations and of course other birders would describe the sounds differently, often depending on their mother tongue. As regards the style of transcription, I have resisted the urge to over-complicate matters and so have not, in most cases, used upper case to convey a louder volume or emphasis. Vowel sounds are all short sounds when written singly, longer vowel sounds are written by combinations of letters such as the "uea" in "squeal". I have used a simple single apostrophe ['] to convey a very short break between notes, or a very short vowel, or glottal stop where it does not feel right to use a consonant. The single apostrophe is also used with a rattling or trilling call to break up the barely discernible consonants. The temporal resolution of humans is some ten times less accurate than birds', with human hearing able to hear only some 20 sound units per second, compared to 200 sound units per second in birds. So, where a bird has a rapid trilling or rattling vocalization, the transcription is suggestive rather than exhaustive, as it would be rather tiresome reading a full version of, for example, a Savi's Warbler song comprising 50 notes per second! For longer breaks and pauses I have used a comma [,] to denote the clear end of a sequence or phrase, a hyphen [-] to show a similar clear end but one that is more connected to the sound of the following phrase, and a series of full stops or an ellipsis [...] to show a trailing off to the sound or a marked pause between phrases, respectively. Exclamation marks [!] denote either an abrupt end or the end of an emphatic phrase. I have avoided musical interpretations and descriptive terms, not because they are not useful, but because they are another language that many (including myself!) would have difficulty relating to.

Among the most regularly used terms in this book are **pitch and frequency**, which are basically two different words for what is essentially the same thing (although pitch really refers to sound that is audible). To describe this accurately I have used the Hertz (Hz) system of measurement for sound wavelengths. At best, the range of human hearing covers 20Hz up to 20,000Hz (ie. 20kHz), although at the extremes of that range the sound may be discernible only when at considerable volume. Most bird sound that we hear ranges from the low frequency booming of the Bittern at 160Hz, up to the high-pitched song and calls of the Goldcrest at 7–8kHz.

Adjectives are used freely to describe the general sentiment of a call or song, such as plaintive,

scolding etc. Other words used in the text include **harmonics**, which refer to the additional layer of sound within a call; this is of a different frequency and not clearly discernible to the human ear, as it is laid over the top of the most audible frequency of the call. Put together, they give the sound a different quality or tone. The word **tone** is used to describe the general quality and character of the sound.

I have mostly avoided using **mnemonics**, but this is not to say that they cannot be very useful for the individual as a way of remembering bird sounds. Mnemonics are a way of converting a complex sound into recognizable words, such as the Yellowhammer saying "a-little-bit-of-bread-and-no-cheese", or a Common Rosefinch saying "pleased-to-meet-you". I would, however, encourage individuals to make up their own mnemonics as a way of learning particular bird sounds.

To fully appreciate the author's efforts in transcription, I would urge readers to do some sound recording themselves! It is a wonderful pastime and, rather like photography, can be used as an identification aid. A sound recording constitutes hard data that can provide clear proof of an encounter, free from opinion or desire. Armed with the recordings provided on the CDs accompanying this book, try sitting down and transcribing the calls into your own words. If you make digital recordings and have the software to view an oscillogram of a bird's call on the screen, then you can study the call at your leisure and try to dissect its various parts.

The Terminology of Bird Song, Calls, Language and Communication

The understanding and interpretation of bird vocalizations is a much less well-explored field than the visual understanding of birds, and traditionally has had a narrower appeal, with fewer field observers focusing on the subject of bird calls.

There are difficulties associated with the subject, even for those with perfect hearing! Often the sound coming from a bird is of very short duration, and the recall or memory of the sound is a rather inexact science, exaggerated by a wide variation in the ability of individual observers to reproduce or describe the sound they have heard. This book is no exception in this respect, with the author's attempts to transcribe the calls and songs having to assume a uniformity of sound. Many of the transcriptions cannot, therefore, avoid being ambiguous, and in spite of almost all of the described vocalizations being transcribed from recordings, it is still a fallible system and at worst perhaps comprehensible only to those who speak in the same way that I do! The description of sounds is further complicated by their pitch (frequency), loudness, duration, tonal quality and the pauses in between, and by the

fact that different calls are given depending on age, sex, emotional or hormonal state, individuality and regional variation. Each vocalization has to be examined in the context of its particular situation, and it can be said that all calls are inextricably linked to social pattern and behaviour.

The vocalizations described in this book can be simplified into calls and songs. **Calls** are usually a brief vocalization, and are not typically affected by seasonal hormonal variation in the way that songs are (although this is a rather broad generalization.) They are often given as signals to other birds of the same species – such as alarm calls to alert others to danger – or to coordinate group behaviour, in the case of contact calls. Other less elaborate or un-emphatic calls often have a distinct purpose, but are less noticeable or significant to the observer; in such cases I have used the rather general term of "conversational" calls, because that is what they sound like from the subjective viewpoint of the observer (rather than

GREY WAGTAIL
(SEE PAGE 124)

having much to do with the birds engaging in an actual conversation). The term "chuntering" has also been used here and there – a rather colloquial English term for inconsequential muttering or chatting in a monotonous and rhythmic fashion.

Alarm calls, from a rather anthropophonic viewpoint, often sound exactly as that, clues perhaps being a sudden diversion from the normal pace and rhythm of calls. It is true, however, that many birds give different levels and types of alarm notes, and where a lower level of threat is detected, a quieter and less emphatic call may be given, for which I have used the term **anxiety call**.

Contact calls are exactly that, and range from short, quiet and unobtrusive little notes, given when birds are in fairly close proximity to each other, through to loud and distinct calls such as those given by many species (waders being a good example) when contact is being attempted over a wider area and distance. **Flight calls** exemplify this, serving to keep airborne flocks together.

Songs are more elaborate than calls and often excited by hormones. Their function is to advertise territory and attract a mate in the early stages of breeding, and they are often continued throughout the breeding season to express territorial dominance over the nest site and feeding territory. Songs are typically given in the run-up to and during the breeding season, but are also used at any time of year to define territory, such as when wintering quarters are newly reached and feeding territories are announced with song. For birds (primarily non-passerines) with no recognizable "song", the term **advertising call** is used, as the function is essentially the same. **Sub-songs** are quieter, less-developed versions of the recognizable primary song, sometimes delivered with the bill closed, and often given by migrants who are not setting up a long-term territory, or immature birds who are just having a "practice".

Recording bird sounds provides the audio equivalent of a photograph, providing hard data that is to a large extent incontrovertible and will not degrade as the memory so often does. For example, if a rare bird is discovered but only brief views are obtained, if it is calling and a recording is made, then this can be as important as getting a photograph. Not only that, with sound recording you do not necessarily require a line of sight on the bird – it can be hidden out of sight in dense bushes, yet if it is vocal a recording can still be obtained.

As recording bird sounds has become easier and more accessible to all, so it has expanded in popularity. From the introduction of portable recording devices through to personal HiFi systems, the Sony Walkman and the digital revolution, it has never been easier to record and collect bird sounds, allowing much closer study and analysis. Digital recordings can be examined closely and in detail using any home computer, whether it be by ear or more elaborate and technical methods, such as with software that can produce sonograms, pinpointing exact frequencies and timings. Sonograms are difficult to read for the casual user, but for the more serious researcher they can provide a picture of the sound that can be read like a graph, using the time and frequency scales along the two axes. While they may not provide a useful tool for many, when a sound requires closer study sonograms can be very useful. Similar to the way a photograph provides hard evidence of the visual, they provide accurate and readable evidence of the sound.

Avian Topography

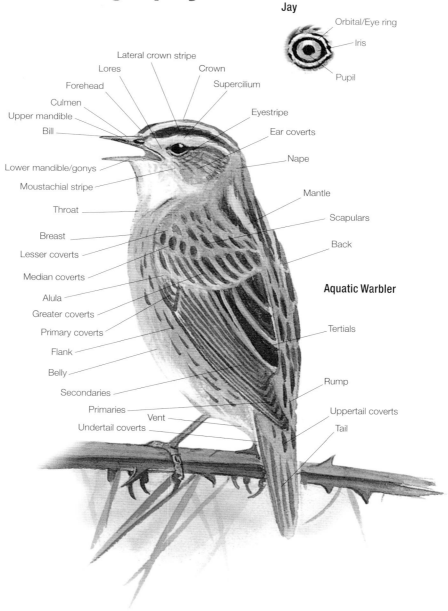

Jay

Orbital/Eye ring
Iris
Pupil

Lateral crown stripe
Lores
Crown
Forehead
Supercilium
Culmen
Upper mandible
Eyestripe
Bill
Ear coverts
Lower mandible/gonys
Nape
Moustachial stripe
Mantle
Throat
Scapulars
Breast
Back
Lesser coverts
Median coverts
Aquatic Warbler
Alula
Greater coverts
Primary coverts
Tertials
Flank
Belly
Secondaries
Rump
Primaries
Vent
Uppertail coverts
Undertail coverts
Tail

Track listing

Disc 1

1: Bewick's Swan
(0–23) triumph and greeting calls; (23–41) flock calls in flight.

2: Whooper Swan
(0–29) sounds from migrating flock; (30–43) warning pair.

3: Pink-footed Goose
(0–10) flight calls; (10–26) various conversation calls; (27–39) calls of large flying flock.

4: Greylag Goose
(0–24) single notes followed by sound of flock in flight.

5: Brent Goose
(0–20) various calls on land; (20–41) calls of large flying flock.

6: Wigeon
(0–14) whistle of male; (14–21) calls of female; (21–42) calls uttered during antagonistic encounter in flight.

7: Teal
(0–29) calls of males in flock.

8: Mallard
(0–11) calls of female; (11–20) calls of male; (20–42) calls of a displaying flock on water.

9: Eider
(0–18) courtship calls of males; (18–41) clucking calls of females defending young.

10: Red Grouse
(0–17) calls from running bird; (17–41) calls in display flight.

11: Ptarmigan
(0–23) perch song and threat calls of two males in dispute; (23–28) flight song turning to cackling; (28–39) calls when flushed.

12: Black Grouse
(0–32) normal display of bubbling and "spitting" calls; 32–46) threat/aggression calls of male.

13: Capercaillie
(0–23) normal display call of male; (23–34) cackling of female and males' response by jump display; (35–43) low-intensity display from male.

14: Red-legged Partridge
(0–42) various calls.

15: Grey Partridge
(0–22) creaky courtship calls by males and some quiet feeding calls; (22–37) gathering calls of adults and "rattle peep" calls of chicks; (37–39) call when flushed.

16: Quail
(0–34) song of male with quiet pre-song growl before third song phrase; (34–38) pre-song growl amplified.

17: Pheasant
(0–14) display call and wing flutter of male; (14–35) single "roosting" call of male; (35–41) call of startled female.

18: Great Northern Diver
(0–42) various courtship and territorial calls.

19: Little Grebe
(0–20) trilling calls.

20: Great Crested Grebe
(0–42) sounds from breeding colony.

21: Manx Shearwater
(0–42) various calls at breeding colony.

22: Storm Petrel
(0–42) various calls at breeding colony.

23: Bittern
(0–29) "booming" song; (29–34) flight calls.

24: Grey Heron
(0–9) perch calls; (9–19) flight call.

25: Black Kite
(0–42) typical "whinnying" calls from perch or in flight.

26: Red Kite
(0–37) typical "whinnying" calls.

27: Marsh Harrier
(0 –16) call of male during display flight; (16–30) excited soliciting perch calls of female; (30–42); chattering calls of male.

28: Sparrowhawk
0–27) weak calls of nest-building adult; (27–44) begging calls of juveniles.

29: Buzzard
(0–42) typical calls with various degrees of excitement.

30: Osprey
(0–15) typical contact calls; (15–30) various yelping calls uttered during trespassing of intruder; (30–41) mild alarm calls.

31: Kestrel
(0–14) threat calls of male to intruder near nest; (15–24) calls of female; (24–41) "whinnying" courtship greeting call.

32: Hobby

(0–11) slow courtship call turning to rapid scolding call; (11–24) slow courtship calls; (24–42) calls uttered when territorial male prepares to attack intrusive male.

33: Peregrine

(0–17) threat calls of male to intruder near nest; (17–42) threat calls of female to intruder near nest.

34: Water Rail

(0–13) screaming call of male; (13–27) screaming call of male followed by grunting announcement calls (with another male singing in background); (27–42) "kikking" song of male.

35: Spotted Crake

(0–42) territorial "song" of male calling at dusk.

36: Corncrake

(0–41) song of male in spring.

37: Moorhen

(0–18) advertising call of male; (18–28) crowing calls;(28–32) mild alarm call; (32–42) confrontation calls.

38: Coot

(0–31) various spring calls.

39: Crane

(0–17) display calls; (17–31) flight calls.

40: Oystercatcher

(0–5) single alarm notes; (5–42) "piping chorus".

41: Avocet

(0–23) typical calls.

42: Stone Curlew

(0–42) typical harsh and "coo'i'lee" calls from birds at dusk.

43: Little Ringed Plover

(0–21) song during display flight; (21–42) typical "peeoo" calls, plus variants given in alarm close to nest.

44: Ringed Plover

(0–28) song during display flight and on ground; (28–41) typical "poo'ip" call.

45: Golden Plover

(0–16) rhythmical wailing song given by male in display flight; (16–30) trilling song, typically heard as bird prepares to land; (30–42) alarm calls uttered when disturbed by intruder in territory.

46: Grey Plover

(0–18) typical call.

47: Lapwing

(0–24) Song and sound of wingbeats from male in display flight; (24–34) mild alarm calls often uttered before roosting on feeding grounds; (34–42) alarm calls given in flight against intruder.

48: Dunlin

(0–20) courting trill given during display flight or on ground; (20–28) long trill often given in combination of courting trill; (28–35) commonly heard contact calls; (35–42) alarm calls.

49: Snipe

(0–20) "drumming" sound in display flight; (20–30) "chipper" excitement/advertising calls given in breeding season; (30–42) flight calls.

50: Woodcock

(0–26) calls of "roding" bird.

51: Black-tailed Godwit

(0–12) calls given during display flight; (12–19) attack call; (19–43) various Lapwing-like calls given during display flight.

52: Bar-tailed Godwit

(0–14) song mixed with very rapid "pre-display calls"; (14–30) advertising call given by feeding bird; (30–35) calls of migrating bird; (35–41) alarm calls.

53: Whimbrel

(0–25) display call series given on the ground; (25–32) "whining" call; (32–39) flight call of migrating bird; (39–45) alarm call against an intruder.

54: Curlew

(0–34) typical "curlew" calls, plus barking alarm notes and bubbling trills; (34–46) repeated "curlew" song notes.

55: Spotted Redshank

(0–21) display call series, first given on ground and then in flight; (21–30) typical flight or contact call; (30–42) alarm calls.

56: Redshank

(0–21) single notes and display calls; (21–42) typical 3–4-note flight calls.

57: Greenshank

(0–23) rhythmic song, normally given on wing and high up – here two phrases are uttered on ground; (23–31) typical loud contact calls; (31–42) alarm calls.

58: Green Sandpiper

(0–22) far-carrying song given during display flight; (22–42) typical flight calls.

59: Wood Sandpiper

(0–20) rapidly ringing yodel uttered during display flight; (20–30) excitedly repeated contact calls, mostly given in flight; (30–42) alarm calls.

60: Common Sandpiper

(0–29) display call series, first given on the ground and then in flight; (29–42) typical 3–4-note call, plus a single anxiety note, given in proximity to a fledgling.

61: Turnstone

(0–25) purring rattle of group in breeding season; (25–32) conversation calls of two feeding birds; (32–36) alert calls; (36–42) chattering alarm call uttered on breeding grounds.

62: Arctic Skua

(0–44) various calls given on breeding grounds.

63: Black-headed Gull

(0–11) various spring sounds; (11–21) various raucous calls; (21–34) sounds of breeding colony; (34–41) squabbling calls of foraging birds.

64: Common Gull

(0–44) single calls and long calls.

65: Lesser Black-backed Gull

(*L. fuscus fuscus*) (0–8) display call given in duet by sitting pair; (8–17) call notes and wailing calls uttered in association with courtship; (17–24) "kaw" calls expressing anger or anxiety; (24–28) "gaga" calls of an alarmed bird; (*L. fuscus graellsi*) (28–40) long call; (40–45) single calls.

66: Herring Gull

(0–23) various calls including long call; (22–28) long call; (28–43) cackling alarm call and single flight calls.

67: Great Black-backed Gull

(0–15) long call; (15–30) single call notes; (30–41) "gaga" calls of alarmed bird.

68: Kittiwake

(0–43) calls at breeding colony.

69: Little Tern

(0–42) short, sharp alarm and anxiety calls, plus "yickering" calls at breeding colony.

70: Sandwich Tern

(0–42) typical calls, plus cackling notes and "pee-pee" begging notes from juveniles.

71: Common Tern

(0–15) advertising calls uttered during display flight; (15–42) "keeyar" calls and single "kik" calls given in alarm near breeding colony.

72: Arctic Tern

(0–8) advertising "kree-ah" call; (8–33) advertising calls uttered by male, and female "ke-ke-ke" begging call; (33–42) alarm calls.

73: Puffin

(0–41) calls given on breeding grounds.

74: Stock Dove

(0–18) two song sequences.

75: Woodpigeon

(0–40) typical 4–5-note song phrases.

76: Collared Dove

(0–38) advertising calls with different pitch; (38–43) excitement calls, often given by male in display flight.

77: Turtle Dove

(0–41) advertising call of male.

78: Cuckoo

(0–26) advertising call of male; (26–32) excitement calls of male; (32–42) bubbling call of female.

79: Barn Owl

(0–16) typical screeching call; (16–33) advertising call of male; (33–41) calls of young in nest.

80: Eagle Owl

(0–30) advertising call of male.

81: Little Owl

(0–22) song; (22–43) various call notes.

82: Tawny Owl

(0–26) advertising call of male; (26–45) typical call note – in this case female responding to excited male.

83: Long-eared Owl

(0–34) advertising call of male; (34–44) begging call of juvenile.

84: Tengmalm's Owl

(0–24) advertising call of male; (24–41) food call and twittering of fledged young.

85: Nightjar

(0–38) churring song of male; (38–42) "coo'ic" flight call.

86: Swift

(0–42) calls of evening "screaming party".

87: Kingfisher
(0–15) various piping calls.

88: Hoopoe
(0–20) advertising call of male; (20–41) cawing and rattling calls uttered in courtship chase.

89: Wryneck
(0–30) advertising call of male, with female answering in duet; (30–42) alarm calls.

90: Black Woodpecker
(0–20) drumming; (20–29) "yaffling" call; (29–45) "kleeuw" single note call.

91: Grey-headed Woodpecker
(0–18) drumming; (18–32) advertising song; (32–43) single call notes.

92: Green Woodpecker
(0–23) "yaffling" advertising call; (23–36) sharp notes of flight call.

93: Great Spotted Woodpecker
(0–23) drumming; (23–38) typical single note call.

94: Lesser Spotted Woodpecker
(0–22) drumming; (22–46) various single and advertising calls.

95: Woodlark
(0–29) typical song sequence from bird singing from ground; (29–32) calls uttered on autumn migration; (32–43) contact alarm calls given by adult on breeding grounds.

96: Skylark
(0–39) song given in song flight; (39–42) dry chirruping calls.

97: Shore Lark
(0–18) jingling, irregular song phrases of male; (18–33) calls uttered by males during territorial fight; (33–42) various calls heard from feeding birds during autumn.

98: Sand Martin
(0–42) song and calls from birds at colony.

99a: Swallow
(0–42) perch song and calls.

99b: House Martin
(44–1:26) song and typical chirruping perch and flight calls.

Disc 2

1: Tree Pipit
(0–33): perch song, then songflight; (33–42) call notes.

2: Meadow Pipit
(0–34) perch song, then songflight; (34–38) alarm call near nest; (38–45) typical calls.

3: Rock Pipit
(0–12) short song given on ground; (13–28) songflight with strong echo from cliffs; (28–42) calls of adults and juveniles.

4: Yellow Wagtail
(0–31) calls; (31–42) perch calls.

5: Grey Wagtail
(0–29) song; (30–38) typical calls.

6: Pied/White Wagtail
(0–27) song and calls of White Wagtail; (27–42) calls of Pied Wagtail.

7: Waxwing
(0–47) calls from a flock.

8: Dipper
(0–30) rippling song of bird sitting on edge of river ice; (30–38) penetrating contact calls given in flight.

9: Wren
(0–7) typical scolding call; (7–18) dry ticking scolding calls; (18–42) song.

10: Dunnock
(0–33) song; (33–38) calls; (38–44) single alarm-type calls.

11: Robin
(0–32) song; (32–42) dry "ticking" calls.

12: Thrush Nightingale
(0–50) song.

13: Nightingale
(0–34) song; (34–42) "eep" anxiety call.

14: Bluethroat
(0–34) perch song; (34–46) calls.

15: Black Redstart
(0–36) song.

16: Redstart
(0–37) song; (37–44) calls.

17: Whinchat
(0–35) song; (35–42) typical "chacking" calls from a male.

18: Stonechat
(0–30) song; (30–42) typical "chacking" calls.

19: Wheatear
(0–9) territorial song of male; (9–30) intense song in territorial dispute; (30–41) contact/alarm calls.

20: Ring Ouzel
(0–32) song with short quiet twittering; (32–42) hard contact/alarm calls from migrant bird.

21: Blackbird
(0–32) song; (32–42) typical "clacking" evening calls.

22: Fieldfare
(0–18) slow song; (18–35) "ecstatic" song; (35–46) calls.

23: Song Thrush
(0–43) typical song.

24: Redwing
(0–31) two song variants; (31–37) threat calls given in mild alarm; (37–41) contact call typically given in flight; (41–45) alarm calls given on territory.

25: Mistle Thrush
(0–32) song; (32–42) chattering call.

26: Cetti's Warbler
(0–12) song; (12–35) song variant; (35–42) alarm/contact calls.

27: Grasshopper Warbler
(0–18) song; (18–34) contact/alarm calls.

28: River Warbler
(0–28) song; (28–36) contact/

alarm calls of male; (36–41) single "excitement" notes.

29: Savi's Warbler
(0–22) song; (22–30) contact/alarm call.

30: Aquatic Warbler
(0–41) typical understated song.

31: Sedge Warbler
(0–37) song; (37–44) calls.

32: Blyth's Reed Warbler
(0–34) song; (34–40) churring calls given by migrants.

33: Marsh Warbler
(0–35) song; (35–42) contact/alarm calls.

34: Reed Warbler
(0–38) song; (38–45) calls.

35: Great Reed Warbler
(0–36) song; (36–42) contact/alarm calls.

36: Icterine Warbler
(0–34) song; (34–46) contact/alarm calls.

37: Blackcap
(0–36) song; (36–42) contact/alarm calls.

38: Garden Warbler
(0–38) song; (38–43) calls.

39: Barred Warbler
(0–33) song from two individuals; (33–36) rattling call

40: Lesser Whitethroat
(0–19) song; (19–36) song; (36–43) calls.

41: Common Whitethroat
(0–33) song; (33–43) calls.

42: Dartford Warbler
(0–36) song; (36–46) calls.

43: Greenish Warbler
(0–31) song; (31–42) call.

44: Wood Warbler
(0–24) trilling song; (24–29) piping song; (29–42) call.

45: Chiffchaff
(0–35) song; (35–42) call.

46: Willow Warbler
(0–32) song; (32–42) call.

47: Goldcrest
(0–35) song; (35–44) calls.

48: Firecrest
(0–33) song; (33–42) calls.

49: Spotted Flycatcher
(0–33) song; (33–47) calls.

50: Red-breasted Flycatcher
(0–26) song; (26–43) calls.

51: Collared Flycatcher
(0–40) song.

52: Pied Flycatcher
(0–43) song.

53: Bearded Tit
(0–30) various calls.

54: Long-tailed Tit
(0–41) various calls.

55: Blue Tit
(0–25) two forms of song; (25–43) various calls.

56: Great Tit
(0–18) typical slow song; (18–33) typical fast song; (33–43) calls.

57: Crested Tit
(0–30) song; (30–42) contact/alarm calls.

58: Coal Tit
(0–30) two forms of song; (31–42) various calls.

59: Willow Tit
(0–20) song; (20–41) calls.

60: Marsh Tit
(0–20) two types of song; (20–41) calls.

61: Nuthatch
(0–13) alarm/contact call; (13–36) two song variants; (36–42) high-pitched contact calls.

62: Eurasian Treecreeper
(0–30) song; (30–43) calls.

63: Short-toed Treecreeper
(0–20) song/calls; (20–42) calls.

64: Penduline Tit
(0–24) calls; (24–31) simple
song from nest-building pair;
(31–41) calls from family party.

65: Golden Oriole
(0–41) song interspersed with
harsh call notes.

66: Red-backed Shrike
(0–28) threat and excitement
calls and song with mimicked
Swallow, Whinchat and
Chaffinch phrases; (28–42)
alarm calls.

67: Great Grey Shrike
(0–22) three types of advertising call; (22–41) threat calls.

68: Jay
(0–16) quiet courtship-song
of male to female; (16–34)
mimicry of Goshawk and
Crow given while foraging,
resting and also when excited;
(34–42) typical alarm calls.

69: Magpie
(0–45) various calls.

70: Nutcracker
(0–22) song; (22–41)

rasping excitement calls.

71: Chough
(0–40) various calls.

72: Jackdaw
(0–37) various calls.

73: Rook
(0–41) various calls.

74: Carrion Crow
(0–41) various calls.

75: Raven
(0–39) various flight calls.

76: Starling
(0–30) song; (30–42) various
calls.

77: House Sparrow
(0–30) song and calls;
(30–42) various calls.

78: Tree Sparrow
(0–24) song; (24–41)
calls from flock.

79: Chaffinch
(0–23) song; (23–42)
various calls.

80: Brambling
(0–26) song; (26–37) typical
call; (37–44) flight calls.

81: Serin
(0–29) song; (29–41) calls.

82: Greenfinch
(0–19) elaborate song;
(19–29) simple song; (29–42)
calls of flock.

83: Goldfinch
(0–12) song; (12–27) song
and calls; (27–42) calls.

84: Siskin
(0–36) song; (36–45) calls.

85: Linnet
(0–37) song; (37–45) flight call.

86: Twite
(0–25) song plus nasal call
notes; (25–40) flight calls.

87: Lesser Redpoll
(0–12) call; (12–42) song
and calls.

88: Common Crossbill
(0–17) song; (17–32) contact
calls of perched bird prior
to flying off; (32–46) song
and calls.

89: Scottish Crossbill
(0–25) song; (25–34)
calls; (34–45) calls.

90: Parrot Crossbill
(0–24) calls; (24–44): song.

91: Common Rosefinch
(0–32) two examples of song;
(32–42) call.

92: Bullfinch
(0–9) calls from "British"
Bullfinch; (9–29) quiet song
from "British" Bullfinch; (29–42)
calls from "Northern" Bullfinch.

93: Hawfinch
(0–42) High-pitched,
explosive contact calls and
quiet, lower pitched, drawn-
out sounds indicating song.

94: Lapland Bunting
(0–31) song; (31–41)
contact/alarm calls.

95: Snow Bunting
(0–27) song; (27–33) contact/
alarm calls; (33–45) calls from
feeding flock.

96: Yellowhammer
(0–22) song; (22–35) call.

97: Cirl Bunting
(0–19) song.

98: Ortolan Bunting
(0–28) song; (28–40)
contact/alarm calls.

99a: Reed Bunting
(0–22) full song of unpaired
male; (22–35) simple slow
song of paired male.
(35–45) calls.

99b: Corn Bunting
(47–1.29) song.

Bewick's Swan
Cygnus columbianus

LENGTH: 115–127cm

WINGSPAN: 180–211cm

🔊 **CALL:** "waah'h waah'h"

⏺ **TRACK:** 1:1

IDENTIFICATION

Only really confusable with our other two swan species, with an obvious difference from Mute Swan (not included here) in that it has a yellow-and-black bill (as opposed to orange-and-black) and holds its neck straighter and not in an S-shape. Closer attention must be paid to separating it from Whooper Swan, however. The bill of Bewick's is black with a yellow patch on the bill sides which is rounded on its anterior edge, extending less than 50 per cent of the length of the bill. Bill patterns vary greatly,

so much so that individual birds can be recognized by their bills alone. In comparison to Whooper, Bewick's is smaller, shorter-necked and dumpier, appearing more goose-like in shape. Juveniles are greyish in plumage, the bill again variable but mainly pink with black parts increasing with maturity.

HABITAT

In the breeding season, they nest in the Arctic tundra, in lowland swampy areas with numerous pools and lakes. Outside this season, en route to and from their wintering areas, they will use lakes, rivers and pools, while in their winter quarters they prefer low-elevation lakes, reservoirs, and rivers with nearby flooded grassland and pastures. They have a strong attachment to regular inland wintering sites, although can vary these over time depending on food supply and climatic conditions. In England they have become habituated to being fed grain at Welney and Slimbridge, in atypically close proximity to humans.

CALL/SONG

Various calls are given; the most familiar to observers in our region are the flight calls, and calls of a flock at rest. In flight a repeated monosyllabic honking is given, difficult to describe but approximating to "waah'h waah'h", "haap haap", "uh-rrh uh-raa". When several birds call simultaneously this merges into a multisyllabic barking "wooh wow waow aaoo how", somewhat like a cinematic version of a 'Red' Indian war party. At rest a flock gives a conversational chuntering of birds calling to their mates and young, making a musical babble of variously pitched sounds such as "oo-oo-ow-ow…".

Whooper Swan
Cygnus cygnus

LENGTH: 145–160cm
WINGSPAN: 218–243cm
🔊 **CALL:** "ahng-ahng"
⏺ **TRACK:** 1:2

IDENTIFICATION

Given a reasonable view, the differences between this and the superficially similar Bewick's Swan are obvious. The Whooper is a bigger bird, some 25–30 per cent heavier, with a longer straight neck and a flattened forehead that gives its head a distinctive profile. These features are useful for distinguishing the birds both flying and at rest. However, the diagnostic feature is the bill pattern, with a longer, deeper bill showing more yellow than Bewick's, a large wedge of yellow on the bill sides extending to a point towards the bill tip. The juveniles tend to be browner than Bewick's juveniles, with a similarly coloured bill of pinkish and black. Juveniles gradually acquire the white plumage of adulthood at 15–20 months old.

CALL/SONG

Similar in general to the vocalizations of Bewick's Swan, but Whoopers typically sound stronger, deeper and more trumpeting. The flight call is a double bugle or toy trumpet-like "ahng ahng", "barp barp baah-hp!", "raaahng haaangh" or "whoop-whoop", repeated several times and with the second syllable slightly higher in pitch. A flock in flight sounds louder than Bewick's, while at rest the varied calls produce a chorus of harmonious babbling.

HABITAT

More widely distributed than Bewick's Swan, favouring a more sub-Arctic breeding environment, although there is a good population in Iceland. It nests on a variety of wetlands, favouring undisturbed reed-fringed lakes, swamps and pools in moorlands and in low-lying steppe and grassland areas. A very rare occasional breeder in Britain, it is most regularly encountered in the north and west, though in winter it occurs more widely and can be found on lakes and flooded pastures, (such as the large wintering population found on the Ouse Washes in Cambridgeshire) and often along the coast. It requires aquatic vegetation on which to feed, but can often be seen grazing in arable fields.

Pink-footed Goose
Anser brachyrhynchus

LENGTH: 60–75cm

WINGSPAN: 135–170cm

🔊 **CALL:** "ahnk-ahnk-ahnk"

⚫ **TRACK:** 1:3

IDENTIFICATION

A medium-sized goose, appearing rather compact, short-necked and short-billed. The most distinctive features are a dark brown head and neck that contrasts (particularly in flight) with a pale grey forewing. Winter plumage is greyer than the browner summer dress, and all ages show plain unmarked underparts. The vent is white, as are the uppertail coverts and trim around the tail. The bill is small and short, black in colour with a pink band over the culmen near the tip, the band extending up the bill sides in a narrow stripe, although it is variable in size and shape. The legs and feet, as the common name would suggest, are pink.

HABITAT

Breeding only in Greenland, Iceland and Spitzbergen, they nest on upland moors, and in Iceland can be seen along river valleys, particularly when with fledged young. In winter they occur from Denmark to the Low Countries, and gather in large numbers in Britain, where they prefer arable fields for feeding, roosting near lakes, estuaries and other coastal features.

CALL/SONG

Highly vocal. In flight a flock gives a continuous cackling, with a medley of calls at different pitches that is often likened to the yapping of puppies! The calls are a two- or three-syllable "ahng-ahng-ahng", a difficult-to-transcribe sound variously written as "wink-wink", "aa'aa'aa" and "aaahh-aaahng", higher pitched than larger species of goose but lower than the laughing of Greater White-fronted Geese. They also give an alarm call, a sharper higher-pitched note.

Greylag Goose
Anser anser

LENGTH: 75–90cm
WINGSPAN: 147–180cm
🔊 **CALL:** "aahng-ung-ung"
⏺ **TRACK:** 1:4

IDENTIFICATION

The largest geese native to our region, with a large heavy head and a large, triangular, completely orange bill. The plumage is greyish-brown overall, with upperpart feathers tipped buffish-white, forming pale lines. The belly is buffish-grey in colour and is predominantly plain, although sometimes with some darker blotching. In flight the bird shows obviously contrasting pale blue-grey forewings. The vent, uppertail coverts and rim of the grey-centred tail are white. The legs are thick and pink. The race *rubirostris*, found from south-eastern Europe to Siberia, has a wholly pink bill and is paler and greyer overall.

HABITAT

Favours wetlands such as lochs, lakes, swamps and reedbeds, which are close to the meadows and pastures that provide its feeding habitat. In England introduced birds are often seen around lakes and reservoirs, whereas wild populations favour similar habitats but where there is less disturbance from man and his activities. In winter Greylag Geese frequent estuaries, floods and marshes, and feed in arable fields on grass and roots.

CALL/SONG

Their calls are a familiar – if annoying! – sound around wetlands in England (where the population is feral), not least because of the similarity to the sounds of domestic farmyard geese. A variety of loud and rather rough honking calls are given, and the typical flight call can be described as "aahng-ung-ung". When birds are in a group on the ground they give a low conversational cackling, such as "a'uuh'aauk'uuh'aah'uh'ah'a" and "nga'nga'nga'gug", which changes into shorter, sharper "ghang" notes if birds are alarmed, or a series of short sharp notes if they have a strong urge to fly.

Brent Goose
Branta bernicla

LENGTH: 56–61cm

WINGSPAN: 110–120cm

🔊 **CALL:** "aaanghrr"

⏺ **TRACK:** 1:5

ADULT 'DARK-BELLIED'
BRENT GOOSE

IDENTIFICATION

The smallest and darkest of our geese, the Brent Goose is rather duck-like in flight, and shows a black head, neck and breast. Two forms occur, Dark-bellied *B. (b.) bernicla* and Pale-bellied *B. (b.). hrota.* The former has a smoky-grey belly and flanks with a whitish trim on the upper flank feathers. The Pale-bellied has paler flanks, as the name would suggest, and although both forms are subject to variation, it has paler underparts contrasting strongly with the black breast. The upperparts are a plain dark grey, the vent or 'stern' is white, as is much of the tail. Both forms show a white neck 'flare' on each side. The North American form B. (b) *nigricans*, also known as the Black Brant, is a vagrant now recorded annually in Britain. This shows very dark underparts with a strongly contrasting white blaze along the flank, plus a more extensive white neck patch.

HABITAT

This species breeds in low-lying Arctic tundra with many pools, but non-breeding birds in Europe favour shallow sea coasts, estuaries and saltmarshes, especially those that are rich in green littoral plants such as Eelgrass *Zostera marina*, feeding on this and also on algae and saltmarsh plants. It is strongly attached to the intertidal zone and stays faithful to regular routes and stopping places on migration. It can also be found grazing in arable fields close to the coast. Often seen in sizeable flocks, flying in ragged formation.

CALL/SONG

Although they have a rather limited repertoire and can be quite silent, Brents can be noisy when in a flock and are a familiar sound in winter around parts of our region. They have a single-syllable call – a deep rolling "aaanghrr", a difficult sound to describe but which can be transcribed variously as a soft "raunk", "rronk" or "krrowk". They also give a more gutteral "k'k'rrrot", and when a large number of birds are calling together, either in flight or when resting on water, this becomes a cacophony of far-carrying metallic honking.

ADULT 'PALE-BELLIED' BRENT GOOSE

FEMALE

Wigeon
Anas penelope

LENGTH: 45–51cm

WINGSPAN: 75–86cm

🔊 **CALL:** "whee-OO-oo"

⏺ **TRACK:** 1:6

IDENTIFICATION

The male is strikingly coloured, with a yellow blaze on the crown, rich rufous head, salmon-coloured breast and pearl-grey back and flanks, and with a bold pattern around the stern of a black vent and tail with white side panels on the rear flank. After the breeding season the eclipse plumage is duller, more like the female but with darker upperparts and richer rufous flanks, but at all seasons the male shows a striking white wing-patch that is visible at rest. The female is more demure, typically paler dull rufous on the flanks contrasting with a white belly, a grey-brown head and brown upperparts. This species has a distinctive shape, with a small, pale blue, black-tipped bill, peaked head and compact, short-necked form.

HABITAT

Typically breeding above 55 degrees north, and favouring shallow freshwater lakes and ponds in the boreal zone, especially where there is tree cover nearby (although it avoids densely forested areas). In winter this gregarious bird can be found on a variety of wetland habitats, ideally close to the coast where it utilizes tidal mud, shallow bays and saltmarshes, although it is often found grazing on inland flooded grasslands and pastures.

CALL/SONG

A typical sound of coastal marshes in winter, when flocks can be heard making a cacophony of musical whistles. The male is highly vocal on the ground, on water and in flight, uttering a loud, excited "whee-OO-oo". At close range one or two short additional syllables can be heard preceding this whistle call, such as "uh-uh-wheooow". The female has a growling purr, which can be described as "urrr-urrr-urrr-urrr", "rerr rerr rerr" or "krrr'krrr'krrr".

MALE

Teal
Anas crecca

MALE

LENGTH: 34–38cm

WINGSPAN: 58–64cm

CALL: "preep-preep"

TRACK: 1:7

IDENTIFICATION

The smallest of the dabbling ducks. The main feature of the male in breeding plumage is a chestnut head with side panels of glossy green around the eye and extending to the rear, rimmed with pale yellow which also extends forwards to the bill. The body appears grey, and on close inspection can be seen to be finely vermiculated with dark grey on cream, and with a prominent horizontal slash of white on the folded wing that is actually the white of the scapulars showing. The stern is boldly patterned with a black-framed yellow patch on the rear flanks. The female is brown, uniformly patterned darker. The speculum is half-green, half-black.

HABITAT

Found on ponds, lagoons and other small wetlands in the breeding season, and sometimes nests far from water. In its wintering and migration areas it occurs on a wide variety of water bodies, ideally where shallow water meets emergent vegetation. In Britain it is often seen on flooded pastures, marshy areas and around the margins of larger wetland habitats.

CALL/SONG

In winter and spring Teal can be quite vocal, the males calling with a far-carrying but discreet little call "preep-preep", "plilp-plilp" or "rrhlew rrhlew", high (3kHz) in pitch yet very short (about 0.2–0.5 sec) in length. When coming from a flock of birds it is often heard in a chorus of repeated calls and becomes a melodic peeping. The females are less vocal, but their main call is similar in pattern to that of female Mallard, a series of quacking notes but higher pitched and more rapid, "uuaap uuaap uuaap", sometimes with a harsh or strangled sound.

MALE

FEMALE

IDENTIFICATION

The most familiar duck in our region, with very differently plumaged sexes. The male is distinctive, a fairly robust long-necked bird with a dirty yellow bill, a glossy bottle-green head, white neck ring, purple-brown breast and ash-grey belly sides and upperparts. The wing has a bold speculum of blue or purple, depending on the light, bordered with black and white lines – a feature shared by both sexes. The female is brown, streaked and spotted overall with black, with a darker crown and eye-stripe. The bill is dull orangey or olive-coloured, with a dark culmen and tip.

HABITAT

The ancestor of the domestic or 'farmyard' duck, the Mallard is widespread, common, extremely tolerant of humans and very adaptable. It is found in an amazingly wide range of wetland habitats, such as shallow coasts, rivers, lakes, marshes, ditches, man-made water bodies such as reservoirs, parks, ponds, and will use arable fields for grazing. It always favours shallow water, and can often be seen up-ending as it feeds on underwater vegetation.

CALL/SONG

The calls of the male and female differ somewhat. The male gives a soft nasal "rrheerrb" or "queep", and often when in a group accompanies this with a low quacking "rhu-rhu-rhu-rhu…". The female gives the classic "quack-quack" call. This call is typically in series of 2–10 notes, with the stress on the first two quacks and then tailing off, such as "Qwah Qwah Qwa qwa wha wha wha wha…". It is frequently uttered, often when flushed or when other Mallards are in the air nearby. The female also gives variations of these

Mallard
Anas platyrhynchos

LENGTH: 50–65cm

WINGSPAN: 81–98cm

CALL: "Qwah Qwah Qwa qwa wha wha wha"

TRACK: 1:8

calls, with persistent quacks when advertising, or low chuntering quacks when with young; the latter give a high-pitched "peepee" contact call.

FEMALE

MALE

Eider
Somateria mollissima

FEMALE

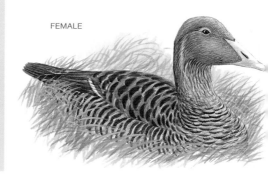

LENGTH: 50–71cm

WINGSPAN: 80–108cm

CALL: "ah-OOO"

TRACK: 1:9

IDENTIFICATION

A rather bulky sea duck, weighing up to 2.5kg. The head has a distinctive profile at all ages, with a large triangular bill that runs straight into the top of the head, giving a 'Roman nose' profile. In early summer the male is unmistakable, with a pattern of black on the crown, belly, flanks and tail, contrasting with the remainder of the body, which is white with a flush of emerald green on the hind-neck. The females are brown all over, with vertically barred flanks. Males in eclipse plumage are blackish-brown with white wing-patches and a white flank-spot. Maturity is reached only after three years, and first-year birds are strikingly plumaged with white breasts and scapulars on a blackish-brown body.

HABITAT

Mostly breeding above 55 degrees north, Eiders frequent shallow inshore coastal waters, often with small islands, rocks and skerries offshore. In winter they stay on the sea, typically dispersing just within their breeding range, wherever they can feed on crustaceans and molluscs, such as mussel beds. The species is accidental on inland waters.

CALL/SONG

The classic call of the male during courtship in spring and autumn is an almost comical "ah-OOO" or "oor-orWhooh", like the sound of appreciative coo-ing, often fusing into a conversation-like noise when multiple callers are in a flock together. The female has other calls, commonly heard when escorting chicks, such as a guttural "grrrar" and a "gog" note, commonly run together as a low grunting "og-og-og-o-og-og". The female also has a cawing "coo-roo" version of the male's call, given during display.

MALE

IDENTIFICATION

The 'famous' grouse of whisky bottles and rich man's 'sport', the Red Grouse is slightly larger than the Ptarmigan and retains dark brown wings throughout the year. Both sexes are similar in general colouration, the male being a deeper rusty-rufous brown all over, subtly marked with darker bars and blotches; it also has a red wattle over the eye and the tail is blackish. The female is a lighter, tawnier shade, showing more fine plumage detail in buff and black and lacking the red wattle. Both sexes show whitish leg feathering, a sure distinction from the superficially similar female Black Grouse.

HABITAT

Favours upland moorland, rich in Heather *Calluna vulgaris*, which provides it with a year-round food supply. It is sedentary and strongly tied to this habitat, so rarely found away from it. It normally avoids forest, although can be found in more grassy areas. The form *L. lagopus scoticus* is endemic to the British Isles and is considered to be just one of fifteen or more subspecies of the circumpolar Willow Grouse. It is frequently found on particular 'grouse moors', where stocks are maintained for shooting, watched over by territorial gamekeepers!

Red Grouse
Lagopus lagopus

LENGTH: 37–42cm

WINGSPAN: 48–54cm

◀)) **CALL:** "k'bow-k'bow-k'bow-k'bow"

● **TRACK:** 1:10

CALL/SONG

The display call of the male is given in a short display flight, with a quick flapping ascent when he calls "eow", followed by a glide down, calling "kakakakakakarrrrr" on the descent, alternatively transcribed as "eow–rka'rka'rka'rka'rka'ak'ak'ak'ak".

He continues the call on the ground with a "koWah-koWah-koWah-koWah", which can last for several seconds. A version of this sound is given when a bird is flushed. Other calls given from the ground include a "kokokokokokgrrrrrrrr" and a loud cackling "k'bow k'bow k'bow..." or "go-bak-go-bak-go-bak…". The female has a range of short, quieter calls.

Ptarmigan
Lagopus muta

MALE SPRING PLUMAGE

LENGTH: 31–36cm

WINGSPAN: 54–60cm

🔊 **CALL:** "aerr-eh-rr gk'gk'gk'gk'gk'r'r'r"

⏺ **TRACK:** 1:11

IDENTIFICATION

The Ptarmigan undergoes remarkable plumage changes with the seasons, in order to have the optimum camouflage for local conditions. In winter the plumage is completely white with a black tail, the male only showing black lores. In spring, he acquires a rather dark grey head, neck and breast, with the remaining upperparts gradually becoming grey, vermiculated black, which in late summer becomes a little blotchy and paler, and with a red wattle over the eye. The female in spring assumes a more yellow-toned plumage, brown spotted with black, buff and white, starting with the head and breast and gradually extending over the remaining upperparts. At all seasons the wings are white.

HABITAT

Found on high mountains on rocky barren tops, typically above 800m in Scotland, although their favoured altitude decreases inversely to latitude, so in Iceland one can encounter them at sea level. Conversely, in southern populations, such as in the Alps, they only occur well above the tree line. Notably confiding, although well camouflaged, Ptarmigan can be reluctant to fly and are often startled at close range, when they either fly or scuttle away from the observer, calling as they go.

CALL/SONG

Some very distinctive cackling and grating calls. The male has a display flight in spring, in which he flies up and then glides down on stiff wings, uttering a hoarse belching and cackling, often finishing in a rolling cackle "aerr-eh-rr gk'gk'gk'gk'gk'r'r'r" or "ahrr-arr-ka-ka-kh-kh-kh-k". Other calls include "arr orr ka-karrr", usually delivered from the ground, as is a shorter "arr-urrr". An alarm note is a short "kwa", and the female also gives a soft, nervous little "kee-a" or "ey-eh" when shepherding chicks.

FEMALE SPRING PLUMAGE

FEMALE

Black Grouse
Tetrao tetrix

LENGTH: 49–56cm (male), 40–45cm (female)	
WINGSPAN: 65–80cm (female 15–20 per cent less)	
CALL: "urr-urr'ur-urr-rhuurrr"	
TRACK: 1:12	

IDENTIFICATION

The male is a striking bird, glossy black over most of the body and with a long lyre-shaped tail that is elevated and spread during lekking displays. The undertail is white, and during display this is fanned upwards to show as a big white nappy. There is a white wingbar visible at rest, and also a couple of isolated white patches at the wing root and on the lesser coverts. The male has a red wattle over the eye. The female is much more subtle, a warm brown overall with barring and freckling in black, less boldly barred and less richly coloured than the female Capercaillie, and with a narrow whitish wingbar and a longer tail in comparison to the female Red Grouse; also, the tail is slightly notched and appears rather square-cut in flight.

HABITAT

Typically but not exclusively favours upland areas, usually in mixed birch and conifer forest, bushy areas with open ground, moorland edges and bogs.

It shies away from open moorland, but can often be seen feeding on open ground, requiring the nearby cover of scrub or tall vegetation to where it can steal away when danger approaches. It is often found perching in trees, and forms flocks outside the breeding season.

CALL/SONG

Often silent, except for the eerie sounds that the males make. They utter a far-carrying repeated five- or six-syllable bubbling sound "urr-urr'ur-urr-rhuurrr", often with a final flourish "arr-arr-awarr!". This call is interspersed with an explosive "khoo-whish!" or a hoarser "tow-wahh!" The males make these sounds when they are advertising or 'lekking', and although it is possible to find males singing alone, typically there will be a group of them gathered in a selected 'lek' where they bubble away, hoping to attract a mate. Another call is a chuntering "eeh-ee-ee-eh-heh", and the females can utter a loud "pluk-pluk-pluk".

MALE 'LEKKING'

Capercaillie
Tetrao urogallus

LENGTH: 74–89cm (male) 54–63cm (female)

WINGSPAN: 87–125cm

🔊 **CALL:** "ka'ko'ka'ko' uk'k'k'kr'r'r'r'r'r"

⏺ **TRACK:** 1:13

FEMALE

IDENTIFICATION

The male is a huge beast of a gamebird, with blackish-slate overall plumage, a big head, shaggy throat and a big, broad black tail that it cocks and spreads turkey-like when displaying. The wing coverts are dark brown and there is a glossy green sheen to the breast. A white patch at the base of the forewing is visible, as is a patch of red skin above the eye, plus it has a pale bill and feathered legs. The female is a third smaller, brown in colour, and finely marked and patterned with blackish and pale bars and scalloping and with an orangey throat and upper breast which distinguish it from the similar female Black Grouse. The tail is more rufous and longer than in that species.

HABITAT

Found in mature coniferous woodland, especially where there is a mixture of spruce, aspen and birch with plenty of shrubby undergrowth. It feeds on buds, leaves and berries in summer and pine needles in winter, when it can occasionally be found in more open terrain. It is sedentary, becoming extinct in Britain in the eighteenth century but re-introduced to Scotland in the 1800s.

CALL/SONG

The male has a very unusual-sounding display call, a series of notes lasting 5–7 seconds and commencing with some clicking or knocking sounds, accelerating to a 'pop' like a cork popping, followed by rasping hissing noises like the grinding of a knife-sharpener, occasionally followed by a noisy wing-whirr. A version of this can be described as "ka'ko'ka'ko' uk'k'k'kr'r'r'r'r'r", the latter part in a descending roll. This remarkable sound is uttered in spring in dawn displays, by singles or in lekking groups of males, from a tree or on the ground. Other calls given by the male include a belching "ogh'ogh'ogh'ogh'ghr", and some low bubbling sounds. Females give a Pheasant-like "kock-kock" sound, often in the lekking season. Very noisy in flight when flushed.

MALE DISPLAYING

Red-legged Partridge
Alectoris rufa

LENGTH: 32–34cm

WINGSPAN: 47–50cm

🔊 **CALL:** "gochok-chok-chokhrrr"

⏺ **TRACK:** 1:14

vegetation that it can both see above and run across. Small parties are often seen scuttling across bare fields or running startled along country roadsides.

IDENTIFICATION

A dumpy gamebird, it differs from the Grey Partridge in having a black bridle through the eye, curving down across the top of the breast to enclose a white throat. A whitish supercilium outlines a grey and brown crown, and the bill, eye-ring and legs are bright red. The upper breast is marked with a necklace of black spots stretching down from the black throat-ring. The flanks are greyish, boldly marked vertically with bands of black and chestnut and thin whitish lines. The lower breast is grey, the belly rich ochre, and the upperparts are a dull olive-brown. In flight it shows a rusty tail, a feature shared with the Grey Partridge, but only the Red-legged has a grey rump.

HABITAT

A sedentary bird restricted to Western Europe, the population in Britain being derived from an introduction from France in the eighteenth century. Frequently found in arable habitats, it can use a diverse range of cultivated and open country, preferring lowlands though extending up to 2000m in the southern part of its range. It enjoys sunny places, with some barren areas and low

CALL/SONG

Commonly heard in farmland, with their gruff calls coming from crops and field margins. The main call begins with a few hoarse notes and accelerates into a "gochok-chok-chokhrrr" or "kaku'kaku'kuk'ukhurr", repeated rhythmically. The advertising call of males is a similar "gochak-chak-chak go-chak go chak-chak", and they also give a "kot'tach'eh" and "uh'uh'akh'akh'aar". When flushed, they can make a sharp harsh "schtregh-schtrregh", also given on the ground as a predator alert call. A number of other conversational chuntering calls are given in various different social situations.

Grey Partridge
Perdix perdix

LENGTH: 29–31cm

WINGSPAN: 45–48cm

🔊 **CALL:** "skieerrrrkkk"

● **TRACK:** 1:15

IDENTIFICATION

A medium-small rotund bird with a small head, short neck and short legs. It has a pencil-grey head, neck and breast, an orange-rufous face, cheek and throat, and vertical chestnut-brown stripes on the flanks. Both sexes show a large horseshoe of dark brown on the lower belly, more strongly defined on the male. The upperparts are dull brown, lightly barred with black and rusty-brown and streaked with cream. The tail is rusty-red, and females are generally duller than the male.

HABITAT

Much declined throughout its range in Western Europe, even before intensive modern farming techniques became commonplace. Wild populations have been supplemented by introduced stock. It favours flat or gently rolling country, preferring continuous grass or other vegetation not taller than the bird itself. In Britain it is mostly found in cultivated land and arable fields, particularly where there is a shelter strip or set-aside of taller undisturbed cover for refuge and nesting. It also frequents pastures, and in the eastern part of its range can be found on steppe.

CALL/SONG

The most commonly heard call is given by both sexes but used often by the male when he is advertising himself. He sometimes does this from a prominent perch and is often heard during the night. Traditionally likened to the sound of a rusty gate, the long harsh note is described as "skie'errrrkkkh", "kierrik" or "iieerrr'ikh!". Other notes include a truncated version of this call, typically given at dawn, a "cheerr-ikh" or "cheerr-ikh'ikh'kh", and a short "khip-khip-khip", given when flushed. The female has various short, harsh contact notes.

Quail
Coturnix coturnix

LENGTH: 16–18cm

WINGSPAN: 32–35cm

🔊 **CALL:** "hwik-hwik'hwik"

⏺ **TRACK:** 1:16

IDENTIFICATION

A summer visitor, which spends the winter months in Africa, and is a surprisingly small bird at just 30–40 per cent of the weight of a Grey Partridge. It is most frequently seen when flushed from dense ground cover, flying fast, direct and low on long wings and quickly dropping back into cover. The back pattern may be seen in such a view, with longitudinal straw-coloured stripes on its brown back. The male differs from the female in having a black centre to the throat, which is otherwise pale cream. The rest of the head in both sexes is boldly marked, with blackish lines on the face and neck sides, and a long straw-coloured supercilium. The underparts are pale buff, more rufous on the breast, with long brown and black stripes on the flanks.

HABITAT

Breeds on wide plains and open farmland, favouring pastures and hay meadows, traditional grasslands and also steppe in the eastern part of its range. In our region it is typically heard singing from arable crops, such as clover and winter wheat, although ideally not where the vegetation is much taller than itself. It migrates on a broad front, often overshooting, and can appear in strange habitats while on passage.

CALL/SONG

The most audible – and therefore most frequently heard – vocalization is the advertising call (or song) of the male in spring, a far-carrying, rhythmic three-syllable "hwik-hwik'hwik", repeated several times. Often rendered as "wet-my-lips", the bird can be devilishly difficult to locate due to the ventriloquistic qualities of the call. There are additional notes that precede this call, a curious low "ma-wow-mawow-mawow", usually audible only at close range. Various other calls are uttered by both sexes, including a "kree-kree-kree", "hooeet-hooeet" and some low purring and piping sounds. The main call can also be given in flight while migrating at night.

Pheasant
Phasianus colchicus

LENGTH: 66–89cm (inc. tail 35–54cm), female 53–63cm

WINGSPAN: 70–90cm

🔊 **CALL:** "karck-kahk!"

⏺ **TRACK:** 1:17

FEMALE

IDENTIFICATION
The male is unmistakable, a big, brightly plumaged bird with a long olive-brown, black-barred tail, a metallic green head with a large red wattle around the eyes, little tufts at the rear of the crown and a copper-coloured body marked with black and pale scallops. The female is a demure brown all over. Introduced into Western Europe many centuries ago, many are bred for shooting. The plumage can be highly variable due to different races having been released, but the common form typically has a white neck-ring. The natural range extends from north Turkey across to China, and there are a large number of different races with varying plumage characteristics.

HABITAT
Commonly encountered in farmland, where it favours crop fields, pastures and rough ground, woodland edges and open woodland, also in scrub and reedbeds, and anywhere that is a little damp with good ground cover. In their natural range they are shy, and can be found in similar habitats, also extending into the foothills of mountain ranges or into semi-desert regions where water is present.

CALL/SONG
The display or advertising call of the male is a loud far-carrying "karck-kahk!" or "aarrkh-ukh", often followed immediately by a quick audible whirr of the wings. This is usually delivered with the head pointing upwards, and sometimes from a raised perch. Sometimes any loud noise, such as the slamming of a car door, can trigger this call. Both sexes can be noisy when flushed, making loud "kh'kh'k!" or "uuk-ukh! uuk-ukh!" calls. The female also has a piping whistle.

MALE

IDENTIFICATION

Large, with a striking breeding plumage of a glossy black head and neck that ends with a sharp line against a white breast and underparts, a ring around the lower neck of vertical white marks, plus a smaller white chinstrap. The sides of the breast are lined with tight parallel black lines. The upperparts are black with a large area of white on the scapulars and mantle forming a loud chequerboard pattern. In summer the bill is blackish, turning a silver-grey in winter with a dark culmen, and is held level while swimming. In all plumages the 'boxy' shape of the head is distinctive with a steep forehead and flat crown. The winter and juvenile plumages are essentially dark above and pale below, whitish from bill to breast, with a dark half-collar on the lower neck.

HABITAT

Essentially a Nearctic breeder, in our region only nesting regularly in Iceland. It requires large undisturbed lakes with reasonably deep water, small islands and islets for safe nesting, and plenty of space for a long take-off run. In winter it is found mainly on the north-western Atlantic coasts, favouring rocky shores and also often in sheltered bays, harbours and estuaries. In winter it occurs occasionally on inland water bodies such as reservoirs.

CALL/SONG

A wide variety of calls is given in the breeding area, the most famous being an evocative laughing tremolo, commencing with a lower pitched note, very difficult to transcribe but which goes something like "aah-hooo-hoo-hoo-hoo-aah" or "uhh'hw'hwa'hw 'hw'hw'hwa'ho". It is often heard in films (and in early 1990s House music!), where it seems to be added randomly to a

Great Northern Diver
Gavia immer

LENGTH: 69–91cm
WINGSPAN: 122–148cm
CALL: "aah-hooo-hoo-hoo-hoo-aah"
TRACK: 1:18

soundtrack to evoke wild places. It also gives a loud rising wail "arrr-ooo-rr-ooooh", and a more strident chorus of clearer syllables "aow-arr'ow'arr'ow'arr' wow-wah, wow'wah, wow'wah…" or "a-a-woo-kuee-kuee-wheeoo-kwee-wheeoo". All these calls serve a territorial or display function on the breeding grounds. In autumn flocks may give a conversational single-syllable moaning call.

ADULT WINTER PLUMAGE

ADULT SUMMER PLUMAGE

Little Grebe
Tachybaptus ruficollis

LENGTH: 25–29cm

WINGSPAN: 40–45cm

🔊 **CALL:** "trr'r'r'r'r'ii'ii'ii'ii..."

● **TRACK:** 1:19

JUVENILE

IDENTIFICATION

The smallest grebe in our region, with a typically small and dumpy shape, a short neck, stubby bill and buoyant appearance, with the flanks often puffed up so that it appears like a floating ball of fluff. The summer plumage consists of rich chestnut on the face and neck, with a blackish crown and a prominent yellow patch on the gape, rather like that of a fledgling. The upperparts are blackish-brown at all seasons, and the flanks are a clean ochre-brown, richer in summer plumage, and the rear of the stern is off-white. In winter it lacks the chestnut colouration, and the face and neck are ochre-brown; the yellow gape spot is also much reduced.

HABITAT

The Little Grebe is adapted to a wide range of habitats and has a huge world distribution covering Europe, Africa and much of Asia. It can be found on a wide variety of water bodies, although in the breeding season it favours shallow water with muddy bottoms and a good amount of emergent vegetation around the margins. It occurs on some of the smallest pools and even along canals and slow-moving rivers, and is expert at remaining concealed in vegetated margins when necessary. In winter it can be seen on more open waters.

CALL/SONG

The most commonly heard call is a loud trill, "trr 'r'r'r'r'ii'ii'ii'ii'ii...", not unlike a human ululation made with the tongue vibrating against the roof of the mouth, albeit higher pitched. It can rise and fall in pitch and tempo, sometimes falling at the end or petering out. Variable in duration, it is generally given in courtship, although birds can give a harder and harsher trill when annoyed. A variety of shorter calls are also made, such as a quick high-pitched "ki-peep", often extended into "kip kipeep peep peep peep", a high "kidli'dli'dli'li'dit", a low "pip" and a loud sharp "ik" or "ih!" when alarmed.

ADULT

IDENTIFICATION

Unmistakable, with a long, low body and a long, slim erect neck. In breeding plumage it has distinctive head plumes, with two bunches of black feathers forming a double crest, or horns, and the cheek feathers are elongated into fan-like 'tippets', chestnut in colour with a wide black trim. These features are raised and fanned during courtship, but otherwise lie flat to the head. The front of the neck and breast are pure white, the upperparts are dark brown and the flanks are paler brown. In winter it loses the head plumes, showing a white face with a black loral line. In flight it shows white secondaries and forewing.

HABITAT

Commonly encountered on inland freshwater bodies such as lakes, gravel pits, reservoirs, fish-ponds and even canals, breeding in these freshwater habitats where the water is reasonably shallow, the bottom is sandy or muddy, and where there is emergent aquatic vegetation, or reedbed margins where it builds a floating nest of reed-stems and other plant material. Outside the breeding season it can also be found on

Great Crested Grebe
Podiceps cristatus

LENGTH: 46–51cm

WINGSPAN: 85–90cm

🔊 **CALL:** "rrek-rrek-rrek"

⏺ **TRACK:** 1:20

COURTSHIP DISPLAY

brackish water or even on the sea, although usually choosing calmer inshore waters, harbours and bays. It can sometimes be seen on passage, flying along the coast, populations further north and east being more strongly dispersive and migratory than birds in temperate latitudes, which are fairly sedentary.

CALL/SONG

Gives a range of grunting and growling calls, the commonest being a grunting "rrek-rrek-rrek" or "rrra-rrra-rrra", and a growling "kraaarr" or "aarrgh aarrgh aarrgh!", which acts as an advertising call and often carries a long way across open water. In spring, pairs can be seen giving an elaborate head-shaking display where the two birds face each other with necks held long, calling with a ticking "ktic-ktic" and "it! it! it! it!". Various shorter and quieter permutations of these calls are also given, plus a Moorhen-like and repeated "geh-geh-geh!" prior to copulation.

ADULT SUMMER PLUMAGE

Manx Shearwater
Puffinus puffinus

LENGTH: 30–35cm

WINGSPAN: 72–83cm

🔊 **CALL:** "chak-ee-ghar-kha"

⬤ **TRACK:** 1:21

IDENTIFICATION

A medium-small shearwater, and the most numerous and frequently seen one on the Atlantic coasts of our region. It is essentially monochrome, with blackish upperparts and white below, identified from similarly plumaged congeners by the black extending below the eye onto the face, contrasting with the underparts which are white, extending to the undertail, with white underwings bordered with black on the trailing edge. In calmer weather it flaps rapidly with shallow wingbeats on stiff straight wings, interspersed with glides on rigid, slightly downturned wings. In a strong breeze it will glide continuously, banking left and right and shearing from the wavetops up to several metres high in the air. At range, birds can seen shearing in arcs above the breakers, alternately flashing black and white.

HABITAT

Exclusively oceanic, coming ashore only to breed on inshore rocky islands, where it nests colonially in burrows, visiting in the hours of darkness. It nests in large numbers around the Atlantic coasts of Britain and Ireland, and winters south to the eastern coasts of South America. In strong onshore winds it can be seen from headlands around the coast, and near breeding colonies can be observed sitting on the surface whilst waiting for night to fall.

CALL/SONG

Rarely heard calling away from breeding colonies, they produce a variety of growls, cackles, screeches and howls which can be heard at night when the birds come ashore to their nesting burrows. These calls are given both in flight and from the ground, as well as from within the nesting burrow itself. Typical phrases are a cackle followed by a cawing sound, sounding like a strangled cockerel or even a Red-legged Partridge, such as "chak-ee-ghar-kha", "uh'eh'i'i'-awwrrr", "aa-oawrr-uh" and "aa-aar'a!", with individuals varying this sound somewhat.

ADULT AT BURROW

Storm Petrel
Hydrobates pelagicus

LENGTH: 14–18cm

WINGSPAN: 36–39cm

🔊 **CALL:** "ker-Chick!"

⏺ **TRACK:** 1:22

IDENTIFICATION

A tiny seabird, weighing a mere 25g or so and bearing a passing resemblance to a large House Martin. The plumage is black and sooty blackish-brown overall, with a short rounded tail, stubby head and tiny bill. The main plumage feature is the extensive white rump that 'folds around' at the sides, extending on to the lateral undertail coverts, but there is also a white band of varying extent running lengthways along the underwing, formed by white tips to the greater underwing coverts. It flies directly and purposefully, with continuous rapid wingbeats, punctuated with short glides and turns, and when feeding it momentarily flutters and hangs with its wings raised in a dihedral, close to the surface of the water, alighting briefly on occasion.

CALL/SONG

It has a range of vocalizations, heard around the breeding colonies which are visited only at night, the birds typically arriving at dusk and leaving before sunrise. When engaged in aerial courtship chases over the colony they give a flight call "chick!" or "ker-Chick!" varying in strength and frequency depending on how excited the birds become. A curious noise is given from the burrows, a low purring growl "arrr-r-r-r-r-r-r-r-r" or "prrrrrr-uh prrrrrr-uh prrrrrr-uh…" at a rate of 30–40 notes per second, sounding like something from a science fiction movie. It also gives another equally odd call during these audio displays, perhaps in duet, such as "i'i'i'ih'ih!" or "ge-ge-gee giggit!". Silent at sea.

HABITAT

Visiting land only to nest, it is at home on the open ocean, where it spends most of its time out of sight of land. It breeds only along the north-western Atlantic coasts and in the western Mediterranean, migrating in winter as far south as South Africa. Favoured places for breeding colonies are cliffs, islands and rocky places free from ground predators and disturbance, the birds nesting fairly close to water in crevices, burrows and even stone walls.

Bittern
Botaurus stellaris

LENGTH: 70–80cm

WINGSPAN: 125–135cm

CALL: "WHOOOUMP"

TRACK: 1:23

IDENTIFICATION

A large, cryptically plumaged and secretive bird, smaller than a Grey Heron but stockier, compact, and with a thick shaggy neck. The plumage is tawny brown all over, heavily marked with black and dark brown, with a black crown and moustachial stripes. The mantle and wings are barred with black arrowheads. The underparts are striped, with the black moustaches framing a whitish-buff throat, a blackish-brown gular stripe, and long stripes of black and whitish-buff continuing down the breast to the pale belly. It uses its camouflage cunningly, and when threatened or disturbed it will stretch its neck upwards and remain motionless, even gently swaying to imitate the movement of the reeds!

HABITAT

Confined to lowland swamps and marshes, requiring extensive stands of tall emergent vegetation and breeding only in *Phragmites* reedbeds. Outside the breeding season, and particularly in severe cold weather, it can appear on a wider variety of wetlands and water bodies. Usually skulking, although occasionally it can become overconfident of its camouflage and appear in open areas.

CALL/SONG

The male makes a remarkable booming sound when advertising during the breeding season, a very low frequency call (about 160Hz) that can carry for long distances in certain atmospheric conditions, in spite of a relatively low volume. It can be rendered as a "WHOOOUMP", and at fairly close range a quieter additional note can be heard preceding the boom, a short gulping inhalation or 'practice' sound, "woup-WHOOOUMP" or "oo-OOOmph", sometimes extended to three or four notes before the boom. It is most frequently heard in the evenings. At all seasons birds of both sexes can give a harsh "kraau" flight call.

IDENTIFICATION

One of the largest commonly encountered birds in our region, it can often be seen fishing at the water's edge. A long-necked and long-legged bird, with mid-grey upperparts, white and greyish below with a white face and throat. The adult has black crown-stripes extending into elongated plumes, with a central white crown-stripe, greyer in immature birds. On the breast it has a chain of black markings forming two vertical lines. In flight it shows grey coverts and blackish flight feathers, with two small whitish patches on the leading edge, and it has a distinctive flight silhouette of wings strongly bowed. The bill is greenish-yellow, turning pale orange in the breeding season, or intense flame orange during courtship.

HABITAT

A colonial breeder, typically nesting in tall trees with up to ten nests per tree, although it will nest singly and occasionally on the ground in undisturbed places. It can be found in a wide variety of habitats, wherever there is water shallow enough, either standing or flowing, in rivers, streams, marshes, estuaries, floods, lakes, ponds, reservoirs, and outside the breeding season on beaches, lagoons and inlets.

Grey Heron
Ardea cinerea

LENGTH: 22–23cm

WINGSPAN: 175–195cm

CALL: "frahnk!"

TRACK: 1:24

CALL/SONG

The most familiar call is a loud "frahnk!" or "raahnk!", given in flight, often repeated by flying birds every few seconds. A less emphatic version of this call is repeated when a bird comes in to land. A variety of other calls are given at the breeding colony, including a sharp yelping "hrow!" or "aaow!", given by the male when advertising for a mate. Various harsh crowing and cooing sounds are given at different stages of courtship and nesting, such as a throaty "ga'ga'ga'ga", a lower-pitched "wark'wark'wark" and a rasping "aaaagh".

ADULT
SPRING
PLUMAGE

Black Kite
Milvus migrans

LENGTH: 55–60cm

WINGSPAN: 160–180cm

🔊 **CALL:** "peeeeh-ee-ee-ee-ee"

● **TRACK:** 1:25

IDENTIFICATION

Shorter and somewhat smaller than the Red Kite, it is comparable in size to a female Marsh Harrier. Apart from plumage differences from that species, the Black Kite always cruises with the wings bowed and hanging heavy, as opposed to holding them up in a shallow 'V'. It is earth-brown overall, the head a little greyer, and it shows a paler brown band on the upperwing coverts. The underwing is a fairly uniform brown, with an indistinct paler panel on the inner primaries. The belly and vent are rufous-brown, and the tail is grey-brown and with a shallower fork (or notch) than Red Kite. The tail appears triangular or square-ended when spread, usually when soaring or foraging at slow speeds, when it twists it around like a rudder.

HABITAT

Similar to Red Kite, although much less disturbed by the activities of man. It favours partly wooded areas and open country, nesting in a tree, and has a strong affinity for wetland habitats, where it scavenges along the margins for fish and other carrion. It is very adaptable and will eat almost any animal food, and also indulges in piracy of other birds' prey. It can be very sociable and forms large gatherings where carrion is plentiful, such as around rubbish tips. It is more frequently found around cultivated areas and human habitation than Red Kite.

CALL/SONG

Similar to Red Kite, but more vocal than that species. It has a rather petulant, urgent-sounding, shrill whinnying "peeeeh-ee-ee-ee-ee" or "aeow-rr'rr'rr", which is variable in length and intensity. It is given more frequently in the breeding season, by both sexes, and both in flight and at rest. The first syllable is emphasized, and the whinnying becomes more staccato when the bird is excited, as in "pew-e'e'e'e'e". It also gives a mewing whistle, a whingeing "peeeee-eeeee...", with this sound sometimes preceding the main call type.

Red Kite
Milvus milvus

LENGTH: 60–66cm

WINGSPAN: 175–195cm

🔊 **CALL:** "peee-ooo-weeoo-weeoo-weeoo"

⏺ **TRACK:** 1:26

it forages for carrion, its main source of food, though it will also hunt small prey. In Britain it has been re-introduced to many former areas of occurrence.

IDENTIFICATION

A large raptor with a distinctive flight silhouette, it has long, fairly narrow wings, held rather loosely in a slightly bowed fashion or with deep elastic wingbeats. Its tail, deeply forked, long auburn-red to buffy-brown with black corners, is twisted and tilted like a rudder when hunting and foraging. While looking for prey it slowly circles and hangs in the wind, its head facing ground-wards. The body is a rich rufous-orange boldly striated with black, while the head is whitish-grey. The mantle is a black-streaked rufous-brown, and in flight the upperwing shows blackish-brown flight feathers and a paler buffy panel across the wing coverts. The underwing is strikingly patterned with black wingtips and blackish secondaries, a large whitish patch on the inner and middle primaries, rusty underwing coverts and a blackish band along the tips of the coverts forming a prominent bar.

HABITAT

Nests in trees in deciduous woodland, and can be found around woods and copses by open country in lowlands and hills below 600m, though it avoids dense forest. It can frequently be seen over open country, as

CALL/SONG

Generally not very vocal, but the main contact call is a mewing "wheee-oo" or a repeated "wee'wee'wee", sometimes extended into a rather tremulous "weee-oo'oo'oo'oo", sounding somewhere between Buzzard and Black Kite in quality. Also gives a longer, high whinnying whistle, a rising and falling "peee-ooo-weeoo-weeoo-weeoo" or "eee-oooo-eee-oooo-eee-oooo", and a plaintive "oo-eeeer". If disturbed at the nest or alarmed in other situations, it will call with a repeated "peee-ee-ee-ee".

Marsh Harrier
Circus aeruginosus

LENGTH: 48–56cm

WINGSPAN: 115–130cm

🔊 **CALL:** "whee-ahh"

⬤ **TRACK:** 1:27

FEMALE

IDENTIFICATION

A medium-sized raptor and the largest of the harriers, with a slim body and head, long tail, and long wings held in a shallow 'V' when hunting low over the ground. The sexes differ, the male having a pencil-grey tail, flight feathers and lesser coverts, contrasting with a rich brown back, rump and upperwing coverts. The outer primaries are black above and below, and the underwing is grey washed with rusty-brown. The underparts of the body are buff with a rich rufous wash on the belly. The female is a uniform chocolate-brown, with contrasting creamy throat, crown and leading edge of the upperwing. Juveniles are similar to females, but darker brown with a ginger-buff crown and throat.

HABITAT

In the breeding season it favours low-lying marshy wetlands, shallow lakes and river valleys, particularly where there are *Phragmites* reedbeds, in which it nests on the ground. Outside the breeding season it occurs around a wide variety of water bodies and wet areas, and also on arable land. The western European population is sedentary, but further east this species is a summer visitor, migrating to Africa or India in winter.

CALL/SONG

Vocal only really during the breeding season, when the male will call with a far-carrying "whee-ahh whee-ahh" while soaring to a great height. This is part of his 'sky-dance' display flight, in which after ascending he plunges earthwards while simultaneously performing aerobatic tumbles and twists, before zooming upwards again to repeat the process. Both sexes have a Kestrel-like chattering call "kek-kek-kek-kek-kek", given as an intruder-alarm when disturbed, as well as a softer "pepepepepepep". When food is exchanged between male and female near the nest, the female gives a sibilant "seeee-oo" call. The male also has a chuckling call.

MALE

FEMALE

Sparrowhawk
Accipiter nisus

LENGTH: 28–38cm

WINGSPAN: 55–70cm

🔊 **CALL:** "kew-kew-kew-kew"

⏺ **TRACK:** 1:28

IDENTIFICATION

A small raptor, with short, broad blunt-tipped wings and a long square-ended tail. It has a distinctive flight pattern, and in level flight makes a few rapid flaps interspersed with a glide. The sexes differ, the female being 25 per cent larger (and 40 per cent heavier), the male quite diminutive and roughly the size of a Mistle Thrush. The male has blue-grey upperparts, orange-rufous cheeks and barring on the underparts, whereas the female has dark brown or slaty upper-parts, with brown bars on the underparts and a prominent pale supercilium. Immature birds are dark brown above, and both sexes show a tail barred with four dark bands. Soaring on flat wings, the presence of a Sparrow-hawk is often announced by the alarm calls of the small birds that form its prey.

HABITAT

Strongly tied to woods and forested areas, selecting both deciduous and coniferous trees for nesting. It hunts by flying low and fast through patches of woodland and along forest edges, hedges, gardens or any areas that provide adequate flying space, often "hedge-hopping" in order to catch prey by surprise attack.

CALL/SONG

Only really vocalizing in the breeding season in the vicinity of the nest, the call is a chattering "eh!eh!eh!eh!eh!" or "kew-kew-kew-kew", which is given in a variety of situations; as a contact call between parents, rapidly by the female as an intruder-alarm call, loudly and slowly by the male as an advertising call, or more quietly when he brings food for the female or chicks at the nest. Another call is a high, shrill "peeeee-peeeee-peeeee" or "wheee'wheee'wheee…", often uttered as an alarm near the nest or as a contact call from fledged young.

MALE

Buzzard
Buteo buteo

LENGTH: 51–57cm

WINGSPAN: 113–128cm

🔊 **CALL:** "peeee'yahh"

⏺ **TRACK:** 1:29

IDENTIFICATION

The commonest and most widespread medium-sized raptor in our region. In soaring flight it holds its broad wings pressed forward slightly in a shallow 'V', and the short broad tail is spread. It glides with wings held flat, or cruises with them cranked and angled at the carpal joint. It has a compact body, thick neck and short rounded head, and the plumage is variable – typically uniform dark brown above with a dark brown head and chest, a lighter patch on the breast that is always paler than the brown belly or belly sides. The tail is greyish or paler brown, and adults have a darker terminal band. The carpal patches are obviously darker, flight feathers are greyish and the primary and secondary tips are dark, forming a dark wingtip and trailing edge.

HABITAT

Preferred habitat is a mosaic of woodland and open areas, the former for breeding and refuge, the latter for hunting, which takes place over clearings, farmland, grassland, pastures and forest edge. This species is often seen and heard in hilly country, soaring around on updrafts, and not infrequently hovers rather awkwardly. It typically nests in a tree in woodland, both deciduous and coniferous, although it may nest on the ground, such as on a cliff or bluff when in treeless habitats such as moorland.

CALL/SONG

Quite vocal, particularly while around its territory in the breeding season. It gives a loud plaintive disyllabic cry "peeee'yahh" and "peeeeooh", uttered usually on the wing but also while perched. Various permutations are given in different situations, and around the nest or during courtship it can be heard to make a very high-pitched shrill "eeee'o 'eeee'o 'eeee'o", a begging "iihp iihp iihp iihp" and a rather corvid-like "how! how!", but generally the vocabulary is limited. It makes up for its lack of vocal range by calling frequently!

Osprey
Pandion haliaetus

LENGTH: 55–58cm

WINGSPAN: 145–170cm

🔊 **CALL:** "piou-piou-piou-piou"

⏺ **TRACK:** 1:30

IDENTIFICATION

A large raptor with unique plumage and a distinctive silhouette. It has a slim body, shortish tail and long wings that are cranked at the carpal, which is pushed forwards. When soaring, the long forewing is drooped and the secondaries raised. The small head is white, with a brown line through the eye, and the underparts are pure white with a brownish wash across the breast, darker in the female. The upperparts are uniform deep brown, while the underwing is well marked with white underwing coverts, grey flight feathers (which are barred), and there is a strong blackish bar along the tips of the wing coverts. It also shows a prominent black carpal patch and black primary tips.

HABITAT

Dependent on its food source of medium-sized fish, it can be found around unpolluted lakes, rivers, estuaries, reservoirs and other freshwater bodies, and while on passage can visit an even wider variety of wetlands and coastal habitats. It has a global distribution, with northern breeders migrating south in winter, and some populations have adapted to marine habitats. It often nests in a large tree such as a pine, although in some parts of the world it breeds commonly on a cliff or on the ground.

CALL/SONG

Calls are typically restricted to the breeding season and usually within the nest territory, where it can be quite vocal. A variety of whistles and yelping calls is given, these typically getting faster and sharper if the bird is excited. The male's flight display in spring is an undulating "sky-dance" with legs dangling, calling with a repeated shrill drawn-out "pyeep-pyeep". Other calls include a peeping "piou-piou-piou-piou" or "eeh-eeh-eeh" whistle, given as an alarm, speeding up if the bird becomes more agitated, also "peop-peop-peowp-pewp" and a high, short and descending "siew! siew! siew!". It also has a sharp "kyep" contact call.

ADULT

Kestrel
Falco tinnunculus

LENGTH: 32–35cm

WINGSPAN: 71–80cm

🔊 **CALL:** "kee-kee-kee-kee"

⏺ **TRACK:** 1:31

FEMALE
HOVERING

IDENTIFICATION

A medium-small falcon with a long tail and wings, and the only falcon to habitually hover. It fans the tail while doing so, angling the body at 45 degrees as it scans the ground for prey. In level flight it flaps rapidly and rather weakly, the slim body and long tail giving it a distinctive silhouette. The sexes differ: the male is brick-red on the mantle and wing coverts with black primaries and primary coverts making a distinctive and readily identifiable upperwing pattern. The head is grey, with a weak black moustache below the eye, the tail is grey with a broad black terminal band. The underparts are buffy and spotted black, as are the pale underwings. The female is less reddish, with a brown head, browner wings, a duller black-barred tail and overall is more spotted and barred than the male.

HABITAT

Resident in Western Europe, and ranging right across Asia and Africa. It avoids dense forests, desert, barren mountains and large treeless wetlands, but can be found virtually anywhere else. It is able to take advantage of almost every habitat, is often to be seen hunting along motorways, and even penetrates into urban areas. It is an efficient and adaptable hunter, and will nest most often in an old crow's nest, although it can utilize many different nest sites.

CALL/SONG

Like many other raptors, the Kestrel is only really vocal in the breeding season and around the nest. The most frequently heard call is a rapid series of sharp "kee-kee-kee-kee" notes, sometimes as "kik-kik-kik" or "i'i'i'i'i'i", becoming sharper and shorter when excited or alarmed. Other calls include a tremulous trilling cry "kri-ee-ee-ee-ee-ee" or "trree-r-r-r-r-eee", variable in length and intensity, and also a more plaintive "whee'u whee'u" and an often repeated sharp "kek" or "pik".

MALE

Hobby
Falco subbuteo

LENGTH: 30–36cm

WINGSPAN: 82–92cm

CALL: "keer-keer-keer-keer-keer"

TRACK: 1:32

IDENTIFICATION

An elegant and dashing falcon, with long wings and a medium-long tail, this species is highly agile in the air, taking prey when on the wing and often eating it while in flight! The upperparts are a uniform dark blue-grey, while the underparts are creamy-white, boldly streaked black from breast to belly. The adult has plain brick-red lower belly, thighs and undertail coverts. The head pattern is striking, with a whitish throat, cheeks and half-collar, and a black mask with long and prominent black moustaches. At rest the wingtips extend beyond the tail.

HABITAT

A summer visitor to our region, exploiting the warmer months when large flying insects are available. It inhabits open country with isolated trees and woods, parkland and savannah-like areas, and nests in a tall tree, often in an old nest of a Carrion Crow. It favours areas where there is a rich food source, ranging widely while feeding, and in addition to insects will feed on a wide variety of small bird species such as hirundines and even Swifts, all caught on the wing. A long-distance migrant wintering in southern Africa, it can be seen on passage in a wider variety of habitats.

CALL/SONG

The most frequently heard call, almost only ever heard near the nest, is a rather high and strangled "kew-kew-kew-kew" or "keer-keer-keer-keer-keer", ascending in pitch and often likened to the song of Wryneck, although that is rarely heard now in Britain! Variations of this call are given in different situations – in alarm the call will become more shrill and chattering, decelerating into softer drawn-out calls such as "ivikh! ivikh! ivikh!". It also gives a short sharp "kipp" call, a "whit-yoo" call when high in the air and excited, and the begging call is a drawn-out urgent "peee-eh".

Peregrine
Falco peregrinus

LENGTH: 38–46cm

WINGSPAN: 89–113cm

🔊 **CALL:** "khhe'khhe'khhhe'khhe"

⏺ **TRACK:** 1:33

IDENTIFICATION

A powerful medium-large falcon, very adept in the air and agile in flight. While there are subtle sexual plumage differences, a greater difference is the size, the female being 15 per cent larger and up to 40 per cent heavier than the male. The upperparts are slate-grey, with a paler blue-grey on the rump that contrasts with the darker, closely banded tail. On the head, the grey of the upperparts merges into the black crown and broad black moustachial stripe, which forms a distinctive black hood. The throat, cheek and remaining underparts are white, and from the lower breast to the vent it is closely barred with black, which may appear grey at range. The female should show a more extensive white breast than the male, contrasting quite strongly with the barred belly, a feature which in both sexes is visible at great range.

HABITAT

Widespread and able to utilize a wide variety of habitats, although this is often strongly related to the availability of secure nesting sites. It occurs over all kinds of open country and typically nests on crags and rocky outcrops in moorland and mountainous areas, and also on coastal cliffs. Some pairs will use tall buildings in urban areas, and overall they are very adaptable. Their main prey is small- to medium-sized birds, which are taken on the wing after a chase, often following a very steep and fast stoop with the wings held close to the body.

CALL/SONG

Mostly silent away from breeding areas, where it can be quite vocal, particularly when disturbed. The most frequently heard call is perhaps the harsh persistent "khhe'khhe'khhhe'khhe" or "rehhk-rehhk-rehhk", which becomes faster and shorter when alarmed, such as "kak-kak-kak-kak". There is also a begging "wheeeer-kheeeer-kheeeer…", and another call described as a 'rusty hinge' sound, given in greeting and courtship, such as "ee'Yukh ee'Yukh ee'Yukh" or "ee-chip". A variant on this is used in antagonistic situations, "klee-CHIP" when coming from the male, and "klee-CHUCK" from the female.

IDENTIFICATION

A slender rail with long red legs, a long neck and a long red-and-black bill. The tail is cocked as it walks, exposing a single triangular panel of buffy-white feathers. The upperparts are dark olive-brown from crown to tail, well marked with black feather centres that form long streaks along the back. The face, neck, breast and belly are a dark blue-grey, the flanks boldly marked with black-and-white vertical stripes. Typically seen as it emerges from reedbeds in the evening to forage along muddy edges.

HABITAT

A wetland bird favouring shallow freshwater habitats with tall dense aquatic vegetation such as *Phragmites* reedbeds, with associated shallow margins of exposed mud or muddy breaks and dykes. It can adapt to a variety of smaller wetland habitats, provided cover is available, and wintering birds in Britain can be found on watercress beds, around pools and in ditches. It is usually very skulking, but in hard weather can be pushed into atypical habitats and locations, even leaving cover to walk around on snow or ice.

CALL/SONG

The commonest and most familiar call, often heard coming from a dense reedbed and sometimes in response to a loud noise like a slamming car door, is a far-carrying 'pig squeal'. Typically of up to six notes, rather explosive in delivery and ranging from a hoarse and mournful groaning to a higher-pitched scream, it descends

Water Rail
Rallus aquaticus

LENGTH: 23–28cm

WINGSPAN: 38–45cm

CALL: "wheeah-wheeah-wheeah-wheeah"

TRACK: 1:34

and trails off towards the end: "wheeah-wheeah-wheeah-wheeah-wheeoh…". This call is used for advertising, display, alarm and other territorial purposes, and often by a pair calling antiphonally. The courtship call, used in spring by both sexes, is a long rhythmic series of short sharp notes "ghik-ghik-ghik-ghik", delivered in groups of notes that accelerate slightly, the female adding a short rolling trill to the end of her phrases, such as "eerrrrr'eeeew". A variety of other short grunts and squeals are uttered in different circumstances, such as "kik-kik-ke'weew" and "eevip" or "eeeyip".

Spotted Crake
Porzana porzana

LENGTH: 22–24cm

WINGSPAN: 37–42cm

🔊 **CALL:** "hwhitt! hwhitt! hwhitt!"

⏺ **TRACK:** 1:35

IDENTIFICATION

Slightly smaller than Water Rail, with rather long wings and a longish tail which is often cocked. The bill is short, orange-yellow with a red base of varying intensity in adults, and brownish in juveniles. The upperparts and wings are a warm olive-brown, boldly marked with blackish feather centres and covered with a profusion of white spots and arrowheads, appearing both singly and arranged in lines. The crown is brown streaked black, the lores are blackish, and the eyebrow, face, throat and breast are grey, washed brown on the cheeks and breast sides and flecked with small white spots. This spotting extends all the way down the underparts and become larger on the flanks, where they are arranged in vague vertical bars. The undertail coverts are buff and clearly visible when the tail is cocked. The legs are a rather pale green.

HABITAT

Found in swampy habitats, such as fens and marshes, where it favours dense vegetation, typically of rush (*Juncus* sp.) together with various grasses and other aquatic plants of low to medium stature (although in Britain it can frequent large reedbeds). It requires shallow water and muddy margins alongside thick vegetation, from which it can sometimes be seen emerging at dawn and dusk.

CALL/SONG

The advertising call or 'song' is very distinctive and produced by both sexes, although more commonly by the male. It consists of a loud repeated "hwhitt!" or "hwatth!", slightly ascending and like a loud echoing drip of water or the sound of a whip cutting through the air. It is repeated continually at a rate of one note per second, particularly at night during the breeding season. Occasionally the female will duet with a male, uttering a similar, softer call. Other vocalizations include a croaking "kwe-kwe-kwe", a sharp "kyak" given when distressed, and another repeated call, "chick-chuck chick-chuck chick-chuck", said to resemble the ticking of a clock. The calls are often the only evidence of this notoriously elusive bird.

Corncrake
Crex crex

LENGTH: 27–30cm

WINGSPAN: 46–53cm

CALL: "crex-crex, crex-crex"

TRACK: 1:36

IDENTIFICATION

In size and shape the Corncrake resembles a thickset, short-billed Water Rail, with long legs and a fairly long neck, which is craned upwards when calling. The wings are chestnut, and their colour obvious when seen in flight. The forehead, eyebrow and breast are pale blue-grey, the eye is beady, and the upperparts are brown with the bold blackish centres of the feathers forming strong lines from nape to tail. The flanks are rufous-brown, with white feather tips forming clear vertical bars. A very skulking bird.

HABITAT

A summer visitor, wintering in Africa. Unlike other crakes, it is not found in marshy and wetland areas but instead favours grassland, damp meadows and pastures, also getting into crops such as clover and cereals. In Britain it occurs mainly in traditionally harvested hay meadows, its survival not being compatible with modern farming methods. Much declined in Britain, and mostly restricted to the Western Isles of Scotland.

CALL/SONG

This bird takes its scientific name from its call, a loud and continuous rasping "crex-crex, crex-crex, crex-crex", given by the male in spring. To different ears it can sound like "grrehhk-grrehhk", "rehhrp-rehhrp" or "eeerkh-eekh". Used as an advertising and territorial call, and also to attract a mate, it can be heard in spring when males often call continually through the night. The call covers a wide spectrum of frequency, and when calling close by, the lower frequencies sound very loud and have a 'ripping' quality. The bird can be lured by imitations such as drawing a fingernail across the tips of a comb, although the first one ever encountered by the author was lured closer using an accordion! Other calls are given – the male has a mewing, grunting growl, the female a cheeping call and a sharp quacking "ook-ook-ook-ack-ack-ack", plus a Moorhen-like call given by either parent in alarm to their young.

Moorhen
Gallinula chloropus

LENGTH: 32–35cm

WINGSPAN: 50–55cm

🔊 **CALL:** "prrrruwk!"

⏺ **TRACK:** 1:37

IDENTIFICATION

A familiar medium sized rail, roughly between Coot and Water Rail in size. It is a dark slaty-grey on the neck and underparts, blacker on the head, and shows two striking white flashes on the undertail, separated centrally by black. The upperparts are dark olive-brown, and along the flanks it shows a prominent white stripe. The bill is red, tipped yellow, with a red-frontal shield, and the legs are green. Juveniles are paler and grey-brown.

HABITAT

Common and widespread, successfully adapting to almost any wetland habitat where dense cover exists in conjunction with freshwater, right down to the smallest dykes, ditches, ponds, slow-moving rivers and even in city parks. It is often not skulking, and can frequently be seen walking and grazing in open areas such as fields, pastures and other dry land, always within easy reach of cover if alarmed or disturbed. It is quite arboreal, roosting in bushes and trees, and is equally at home flying, walking or swimming, which it does with a characteristic head-jerking movement.

CALL/SONG

The common sound indicating the presence of this bird is a rather explosive "prrrruwk!", sometimes delivered in a two-syllable variant "kurr-rruck" or "kirr'rr'rk". It has a variety of similar abrupt and sometimes murmuring calls, such as a quiet "pook-pook-pook" etc., and a sharp "keh-keh!", "ik'ik'ik'ik" and "kittick!", delivered in alarm. It calls in flight, a sound that can be heard sometimes from wandering birds at night over urban areas, an "eggkh-eggkh-kehk", not dissimilar to the call of the Black-tailed Godwit.

TERRITORIAL
SQUABBLING

Coot
Fulica atra

LENGTH: 36–42cm	
WINGSPAN: 70–80cm	
🔊 **CALL:** "kuhk!"	
⏺ **TRACK:** 1:38	

IDENTIFICATION

A rather buoyant, fat-looking bird, completely uniform charcoal-black with an obvious white bill and frontal shield on the forehead. In flight it shows grey flight feathers with a white trailing edge to the secondaries. The eye is red and the feet greyish-pink. Often in large groups on lakes, diving or up-ending, but will also graze on grassy margins. It flies well, with its curious flat-lobed feet trailing behind, but take-off is rather messy with lots of splashing and pattering on the surface before lift-off is achieved.

HABITAT

Very common and widespread over much of our region, Coot can be found on a variety of freshwater habitats, preferring rather shallow water where they can feed on submerged or emergent vegetation. They avoid water bodies with confined spaces, requiring a reasonable amount of open water, and outside the breeding season can congregate in large numbers on larger lakes and reservoirs.

CALL/SONG

The most commonly heard call, and the one that it supposedly takes its name from, is a short sharp "kuhk!" or "geowh!", quite loud and often repeated, variable in tone and volume and given more conversationally as "egh-ekh-egh-ekh" . Another similar call is a harder sequence of pairs of sharp notes, "uk-owk uk-owk uk-owk", plus it gives a very short, high-pitched explosive "ihh!" or "pip!", given in aggression or intimidation towards fellow Coots. It often makes quite a lot of noise by splashing about, and also gives a strangled "gheeo" when flying around its territory on spring nights. Juveniles and small chicks can often be heard calling, with a weak and plaintive "whee-ip".

Crane
Grus grus

LENGTH: 110–120cm

WINGSPAN: 220–245cm

🔊 **CALL:** "krrruuh"

⚫ **TRACK:** 1:39

IDENTIFICATION

A large elegant bird, standing tall on long legs or forming a large silhouette in flight. It is distinctive in shape, with a small head, short pointed bill, long neck, long legs and a cloak of loose tertial feathers, known as a bustle, hanging over the tail and wingtips. In flight it carries the neck outstretched and the broad wings are held rigid and flat, with a strong upstroke. The head and neck are black, with a discrete small red crown patch and a bold white band from the rear of the eye down the length of the neck. The remaining upperparts are ash-grey, often becoming stained with brown, and the flight feathers are black, visible at rest on the tip of the bustle.

HABITAT

Breeds in bogs, damp moors, swampy clearings in forest and in reedbeds, wet areas such as pools or lakes, and always where undisturbed by humans. Migrates along narrow traditional flyways with regular stop-off points, and winters in open country around lakes or marshes, or on and around arable land.

CALL/SONG

The call of the Crane gives the bird its name in several languages, such as *Grue* in French or *Daru* in Hungarian. It is a loud, far-carrying trumpeting sound that is variable in pitch and strength depending on the situation, and can be described as a "krrruuh", "krRRuuooh" or a more gutteral "krrraa". It is used as a contact call, in greeting or in excitement, and can be given singly or in a repeated sequence of notes. A pair will duet with a more musical alternating and repeated "krroo 'krree 'krroo 'krree" or "errkh'rr ekhrr'o" etc. Cranes in flight give similar notes, and when made by a flock these become a cacophony of differently pitched "krrruuh" notes running together. Young birds accompanying such flocks are also quite audible, making a plaintive high-pitched and slightly hoarse "peee-ee" or "cheeerp".

ADULT WINTER PLUMAGE

Oystercatcher
Haematopus ostralegus

LENGTH: 40–46cm

WINGSPAN: 80–86cm

🔊 **CALL:** "kleeep!"

⬤ **TRACK:** 1:40

IDENTIFICATION

A large, bulky and strikingly coloured wader, with a long stout, blunt-tipped, orangey-red bill used for chiselling open molluscs, medium-length pink legs, and an orange-red eye-ring. At rest it shows a white belly and lower breast, and in flight the broad white wingbar, back and rump become obvious. The remainder of the plumage is a glossy black, although in winter plumage it acquires a whitish throat-strap. First-winter birds are browner above with a dark tip to the bill.

HABITAT

Most commonly found along coasts, where it favours shingle and pebbly beaches, seaweed-rich rocks, tidal mud, sandy flats, beaches, and any intertidal areas where it can find its favourite food of molluscs. It is also found breeding inland, particularly along river valleys, lakes with suitable shingle islands, and also in grassy fields and pastures. A ground nester like most shorebirds, it lays its eggs in a shallow depression on bare ground or shingle.

CALL/SONG

A noisy and obvious bird, with a range of loud shrill piping calls. The common call is a "kleeep!" or a two-syllable "ke-beeep!", often heard in flight. Other commonly heard calls are a sharper repeated "kip"or "keep", given excitedly in alarm when the nest or young are approached by intruders. Further calls include a higher-pitched "keeuup" and "kepiouw", with these and the "ke-beeep" calls often run together with a Curlew-like trilling when in a pair or a small gathering to make a 'piping song', such as "kip'kip'kip'kip'ke-beep' ke-beep' ke-beep' klikliklikliklikli' krrrrrr…".

ADULT SUMMER PLUMAGE

Avocet
Recurvirostra avosetta

LENGTH: 42–46cm

WINGSPAN: 77–80cm

🔊 **CALL:** "kluut"

⏺ **TRACK:** 1:41

male is blacker, the female often having a browner tinge. The legs are pale bluish-grey.

IDENTIFICATION

An unmistakable, graceful and elegant bird, with a striking plumage of black patterns on white. It has a unique slender upcurved bill which accounts for 20 per cent of the bird's total length and is used to make distinctive lateral sweeping motions when feeding. The plumage is white overall, with a black cap and rear of neck, broad black brace-like lines across its back, a pair of broad black transverse lines on the wing coverts and black wingtips. The

HABITAT

Very much a coastal bird in Europe, in the breeding season preferring shallow saline and brackish lagoons, saltpans, deltas, estuaries and flat open seashores with dry sandy or muddy flats, usually with a minimum of vegetation where it can nest. It can also be found well inland where there are saline lakes. Outside the breeding season it can be found commonly on estuaries, mudflats and other tidal areas, and occasionally on large lakes and reservoirs with shallow edges.

CALL/SONG

The main call is a rather clipped, slightly ascending fluty whistle "kluut", (which is in fact the Dutch name of the bird) or "hlout! hlout!", often repeated as "kluut' kluut' kluut' kluut' kluut", becoming rather shrill as birds become more agitated. Frequently noisy, very much so near their colonial nest clusters where they behave aggressively to any inbound predators, or indeed any other bird, so much so that their calling can become a continuous cacophony. Also calls with a shorter, lower-pitched "kup", a higher-pitched "kleeup" and an even higher "klitp!".

IDENTIFICATION

A cryptically plumaged bird, with a strange reptilian appearance due to the large yellow eyes set in a rather small head. Fairly sizeable, and resembling a large plover, the Stone Curlew has long yellowish legs with a prominent tibiotarsal joint, from which is derived its other name of Thick-knee. It has a shortish yellow bill with a black distal half. The plumage is a sandy-brown streaked with black, and at rest it has a prominent wingbar, a white stripe bordered above and below in black. In flight this is also quite striking, as are the black wingtips. Crepuscular, it is mostly active at twilight and night.

HABITAT

Essentially a bird of semi-desert and arid areas within the temperate zone, it favours sandy plains and heaths, stony bare ground, fallow or dry fields and anywhere with bare and dry open areas without vegetation or with a very short sward. In Britain it is found on sandy heaths and on sandy or stony arable land in the south-east of England, and in autumn can form large gatherings on similar habitats prior to southward migration for the winter.

CALL/SONG

The common English nomenclature uses the "Curlew" name due to the similarity of some of the calls to those of the unrelated Curlew *Numenius*

Stone Curlew
Burhinus oedicnemus

LENGTH: 38–45cm

WINGSPAN: 77–85cm

CALL: "kee-oo-lee"

TRACK: 1:42

arquata. Most commonly heard at night or at twilight, when it can be very vocal, particularly on the breeding grounds. There is a similarity to Oystercatcher and Avocet in the quality of the voice, and the main call is a clear loud trisyllabic "kee-oo-lee". The display call or song is a long and rising sequence with a Barn Owl-like hoarse rasping sound "ukhhhhh-lipp" ascending on the second note, preceding a chorus of this sound added to the main call, such as "ki-ukhhhh-lee ki-ukhhhh-lee ki-ukhhhh-lee ki-ukhhhh-lee ki-ukhhhh-lee". It also has a thin piping "kiiiiie", and in alarm gives a series of "ku-vuee-vuue" notes.

Little Ringed Plover
Charadrius dubius

LENGTH: 14–17cm
WINGSPAN: 42–48cm
🔊 **CALL:** "pee-oo"
⬤ **TRACK:** 1:43

JUVENILE

IDENTIFICATION

Very similar to the Ringed Plover at first glance, but is smaller, slimmer and more attenuated, with a bold yellow eye-ring. Although it has a pattern of black rings and bands similar to Ringed, with black cheeks, lores and band over the forecrown, Little Ringed shows a white band across the posterior edge of the black on the crown that connects with the white over and behind the eye. The breast and collar band is also narrower. The legs are pinkish-grey, and the upperwing is plain and lacks any wingbar. The bill is thinner and longer than that of Ringed, and black in summer.

HABITAT

Essentially a freshwater version of Ringed Plover, this is a summer visitor that breeds on sandy and gravelly banks and along the borders of pools, lakes, reservoirs, salt pans and gravel pits, as well as on river banks. It can occasionally be found on industrial sites and at quarries where open sandy or dry areas exist adjacent to a little freshwater and mud. On passage it occurs more widely, but tends to avoid coastal habitats.

CALL/SONG

The main call is distinctly different from that of Ringed Plover, a descending "pee-oo" with the emphasis on the first syllable and with a short second syllable. Typically a clear piping sound, it can acquire a gravelly quality when given in different situations, as do some of its other calls. The note given in alarm is a shorter and more urgent "peeau!" or "ee-eau!", sometimes in a trisyllabic "peeo! ee-oo' ee-oo", the latter two notes lower in pitch. The display song is a deeper "pee-po pee-po pee-po pee-po", interspersed with a higher "kip kip kip" and a more gravelly "gree-yo gree-yo gree-yo gree-yo", with repeated phrases of "ip'ip'gree-yo" or "ip'ip'pee-boh". Also breaks into a hard chipping and trilling not unlike the call of the Oystercatcher.

ADULT SUMMER PLUMAGE

Ringed Plover
Charadrius hiaticula

LENGTH: 18–20cm

WINGSPAN: 48–57cm

CALL: "tooo-i"

TRACK: 1:44

IDENTIFICATION

A small but stocky and robust-looking plover, with a typical feeding action of running a few paces and then pausing, running and pausing, and tilting downwards to take food from the ground. It has a short orange black-tipped bill and orange legs. The striking head pattern consists of black cheeks (duller in the female) with black bridles over the crown and over the top of the bill, enclosing a white forehead. It has a small white patch behind the eye, and a broad black ring across the breast, narrowing but connecting around the back of the neck. It has sandy-brown upperparts, is white below, and has a long white wingbar in flight.

HABITAT

A common bird of coastal regions, favouring coastal habitats such as sandy and muddy beaches and, for breeding, sandy or gravelly beaches with sparse short-stature vegetation. Occasionally it can be found on sandy heaths, meadows and cultivation, and in higher latitudes can be found breeding above the tree line and on tundra. Outside the breeding season it can be found in a wide variety of coastal habitats, such as mudflats, estuaries, shallow lagoons with exposed mud, marshes and even rocky coastlines. It is less frequently encountered inland, on lakes, reservoirs and rivers.

CALL/SONG

The typical call is a soft rising "poo-eep" or "tooo-i", with more emphasis on the second syllable. The alarm call is a similar but shorter monosyllabic piping "wheep!" or "whilp!", typically given repeatedly by an agitated bird, and sounding a little like the call of an Avocet. The song or display call is given together with a display flight, in which the bird will fly in a circuit low over the ground with slow, deliberate and rather bat-like wingbeats, calling "te-wheuoo te-wheuoo te-wheuoo te-wheuoo te-wheuoo te-wheuoo…" and "t'wheedle t'wheedle t'wheedle…" or "wheedly-wheedly-wheedly…", plus a chorus that sounds more like a series of single notes, such as "irr'h'irr'h 'irr'h'irr'h'irr'h…" or "te-too-ee te-too-ee te-too-ee te-too-ee te-too-ee…".

ADULT SUMMER PLUMAGE

ADULT WINTER PLUMAGE

Golden Plover
Pluvialis apricaria

LENGTH: 25–29cm

WINGSPAN: 67–76cm

🔊 **CALL:** "tlui"

⏺ **TRACK:** 1:45

ADULT WINTER
PLUMAGE

IDENTIFICATION

It shares the same overall shape with the Grey Plover, but is a slimmer and more elegant bird, and usually found in different habitats. It is shorter-legged and narrower-winged, and has a strong yellowish tone to the upperparts, which in summer are strongly spangled black and gold. In winter the plumage is fairly uniform, with paler underparts finely marked with golden and dusky mottling. In summer the face, central neck and belly are black, surrounded with a broad white rim. The extent of black is variable, northern populations showing much more than southern populations, and southern females having the least black of all.

ADULT SUMMER
PLUMAGE

HABITAT

Breeds on upland moors and peat bogs with short heather and grass, preferring an open habitat where it can see and run unhindered. It also breeds on tundra, on mountains above the tree line, and on upland pastures. For the remainder of the year it is commonly found in large flocks on bare fields, in stubble or in short-stature crops, on pastures and other similar areas away from wetlands and the coast, although it commonly uses intertidal mud-flats and sand banks for roosting, commuting back to fields for feeding.

CALL/SONG

The common flight call heard at all seasons is a plaintive mellow "tlui" or "too-ee", typically monosyllabic but sometimes extended with a slight descent in the note. This can also be given from the ground as a flatter, more insistent note "pl'eeh", and on the breeding grounds is given as an alarm when parents will start calling upon spying an intruder at considerable distance. The song is a far-carrying call given in a song flight, where normal flight is replaced by slow, deep, deliberate wingbeats, at a slower speed, calling "per-wheo per-wheo" or "pu'peee-oo pu'peee-oo", repeated a number of times. In addition to this call is a bright cyclical "whe-wheedli'whe-wheedli'whe-wheedli…" or "ihrrulya'ihrrulya'ihrrulya'ihrrulya…", an almost bubbling sound that can sometimes be heard at other seasons.

IDENTIFICATION

A large robust plover, with a stout body, rather bold eye, large head and short stout bill. It feeds in typical plover fashion, running a few paces and pausing before tilting down to pick up food items. In winter it looks very grey, rather plain on the head with whitish underparts, and vaguely patterned with darker grey on the upperparts. Juveniles are more streaked below and are patterned with buffy-yellow on the upperparts. In summer plumage Grey Plovers are very striking, with jet-black face, neck and breast down to the tarsus, contrasting with brightly patterned upperparts that are spangled with black and silver. In all plumages the diagnostic feature, visible in flight, is an obvious black patch on the 'armpit' or axillaries, plus a white wingbar and rump.

HABITAT

Breeds in the high Arctic, where it favours damp tundra. In the non-breeding months it ranges southwards across the globe, with many wintering in the tropical zone. In our region it is found in coastal habitats such as mudflats, estuaries, saltmarshes, beaches and anywhere with expanses of mud or sand in the intertidal zone. It can congregate in large numbers at high tide roosts, but otherwise is usually seen singly. It is unusual inland or on freshwater habitats.

Grey Plover
Pluvialis squatarola

LENGTH: 26–30cm
WINGSPAN: 56–83cm
🔊 **CALL:** "pee-OO-ee"
⏺ **TRACK:** 1:46

CALL/SONG

The call is a trisyllabic mellow clear whistle "tlee-oo-ee" or "pee-OO-ee", the middle syllable stressed and of lower pitch, and is a typical sound of a winter's day on a saltmarsh. More shrill variants are also heard, usually from juveniles. This is perhaps the only call likely from this species within our region, but on its breeding grounds other calls may be heard, such as an alarm note "pluuuh" and a Curlew-like "pluuu-ee". The song, given in a slow flapping flight with deep wingbeats, consists of another trisyllabic whistle somewhat in reverse to the call note, such as "ploo-ee-oo" with the stress on the lower-pitched first and third syllables.

ADULT WINTER PLUMAGE

ADULT SUMMER PLUMAGE

Lapwing
Vanellus vanellus

LENGTH: 28–31cm

WINGSPAN: 82–87cm

🔊 **CALL:** "wheeeo-wheep!"

⏺ **TRACK:** 1:47

IDENTIFICATION

An unmistakable, medium-sized and dumpy plover, appearing black and white when seen at range. The upperparts are a deep green with a purple iridescence, the underparts white, with a broad black chest band. The head is striking, with a long thin erect crest, a black crown, forehead and lores, and in summer with a black face, chin and throat. The sides of the head and cheeks are pale grey. It has a unique flight silhouette, with very broad blunt-tipped wings and a weak-looking but deep-flapping flight. The underwing coverts are white, creating an alternating black/white flashing pattern when flying.

HABITAT

In the breeding season and throughout the year it can be found on grasslands, meadows, pastures, lakesides, margins of marshes, and also arable fields where the vegetation is not too high, and in winter will flock onto arable land, saltmarshes and tidal habitats. It requires a degree of dampness in the substrate and a richness of invertebrate food, and will avoid hard and arid ground where feeding is difficult.

CALL/SONG

An old common English name relating to the call is "Peewit". These are very vocal birds, either conversationally when in a flock or on the breeding grounds when they make a lot of noise if alarmed. In spring they make a tumbling and dive-bombing display flight over the breeding grounds, accompanied by a more elaborate call sequence or song, "whee'wheedle-wi'up'ee-wip'ee-wip'ee-wip'iyuweeep!" accompanied by a low throbbing sound that emanates from their vigorous wingbeats. The commonly heard call at all seasons is a "whheee'ow", "eeeee'woah", an ascending "wheeeo-wheep!" or a lower and hoarser "eeoo-whep". Slight variations of this call are given depending on their state of anxiety, the alarm note being a shriller and more urgent "eeeeo'whip!".

ADULT SUMMER
PLUMAGE

Dunlin
Calidris alpina

LENGTH: 16–22cm

WINGSPAN: 38–45cm

🔊 **CALL:** "krrreeeep"

⏺ **TRACK:** 1:48

IDENTIFICATION

A small, dumpy wader with medium-short black legs. In summer plumage it has a unique pattern, with a bright rufous mantle, scapulars and cap, the feathers marked centrally with black, plus a large, square black belly patch on white underparts. Also, the whitish breast is finely striped with black. In winter and juvenile plumages it is distinctly unassuming and rather proletarian in appearance, something of a pitfall for the inexperienced. In winter it is a plain grey-brown with narrowly streaked breast sides, but in all plumages it shows a medium-length bill that is gently decurved. The juvenile plumage is more strongly marked, more heavily streaked on the chest and underparts, and with dark-brown, pale-edged upperpart feathers.

HABITAT

The commonest small wader in our region, it breeds on boggy moors where there are pools and wet areas with short grassy vegetation, avoiding rocky or over-grown areas. In Britain it can be found up to 1000m, but at higher latitudes it is found at lower elevations, on tundra, coastal grassland and meadows. Outside the breeding season it is found in a wider range of habitats, such as saltmarshes, rough pasture, shallow brackish lagoons and along river plains. It is very partial to locations where soft mud provides a rich area for feeding on invertebrates, and is commonly found on estuaries, mudflats and other intertidal areas, as well as at shallow lakes, gravel pits, sewage farms and other muddy freshwater wetlands.

CALL/SONG

The most commonly heard call is a rather liquid trilling "prrreeehp" or "krreeep!", rather harsh sounding at times. This call is also given in a more shrill and urgent fashion as a warning or alarm near the nest. Other calls can be heard from feeding flocks, a short conversational chuntering "chup'chup'ip'ip'ip" or "bibi'bibi'bi-bip-beep". There is also a well-defined song, an evocative sound of the moors and mountains, given in a display flight over breeding grounds and also occasionally from the ground. There are two variants: the first is a long, descending growling trill "eeeerrrrr'r'r'r'r'r'r'r'r'r'r", the second is a courtship trill and is a slightly ascending, scolding growling churr "eerrwhrrrrr-eerrwhrrrrr-eerrwhrrrrr".

ADULT
WINTER
PLUMAGE

Snipe
Gallinago gallinago

LENGTH: 25–27cm

WINGSPAN: 44–47cm

🔊 **CALL:** "scaap!"

⏺ **TRACK:** 1:49

'DRUMMING'
DISPLAY
FLIGHT

IDENTIFICATION

The Snipe is a cryptically plumaged bird, with a distinctive pattern of stripes, mottling and barring all over. The most obvious feature is a rather disproportionately long, bicolored bill, combined with rather short legs and a dumpy body. The head is boldly striped with a very broad buffy-yellow supercilium and a black line between bill and eye. The large black eye looks high and to the rear of the head, giving it a unique expression. The crown is black with a buff central streak, and the mantle has thick straw-like yellow stripes. The underparts have a whitish ground colour with neat dark brown barring on the flanks and breast. In flight it shows a distinct white trailing edge to the secondary flight feathers. The sexes are similar. Juvenile birds show narrower bars on the upperparts and unbroken pale edges to the wing coverts.

HABITAT

Relatively common throughout Britain, although declining, and breeds in damp grassy areas, boggy uplands and other wet and marshy areas. In winter it occurs more widely in various wetlands. It can often be seen probing its long bill deep into soft mud along wet edges, although it can be shy and well camouflaged, announcing its presence with a harsh call when flying up in rapid zig-zagging escape flight.

CALL/SONG

Its rough "scaap!" flight call can be heard year-round, but on its breeding grounds it is much more vocal, sitting out on fence posts and making a loud rhythmic "chip-chip-chip-chip…" or "per-chip-per-chip-per-chip-per-chip" sound, lasting for 5–60 seconds and including 4 or 5 notes per second. This call can also be uttered in flight. In addition to these vocalizations, the male makes a remarkable drumming noise in a display flight, not dissimilar to the sound of the distant bleating of a sheep. It can be seen over its breeding areas from March to June making continuous flights, diving steeply down at a 45 degree angle which causes the air to rush through the stiff and extended outer tail feathers, creating the distinctive drumming sound. This sound lasts typically for 1.5–3 seconds, although occasionally for longer.

'RODING' FLIGHT

Woodcock
Scolopax rusticola

LENGTH: 33–35cm

WINGSPAN: 45–51cm

🔊 **CALL:** "wurr'urr'urr'SpiSSp!"

● **TRACK:** 1:50

IDENTIFICATION

A very plump and medium-sized wader, with broad rounded wings and a long bill for probing in soft mud. The legs are short, and the eyes are set very high in the head, giving it 360-degree vision. The plumage is very cryptic, with reddish-brown upperparts intricately barred and marbled with black, white and buff, and dark-barred buff underparts, giving the effect of dead-leaf camouflage. The face is rather pale and plain, and the crown is patterned with broad blackish transverse bars.

HABITAT

It can be found throughout the year in broad-leaved, mixed and coniferous forests, with some undergrowth and shade, especially with soft boggy ground, streams and pools, and it can sometimes be found nesting in more open areas on bracken-rich moorland. Resident across our region, with continental birds supplementing the population in winter, when they can be found in scrub, urban cemeteries, gardens, reedbeds and thickets. It is crepuscular and secretive, usually only encountered when flushed or when 'roding'.

CALL/SONG

Not particularly vocal except on the breeding grounds, when males perform a display flight known as 'roding'. They patrol their woodland territories and beyond, often just at treetop height and flying level with a jerky flight on stiff wings with rapid wingbeats, the bill pointing down at 45 degrees. During this flight they regularly utter a strange combination of sounds, the most audible being a high-pitched (3–14kHz) "SpiSSp!", which is far-carrying, but at closer range some low (0.6–1.5kHz) croaking notes can be heard preceding this sneezing call, such as "wurr'urr'urr'rr'SpiSSp!". With a good close view, the bird can be seen to jerk its legs in time to the rhythm! Little-known calls occur between the sexes on the ground, such as "bibibibibib", plus the female may call down the roding male with a softer and quieter version of the male's roding sneeze, "iiiitz-iiiitz psit". Birds chasing each other around may give a "plip'plip'pissp'psi'plip". The only call that seems to be heard at all seasons is a Snipe-like "scaap", given in flight.

Black-tailed Godwit
Limosa limosa

LENGTH: 40–44cm

WINGSPAN: 70–82cm

🔊 **CALL:** "kip-kip-kip"

⏺ **TRACK:** 1:51

ISLANDICA (ICELAND) RACE SUMMER PLUMAGE

IDENTIFICATION

A big wader, larger, longer-legged and longer-billed than Bar-tailed Godwit, although birds of the *islandica* race (the form most frequently seen in Britain) are much closer in size and measurements to the Bar-tailed than the larger nominate *limosa*. In breeding plumage it shows an orange-rufous head, neck and breast, and a white belly and vent with dark bars extending from the shoulder across the flanks and belly. The upperparts are predominantly a clean grey with a random scattering of feathers patterned with black and rufous, most regular on the upper back. The bill is long and nearly straight, with the basal 60 per cent flesh-pink, but more orangey in spring. In winter the plumage is very plain ashy-grey. Juveniles are washed orange on the neck and breast and have more strongly patterned upperparts. The

summer plumage of *islandica* birds is closer to that of the Bar-tailed, with a darker rufous-chestnut extending further down the belly and flanks, and darker and more strongly patterned upperparts.

HABITAT

In the breeding season it is found in wet meadows, damp grassland, pastures, the margins of fresh-water marshes, damp moorland and blanket bogs, and any kind of marginal open country where water-logged or seasonally flooded. In Iceland it nests in similar habitat but tends towards marshy, hummocky moorland. Outside the breeding season it favours estuaries, sheltered inlets, saltmarshes, coastal mudflats, lagoons and brackish pools, and freshwater habitats such as paddyfields and flooded grassland.

CALL/SONG

On the breeding grounds it is very vocal, excitedly mobbing intruders or displaying in a noisy aerial song flight. The song is a repeated two- or three-note pattern, such as a nasal "uh'uh'werrh' uh'uh'werrh-uh'uh'werrh-uh'uh'werrh-uh'uh' werrh…" or "e'e'e'eh-weouw, eh-weouw, eh-weouw, eh-weouw…", or a strident "wheddu-wheddu-wheddu-wheddu-wheddu…", with variants such as a staccato "i'i'i'i'id-wheeeow". Call notes uttered by birds on the ground or in the air are a peevish Lapwing-like "peeoo", and a sharp nasal "kyep!", "kyep'ep" or "kip-kip-kip". A sociable bird, often seen in flocks, which utter a conversational yapping.

WINTER PLUMAGE

WINTER PLUMAGE

Bar-tailed Godwit
Limosa lapponica

LENGTH: 37–39cm
WINGSPAN: 70–80cm
🔊 **CALL:** "kep!"
⏺ **TRACK:** 1:52

IDENTIFICATION

Similar in many ways to Black-tailed Godwit, this is a large wader with medium-long legs and a long, slightly upcurved bill, which is dark in summer and flesh-coloured on the basal half in winter. The summer plumage is dominated by a dark reddish-chestnut colour over the head, neck and underparts, all the way to the tail and offset by silver-grey wings and a strongly patterned back of black feathers edged in rufous. In winter the upperparts are brownish-grey, the mantle and scapulars have darker centres to the feathers, and it lacks any white wingbar. The underparts are off-white with a buff-brown wash on the chest. The rump is white at all seasons.

HABITAT

A high Arctic breeder which nests on low-lying wet tundra and bogs, also on swampy ground with raised hummocks and scattered trees where birds freely perch. In winter it is primarily coastal, favouring extensive mudflats, estuaries, bays, saltpans, sheltered inlets and sometimes island beaches, where firm mud within the intertidal zone provides rich feeding on invertebrates.

It is occasional inland as a migrant, turning up on freshwater bodies or flooded areas.

CALL/SONG

The common call is a sharp "kep!" or "chet!", sometimes a disyllabic "ki-vip", often repeated, with a range of similar variants including a barking "kak-kak" and a nasal "ki-wuh". On the breeding grounds it sings with a rapid "ke'deu ke'deu ke' deu ke'deu ke'deu" or "i'vidh'i'vidh'i'vidh'i...", which is often accompanied by a nasal laughing "wahwahwah!" or "hweh-hweh weh". This latter call is given in flight at other times of year, and can be heard sometimes at night as birds migrate overhead.

ADULT SUMMER PLUMAGE

Whimbrel
Numenius phaeopus

LENGTH: 40–42cm

WINGSPAN: 76–89cm

CALL: "puhuhuhuhuh"

TRACK: 1:53

IDENTIFICATION

Similar to the Curlew, slightly smaller with a shorter bill that decurves more strongly in its distal third. It has a bolder head pattern, with a prominent narrow pale crown-stripe, contrasting with dark sides to the crown, a pale supercilium offset by the crown pattern, dark lores and eye-stripe in front of the eye. The plumage is very similar to that of the Curlew, with a contrasting white rump, but the Whimbrel has shorter legs and is generally darker.

HABITAT

It breeds in the Arctic and boreal zones, typically in fairly dry areas on mountains and moorland above the tree-line, tundra and taiga bogs, cranberry scrub, and on vegetated lava flows and wetter moorland in Iceland. Outside the breeding season it may be encountered in our region as a migrant, but most birds migrate overland to tropical shores with few stops en route, and can be found on coastal wetlands, saltpans, mangroves, saltmarshes, inlets, marshes, large rivers, sandy beaches, reefs, pastures and coastal short-grass areas.

CALL/SONG

The call heard most frequently is a whinnying whistle of a repeated single note, descending over the whole of the phrase. It can sound quite staccato, as "i'i'i'i'i'i'i'i", or softer and lower, as "puhuhuhuhuh", and is often heard in flight. It is quite far-carrying and may be heard at night as migrant birds head south across both coastal and inland areas. On the breeding grounds this call is often given with a sharper quality and in a longer sequence, particularly when the bird is anxious. It has a repertoire of calls similar to those of Curlew, with a bubbling song starting with low drawling notes then accelerating and rising in pitch "err-errr-errr-er'r'rrrr'rrr'd'd'd'd'd'd' 'r'r'r'r", with a harder and less liquid sound than its larger relative, and often in shorter, flatter sequences. It also gives a sharp "kup!", and a plaintive, Golden Plover-like "weeeh'weeh'weeh'weeh'weeeh!".

Curlew
Numenius arquata

LENGTH: 50–60cm

WINGSPAN: 80–100cm

CALL: "cuh'rr'lee!"

TRACK: 1:54

IDENTIFICATION

The largest wader of our region, with long legs and a long, strong decurved bill. At range the plumage appears demure and plain, but closer up it shows clear black streaking almost uniformly on the upperparts, head, neck, breast and flanks. It is overall rather buffy-brown, with a white belly and vent, a pale supercilium, a rather pale face and lores, and a slightly darker crown, although never approaching the contrast of the Whimbrel's head pattern.

HABITAT

Breeds in grassy moorlands and open country with clear all-round visibility, meadows, pastures, damp grasslands, heathland, bogs, and low-intensity arable land where damp areas occur. After breeding it leaves for marine coastal habitats, such as tidal mud- and sandflats, beaches with rock pools, mangroves and saltmarshes, as well as freshwater wetlands and indeed any habitat where it can feed by probing its bill deep into soft mud.

CALL/SONG

In addition to the clear ascending "cuh'rr'lee!" call note from which the bird takes its name, it has a wide variety of other vocalizations. This commonly heard call can be uttered as "Ouurrr'wheh!" or "churr-WEOEW", and is shorter and harsher when the bird is alarmed. It is heard particularly on the breeding grounds, where birds can be very noisy, along with other calls such as a stammering, barking "Ow'Ow'wow'wow", "urh'urh'urh" or "Aa'wowow!", a "prrr'rr'up", and a rising bubbling "drrr'i! drrr'i! drrr'i!". The bubbling call can be heard at all seasons and starts with slow drawling notes before quickening into rising bubbling phrases, "orrr'whrrrr' prrr'prrr'prr 'prrr'prrr'pr'pr'pr" and "prrr'e'prrrr'e'prrrr'e'prrr'e'prr r'e'prrr". The song on the breeding grounds is given on the wing and has similarities to many of these calls in tone, a forceful repetition of "oouurrr'wheh', ouurrr'wheh', ouurrr'wheh', ouurrr'wheh…".

Spotted Redshank
Tringa erythropus

LENGTH: 29–33cm

WINGSPAN: 61–67cm

🔊 **CALL:** "che'wit"

⬤ **TRACK:** 1:55

ADULT SUMMER PLUMAGE

summer plumage, a bold feature is the prominent whitish supercilium, enhanced by the contrast with a solid black eye-stripe.

IDENTIFICATION

An elegant, long-necked and long-legged wader with two distinct seasonal plumages. The summer plumage of the male is a remarkable almost uniform sooty-black, finely spotted with white on the feather edges of the mantle and wings, with heavier white spotting on the flanks and undertail. The female is less black and more spotted. At all ages this species shows a long white rump patch. The legs are red, turning black in summer, and the bill is long, fine and straight with a red base to the lower mandible. Winter plumage is a rather pure grey with whitish underparts, finely spotted with pale and dark, and the juvenile is more heavily marked with uniform mottled barring below and darker upperparts. Except in

HABITAT

An Arctic breeder that nests on boggy wooded tundra, thinly wooded areas of the taiga forest, and also on open tundra with adjacent swampy areas. On passage and in winter it is found on freshwater more than Redshank, favouring sewage farms, shallow lakes, lagoons, marshes, paddyfields and flooded grassland. Also found on saltpans, estuaries and saltmarshes. Quite adept in the water, wading deeply and often swimming.

CALL/SONG

The most familiar call, often given in flight when flushed, is a quick clear "che'wit", "chi'hee!" or "tee-veet!", higher pitched on the second syllable. The song, typically given in song flight but sometimes from the ground, is a rather simple rolling "gweee-yerh gweee-yerh gweee-yerh" or "oOo-weeee'yeh oOo-weeee'yeh oOo-weeee'yeh", with a gravelly quality not unlike the song of the Dunlin. This is punctuated by bouts of rapid 'chipping' calls, such as "chi'ih'ih'ih'ih'ih" or "chep chep chep chep". It also gives a tern-like rasping "kree' kree' kree".

ADULT WINTER PLUMAGE

Redshank
Tringa totanus

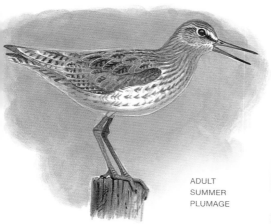

ADULT
SUMMER
PLUMAGE

LENGTH: 27–29cm

WINGSPAN: 59–66cm

🔊 **CALL:** "TEU-huhu"

⏺ **TRACK:** 1:56

IDENTIFICATION

The most common and noticeable medium-sized wader in the region, with medium-long red legs and a straight bill with a red base. It has a striking pattern in flight, with a large white wedge on its rump and white secondaries and inner primaries forming a broad white trailing edge to the wing. The winter plumage is a rather plain grey-brown with a dingy mottled and brown-washed breast, whereas in summer the upperparts are brighter olive-brown finely marked with black; the breast is darker and the white underparts are strongly streaked and blotched with black.

HABITAT

In the breeding season it favours damp ground in open or rolling country, sometimes to a fairly high altitude, on moist meadows and grassland, marshes and open moorland free from tall vegetation, bushes etc and with good all-round visibility. Typical habitats frequented outside the breeding season include mainly coastal areas with soft mud such as intertidal mudflats and estuaries, lagoons, bays, harbours and shorelines. It can also occur on fresh or brackish water bodies, sewage farms and various other wetland margins with rich invertebrate fauna.

CALL/SONG

A noisy and obvious bird, the common and familiar call is a ringing downwards-inflected "TEU-huhu" or "CHEW-tutu", with variants on that theme including a shorter "Tyoo'oo" and a more liquid "TLOOo-dudu". Single sharp notes such as "chet! chet! chet! chet!!" or "kew! kew! kew! kew!" are given in anxiety and in alarm near the nest, together with a less-alarmed and softer "kyup kyup" or a Coot-like "kew, kew, kew". The song, given in a display flight, is a repetitive "teu! teu! teu! teu! teu! teu!" and a rapid liquid fluty "woo'dli-woo'dli-woo'dli-woo'dli…" or "hi-weedly'weedly'weedly'weedly…".

Greenshank
Tringa nebularia

LENGTH: 30–34cm

WINGSPAN: 68–70cm

CALL: "chu! chu! chu!"

TRACK: 1:57

IDENTIFICATION

A large bulky wader with a robust medium-long, slightly upturned bill and medium-length dull green legs. The upperparts are greenish-grey, with the feathers on the mantle and wings patterned irregularly with black in summer, while in winter they are greyer with fine spotting. In all plumages it appears pale-headed, closer inspection revealing fine streaking on the crown and neck. The white underparts are spotted with black in summer. In flight the wings are plain and dark, contrasting with a long and broad white rump and mostly white tail. Juveniles appear darker on the upperparts.

HABITAT

In the breeding season it can be found on moorland and taiga with scattered trees, bogs, wild tracts and uplands, although selecting drier areas than some relatives. On passage, migrant birds en route to Africa for the winter disperse on to freshwater habitats such as lakes, marshes, shallow lagoons and flooded pastures, plus coastal areas such as the seashore, estuaries, lagoons, mangroves and saltpans.

CALL/SONG

The familiar call of the Greenshank is a clear ringing note repeated two or three times, "chu!-chu!-chu!" or "Tiou' Tiou'Tiou!", often given in flight. It gives a shorter, sharper call when more agitated, sometimes running this call into a longer sequence, and in the breeding season often calls with a shrill chipping "chi'chi'chi'chi'…", particularly near the nest when anxious. The song is given in a roving song flight high in the air and is a rather mournful two-syllable "cheh-wher cheh-wher cheh-wher cheh-wher cheh-wher…" or "oo-hwerr oo-hwerr oo-hwerr oo-hwerr oo-hwerr oo-hwerr…", the first note descending and the second ascending, the sequence rising and falling as the sound is carried on the wind.

IDENTIFICATION

An elegant medium-sized sandpiper, larger than the similar Wood and Common Sandpipers, and looking very much broader in the beam and dumpier. It is a very striking blackish and white bird, particularly in flight when the square white rump and underparts contrast with the blackish-green wings and upperparts. It is well marked across the entire breast with diffuse streaking, and has a well-defined lower edge to the breast markings. It has a strong white supercilium in front of the eye, weakly marked behind the eye, and a narrow white eye-ring. The shortish legs are green, the bill is medium length and straight, and it bobs the body in the same manner as the Common Sandpiper.

HABITAT

Nests arboreally, in the old nest of another bird such as a thrush, in flooded forest, boreal bogs, wet willow scrub, along forest streams and in marshes with stands of trees, but always near freshwater, standing pools or swamps with muddy shores that can provide feeding. Outside the breeding season it can use very small water bodies, often rather enclosed, such as woodland pools, ditches, flashes and seasonal floods, sewage farms, streams, lakeshores and marshes. It avoids mudflats, coastal habitats and wide open areas.

Green Sandpiper
Tringa ochropus

LENGTH: 20–24cm
WINGSPAN: 57–61cm
🔊 **CALL:** "tlooeet!"
⏺ **TRACK:** 1:58

CALL/SONG

The most commonly heard vocalization is the flight call, given loudly as the bird climbs steeply away when disturbed from a discrete pool or ditch. It is a clear ringing "klu'uweeet-whit'whit'whit", the first note rising sharply, the others even and higher pitched. This call is variable, often with just a single "tlooeet!" or a longer sequence of several notes. The song, infrequently heard in Britain, is of similar quality to these call notes, with a fluty rhythmic piping and "klid-oo-weet, klid-oo-weet, klid-oo-weet, tluuuee-dee'it, tluuuee-dee'it, tluuuee-dee'it…" etc. It also gives a clipped, flat alarm note, "chut'chut'chut'chut'chut" or a "chep'chep'chep".

Wood Sandpiper
Tringa glareola

JUVENILE

LENGTH: 18–21cm

WINGSPAN: 56–57cm

CALL: "chiff-chiff-chiff"

TRACK: 1:59

IDENTIFICATION

A slim and elegant wader, smaller than Green Sandpiper and with a longer slim neck, longish yellow-ochre legs and a more dainty appearance, approaching Redshank in shape. The upperparts are paler, greyer in adults and browner in juveniles, and in all plumages it is well spotted on the back and wings. The breast is loosely streaked in a more diffuse pattern than the Green, and it lacks any clear breast band. It always shows a well-defined whitish supercilium in front of and behind the eye, bordered below with a blackish eye-stripe. In flight it shows a square white rump, and the underwing is very pale, unlike the black underwing of the Green.

ADULT SUMMER PLUMAGE

HABITAT

Breeds in swampy habitats within the taiga forest zone, favouring forest bogs and lightly wooded marshy areas, or the more open habitats of 'forest-tundra' with scrub of willow and other species and open boggy areas of sedge and grass. A familiar migrant wader in our region, it avoids open exposed habitats like the seashore and mudflats, seeking freshwater pools and marshes, grasslands, paddyfields, shallow lakes and lagoons, and can occur on small temporary pools and muddy habitats.

CALL/SONG

Quite vocal, the commonly heard flight call (which gives the bird its Russian name of "Fifi") being a short, repeated, high-pitched single note "chiff-chiff-chiff", rather soft in quality and occasionally repeated in longer sequences or rising in pitch in a more agitated version, when it may begin to sound more Redshank-like. The song is given on the breeding grounds in a display flight or from a perch, and is a rapid repeated 'wheedling' sound, "chirro o'chirroo'chirroo'chirroo'che!" or "weedl-weedl-weedl-weedl-whiw", interspersed with a lower-pitched "pup'pup'pup'pup" or "chup'chup'chup'chup'chup". It also mixes in a continuous liquid tittering "titt'it'rr'tr'tt'rr'tr't t'rr'tt". The alarm call is a drawn-out peeping note, "hweeeep".

IDENTIFICATION

A dumpy, short-legged wader with some strongly defined characters, such as a continual and exaggerated bobbing of the rear body and a flickering action to the wings, which are held below the horizontal as it flies low over the water, interspersed with short glides on stiff wings. It is rather short-necked, long-bodied and long-tailed, white below, olive-brown above and with a dusky breast that is stronger at the sides and outlined by a white spur on the lower edge that extends up to the shoulder.

HABITAT

An adaptable wader with a wide range covering several climatic zones, it is strongly tied to freshwater and in the breeding season can be found along slow-flowing upland rivers and streams, sheltered rocky and sandy sea coasts, inlets and archipelagos, lakes and pools with sandy or gravel shores, in forested areas where these habitat types can be found, and sometimes in mountains to high altitudes. Outside the breeding season it occurs more widely, on all kinds of freshwater habitats, such as rivers, streams, pools, lakes, lagoons and marshes, and also on more saline areas such as saltmarshes, creeks and rocky shorelines, although it avoids open mudflats.

CALL/SONG

A vocal wader, with a distinctive call of three cheery notes "swee-wee-wee" or "peee'wi'wi", given

Common Sandpiper
Actitis hypoleucos

LENGTH: 18–21cm

WINGSPAN: 38–41cm

🔊 **CALL:** "swee-wee-wee"

⏺ **TRACK:** 1:60

frequently in flight but also from the ground. This may also vary from one single note to several notes strung together, depending on the bird's state of excitement. Migrants can often be heard calling at night as they pass over inland areas. The alarm call is a "peeeee" of similar high pitch although shriller, and rather piercing when heard at close range; it is given in warning, especially when near the nest or chicks. The song, delivered in a song flight of flickering wings over the breeding grounds, is a continual medley of notes similar to the call, "uh'u'wi'wi – uh'u'wi'wi – uh'u'wi'wi…" or "chi'wi'didi – chi'wi'didi – chi'wi'didi…", interspersed with a sharper "chit! chit! chit!".

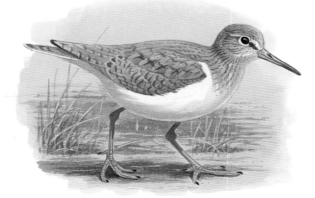

Turnstone
Arenaria interpres

LENGTH: 21–25cm

WINGSPAN: 49–57cm

🔊 **CALL:** "chut-chut'ut'ut'ut"

⏺ **TRACK:** 1:61

ADULT WINTER PLUMAGE

IDENTIFICATION

A small, boldly patterned and dumpy shorebird, with a short neck, short orange legs and a short, strong bill. In breeding plumage it is very colourful, with chestnut-orange upperparts marked with a bold pattern of wide black straps along the scapulars, a black upper mantle and black wingtips. The head and underparts are white with a broad crescent of black on the breast that extends up on to the face and neck in a bridle, plus a black-streaked crown. In winter it loses the red of the upperparts, becoming dark grey-brown and lightly scalloped, but in flight it appears pied and very variegated, a pattern dominated by a bold white back patch. The breast patch becomes more diffuse and the head becomes dusky.

HABITAT

A breeder of high latitudes, favouring islands and archipelagos, dry tundra, rocky and shingly areas around coasts and never more than a few kilometres from shore. Outside the breeding season it can roam widely, even as far as the tropics, and is commonly seen around British coasts, where it is strongly tied to rocky and seaweed-rich places. It can be found on breakwaters and harbour walls, and is well adapted to enduring the high winds, strong wave activity and spray that come with this choice of habitat. Occasionally migrants can be seen on inland water bodies. As its name suggests, it feeds by foraging and lifting small stones, seaweed and other littoral matter with its bill.

CALL/SONG

Often heard calling, partly due to its confiding nature which allows the observer to hear calls at fairly close range. It has a limited repertoire, however, uttering hard 'stony' calls when disturbed along rocky shores. Typical calls are a short sharp "kheew!", a "chut-chut'ut'ut'ut" or a lower-pitched "chup'up'up'up". When its mood is elevated due to alarm or breeding fervour, it extends this call into a rolling chatter, "drrd'du'dr'r'r'r'r'r" or "chit-uk'chit-uk'i-peep-pi'pi'pi'pi'pi" and "weh-whidi'whidi'kikikikikikiki".

ADULT SUMMER PLUMAGE

PALE AND DARK PHASES

Arctic Skua
Stercorarius parasiticus

LENGTH: 41–46cm

WINGSPAN: 110–120cm

🔊 **CALL:** "kioaw'ho!"

⏺ **TRACK:** 1:62

IDENTIFICATION

A dark, sleek bird, gull-like yet with a hint of a falcon. Adults have elongated central tail feathers, and occur in both light and dark colour phases. The pale birds have creamy-coloured underparts and collar, with a contrasting dark cap. Dark-phase birds are uniform dark chocolate-brown, broken only by pale bases to the primaries forming a prominent 'flash', a feature common to all ages. Juveniles are dark all over, although often more rufescent. Agile and aerodynamic, with a fast, buoyant and powerful flight, in strong winds this species tends to 'shear' on stiff wings angled at the carpal.

HABITAT

Breeds at high latitudes, on tundra, coastal moors and inshore islands, favouring coastal locations where it can take advantage of seabird colonies. In the Arctic this species often nests close to Little Auk colonies. It feeds by stealing fish from other seabirds, engaging in long and aggressive aerial chases until the victim drops its meal. It nests in a loose colony, with adults aggressively defending their territories against intruders, dive-bombing humans and attempting to strike them on the head with their feet, sometimes hard enough to draw blood! Outside the breeding season the species is strongly pelagic, migrating to the oceans south of the Equator; on passage it can be seen around the coasts of our region, although only accidentally appearing inland.

CALL/SONG

Mostly silent except when breeding, although outside this season they are at sea and typically out of earshot! On their breeding grounds they are quite vocal, a typical single call being a rather bright-sounding "eeow'eh!" or "kioaw'ho!". They have far-carrying display and territorial calls, a nasal mewing "eeeeee'yah eeeeee'yah eeeeee'yah" that rises, the final syllable higher and even in pitch, and not entirely dissimilar to the call of the Kittiwake. It can be delivered from the ground or in the air, sometimes repeated in long sequences, and is also given as a threat call when intruders approach the nest. When attacking intruders they give a short "cack-cack-cack" call, and another alarm call is a short "pyew". It also gives a short sharp "i'i'i" or "ik'ik'ik", and conversational grunting notes "eeh eeh eeh".

PALE PHASE

Black-headed Gull
Larus ridibundus

LENGTH: 34–37cm

WINGSPAN: 100–110cm

🔊 **CALL:** "krreearr"

⏺ **TRACK:** 1:63

ADULT WINTER PLUMAGE

IDENTIFICATION

The familiar small gull in our region, the adult in summer has a chocolate-brown (not black!) head, with a short transitional state between this and the winter plumage of just a dark smudge over the eye and a bold dark ear-spot on a white head. The upperparts are pearly-grey, with a long white wedge from the primary coverts to the outer primary tips, a black trailing edge to the primaries and smoky-grey underside to the flight feathers. Immature birds take two years to mature, are blotched and marked with dark brown, in decreasing amounts with age, but adults always have a roughly similar pattern of black and white on the primaries.

HABITAT

Common throughout our region and fairly ubiquitous in most wetland habitats. In the breeding season it nests around both shallow brackish and saline marshy pools, lakes, gravel pits, reedbeds, saltmarshes, estuaries, broad slow-moving rivers and flooded areas, often favouring small shingly islands for security, but also on drier areas close to water, such as heather moors and dunes. Outside the breeding season it is found even more widely, in urban areas, parks, playing fields, sewage farms, rubbish tips, reservoirs, inlets, estuaries and intertidal areas.

ADULT SUMMER PLUMAGE

CALL/SONG

Very vocal, particularly around breeding colonies, where the noise can be deafening and often continues through the night. It has a variety of rather unattractive harsh calls, the common call being a slurred screech, "krreearr" or "kaa'aarrr". It gives a harsher and insistent "raaargh!" or "gaaarhh!" when reacting anxiously to the presence of intruders, but also has a softer and less urgent "aaarrrr", an "akh'akh'akh" and singles and multiples of "kik", delivered in a more conversational tone. A longer and more elaborate call, "kre-kre-kreh'kraaa'kraaaa'kraaaa'kraaaa", is given in various social contexts.

IDENTIFICATION

A medium-sized gull, superficially similar to the Herring Gull but intermediate between that and the Black-headed Gull in structure and size. It has a white head, streaked dusky in winter, with a dark eye, a gentle expression and a greenish-yellow bill. The legs are also greenish-yellow, and the wings are long with a large amount of black on the primary tips and a large white panel or 'mirror' on the very tip. The mantle and upperwings are mid-grey with a smokey-bluish tone. Immatures take three years to reach maturity, and from the first winter show mantle and head markings similar to the winter adult, with a gradually decreasing amount of dark brownish markings on the head, body, upperwing coverts and underwing. They also show more black on the primaries, and have pinkish legs and a pink base to the bill.

HABITAT

Breeds colonially or singly, around marshes, lakes, bogs, grassy moorland, in coastal and island habitats, dunes, grassy and rocky slopes, along broad river valleys with shingle banks, and occasionally on cliffs, roofs and other elevated situations. After breeding,

Common Gull
Larus canus

LENGTH: 40–42cm
WINGSPAN: 110–120cm
🔊 **CALL:** "arrrw!"
⏺ **TRACK:** 1:64

IMMATURE

and in winter, it disperses onto grassland and farmland, often following the farmer's plough, and can be found in a wider range of wetland and dry country, such as reservoirs, gravel pits, playing fields, parks, pastures, flooded areas, and coastally in harbours, estuaries and on sandy beaches.

CALL/SONG

The calls are higher-pitched than those of the Herring Gull, which has a similar range of vocalizations, with a whining, mewing quality which gives it its other name of Mew Gull. The long call is a shrill nasal "eh'eh'eh'eh'wheeeee-yow wheeee-yow wheee-yow ee'ya ee'ya ee'ya'eh'eh", with variants such as "aah-ow aa-ow ar'ar'ar'ar'ar" and an excited "wheeyah-wheeyah-wheeyah-wheeyah'wow". These calls are uttered in flight or on the ground, when it stretches the head back and up. Various shorter calls are given, such as a rather knowing "raow!" or "arrrw!", or sharper yelps such as "arr!" and "yaow!", often breaking into sequences of shrill mewing calls.

ADULT

Lesser Black-backed Gull
Larus fuscus

LENGTH: 52–64cm

WINGSPAN: 135–150cm

CALL: "eeeyhhr"

TRACK: 1:65

IMMATURE

IDENTIFICATION

Typically a little smaller, slimmer and more graceful than the Herring Gull. The adult *graellsii* form in Britain has a dark slate-grey back and upperwings, rather extensive black wingtips and a small white 'mirror' on the outer primary tips; in addition, the white head is blotched and streaked in winter. The Scandinavian forms *intermedius* and *fuscus* have very black upperparts, resembling Great Black-backed Gull, but all forms show yellow legs and a smaller and more slender bill. Immatures take four years to mature, and are dark brown, patterned and streaked with blackish, gradually acquiring adult plumage in stages.

HABITAT

Common in our region, it typically nests colonially in similar habitat to Herring Gull, favouring grassy areas on low or rocky islands, sea cliffs, coastal dunes, also inland on moorland, bogs, lakes and increasingly on buildings in urban areas. Outside the breeding season it disperses widely, over offshore and inshore waters such as lagoons, estuaries, harbours, shorelines and tidal areas, reservoirs, gravel pits, flooded pasture, ploughed fields, farmland, urban areas and sports fields. Eastern and northern populations migrate overland to Africa, but western populations travel less far, with many wintering in Britain.

CALL/SONG

The various calls are similar in pattern to both Herring and Great Black-backed Gull. The 'long-call' is deeper and more nasal than that of the Herring, such as "rru'rru'rru'rru'rru'rru…" or "egh-egh-egh-egh-egh…", and may accelerate more towards the end of the sequence. It also has a barking anxiety call, "gow'ow'ow'ow'ow", deeper and gruffer than the Herring. The simple calls are a nasal descending "eeeyhhr" or "ehrrw", or a repeated "owrr owrr owrr", all lower in pitch than Herring. It also has a more plaintive, slightly higher-pitched "i'i'i'errr" or "oo-eeerrr", given by juveniles.

ADULT

IMMATURE

Herring Gull
Larus argentatus

LENGTH: 56–64cm
WINGSPAN: 138–150cm
CALL: "kyaow"
TRACK: 1:66

IDENTIFICATION

The most familiar large 'seagull' in our region, with a pale grey back and upperwings, a white head that is variably streaked in winter, pink legs and a yellow bill with a red spot on the gonys. The wingtips are black with white tips and a white 'mirror' spanning the two outermost primaries. The iris is pale yellow. Immatures take four years to mature, and in the first year are a rather uniform pale brown, blotched and barred, with the feathers of the wing and mantle well marked with black bars and centres. As they mature further, the mantle and wings gradually moult out brown feathers and acquire grey ones.

HABITAT

Common, typically breeding in coastal areas where it prefers sea cliffs and rocky coasts, but it also nests on islands, dunes, moorland and often on buildings in coastal towns and ports, occasionally well inland. During the remainder of the year it uses these same habitats, but also ranges more widely on to arable fields and farmland, harbours, bays, estuaries and saltmarshes, always keeping within range of large water bodies such as reservoirs and lakes for roosting, and seldom very far from the coast. Successful and adaptable, it takes advantage of human food refuse, scavenging from fishing boats, markets, docks and rubbish tips.

CALL/SONG

Quite vocal, especially during the breeding season. The simple and familiar call is a high ringing "eeow!" or "kyaow", often heard as a medley of cries when several birds are present. Variants include a rather high-pitched "eeoow!", sometimes an "eeuurrw!" in a lower pitch, or a shorter, sharper "kliu", etc. A rather deep barking "og'og'og'og" is given in anxiety, as well as a softer, less worried "ah'ah'ah'ow". The long call is "eeo'eeo'eeo'eeoo 'eeoo'eeoo'eu'eu'argh'argh'argh'aa-ow'aa-ow", delivered in a display sequence where the neck stretches down to the ground, is then pulled inwards and slowly raised upwards before relaxing.

ADULT

Great Black-backed Gull

Larus marinus

LENGTH: 64–78cm

WINGSPAN: 150–165cm

◀)) **CALL:** "aaaow"

● **TRACK:** 1:67

IMMATURE

IDENTIFICATION

The largest gull in the world, at all ages showing a heavier structure than other large gull species. It has a very bulky, deep-chested body and a deep, thick bill. The bill is yellow in the adult with a prominent red gonys spot, and the legs are stout and pink. The mantle and upperwing are black, with a white trailing edge to the wing and a bold white 'mirror' on the outer primary tips. The head and remainder of the plumage are white, with little or no head streaking in winter. Immatures take four years to mature, and in the first year are streaked on the head and underparts, with a boldly chequered pattern of black and white on the upperparts.

HABITAT

As its scientific name suggests, this species favours coastal habitats and nests singly or in a loose colony on rocky islands and sea cliffs, often occupying the higher ledges and clifftops. On occasion it will nest on sandy beaches and saltmarshes, or some way inland on the islands of large lakes or on moorland on drier raised ground. It is sedentary, although in winter it ranges more widely along coasts, extending seawards out over the continental shelf or penetrating a short way inland, such as along larger rivers and estuaries, onto rubbish tips and sewage outfalls, and around ports. It will scavenge, but otherwise chases and steals food from other birds.

CALL/SONG

All the calls are very deep and gruff, but follow similar patterns to Herring and Lesser Black-backed Gulls. The laughing 'long' display call never sounds manic or shrill and is shorter, slower and more hoarse than those species, such as "orw'orw'orw'orw'orw" or "arr'rrr'rrr'rrr'rrr'rrr". A frequently heard call is similar to the barking anxiety calls of the other species, but is much deeper and more masculine sounding, such as "ugh-ugh-ugh-ugh" or "ow'ow'ow'ow". Other calls are simple, monosyllabic, and rather strangled sounds like "aarr'ow" or "aaaow", descending at the end of the note as if calling from inside a cardboard box. Also gives an even gruffer, growling "argghhw".

ADULT

IMMATURE

Kittiwake
Rissa tridactyla

LENGTH: 38–40cm

WINGSPAN: 95–120cm

CALL: "kitti-wake"

TRACK: 1:68

IDENTIFICATION

A slightly built and graceful gull, with a gentle expression and buoyant flight. The rounded head is entirely white, the bill yellowish, and the short legs are black. The back and rather long slender wings are mid-grey, with paler flight feathers and distinctive 'dipped-in-ink' black wingtips. It flies with quick wingbeats and is well suited to coping with the marine environment. The immatures have a bold black 'W' across the upperwing and a black terminal band to the tail.

HABITAT

A seabird strongly tied to maritime habitats, it nests in large colonies on stormy exposed coasts, on high sea cliffs and islands, and when in mixed cliff colonies it generally occupies the lower-level sites. Particularly around the North Sea they will nest on low cliffs, windowsills and ledges of warehouses, piers and other buildings close to human activities, such as in ports and harbours. After breeding they disperse to the sea, most wintering in the Atlantic off Africa, and usually stay far from land, although storm-driven birds may appear on inland water bodies.

CALL/SONG

Mostly silent (or out of earshot), except on their breeding grounds, when they call noisily with the sound that gives them their name, the shrill and often-repeated "kitti-wake". Of course, variations do occur, but the call is perhaps better written as "i'i'ee-weeer i'i'ee-weeer" or "i'whicky-weeehk! i'whicky-weeehk! i'whicky-weeehk!", a sound that fills the air at a colony when many birds are calling together. They also give sharp "ik-ik-ik-IK'IK" calls, and in flight a slurred cawing "I-wake" or "ee'yick" call, or a short nasal "kya!". Other described calls are a gruff "vek-vek-vek", a short knocking "kt'kt'kt" in alarm, and a soft wailing "oh", given once per second as a predator-anxiety call.

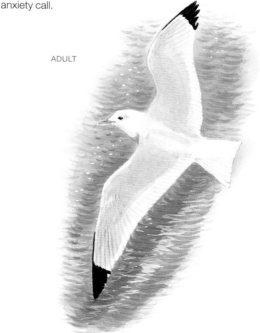

ADULT

Little Tern
Sterna albifrons

LENGTH: 22–24cm

WINGSPAN: 48–55cm

🔊 **CALL:** "yik"

● **TRACK:** 1:69

IDENTIFICATION

The smallest of our terns, typically less than half the weight of Common Tern. It has a rather fine yellow bill with a black tip, orange legs, and a black cap with a prominent white forehead that extends over the eye. It has pale grey upperparts, and in flight shows a short forked tail and a blackish wedge along the outer two or three primaries. The flight action is noticeably quicker, jerkier and more buoyant than its larger relatives, and it hovers rapidly and often close to the water, into which it plunges forcefully.

HABITAT

A summer visitor that in Britain is strongly tied to coastal regions, but elsewhere is often found well inland along large rivers and on some lakes. It nests close to the sea near shallow waters, on low-lying small islands, bare shingle, shell beaches and sand bars above the high-water mark. At inland localities it favours comparable habitats for nesting. Outside the breeding season it migrates southwards to African coasts, and on passage can be found in a wider range of coastal habitats, such as harbours, tidal creeks, estuaries, lagoons and mudflats.

CALL/SONG

Very vocal at breeding colonies and during the nesting season, it gives rather high-pitched and sharp monosyllabic calls, such as a rising "yik", "yeek","krieet!", "yaeep!" and "kyik". Shorter, sharper notes are given in alarm or anxiety, such as "kit kit kit", or combined with the longer call as "kit-kit-kit Yaeep!", accelerating into a sharp dry "kt-kt-kt-kt" and "tt't't't't't". A longer sequence of calls is given, often when birds are chasing each other around in display or dispute, a rapid cyclical 'yickering' such as "keer'ik'ik keer'ik' ik keer'ik'ik keer'ik'ik" or "iirr'i'i'- iirr'i'i'- iirr'i'i".

IDENTIFICATION

Larger and bulkier than the other terns in our region, with long narrow wings and a whiter overall appearance. It has a rather long and large head, and the bill is long and black with a pale yellow tip. It has a black cap and shaggy crest, black legs, and the upperparts are pale grey – often looking very pale at range – with a weakly defined dusky wedge on the wingtip. It has a front-heavy appearance, exaggerated by the large head and shorter tail, and when fishing dives from a reasonable height to catch its prey.

HABITAT

A summer visitor favouring coastal regions, where it nests on inshore sandy islands, rocky islets, sand spits, dunes, undisturbed shingle beaches, shallow bays, deltas and other dry, sandy sites in saline and brackish environments, with adjacent feeding areas in shallow, sandy-bottomed waters rich in surface-level fish. It migrates along the Atlantic coasts and is very rare inland, although some nest locally on islands in freshwater lakes close to the coast. Migrates to warmer waters off Africa for the winter.

Sandwich Tern
Sterna sandvicensis

LENGTH: 36–41cm

WINGSPAN: 95–105cm

CALL: "ear'rink!"

TRACK: 1:70

ADULT SUMMER PLUMAGE

CALL/SONG

Noisy and vocal, especially in the breeding season and around nest colonies, but also when out fishing and foraging or travelling with dependent juveniles in tow. The typical familiar call is a loud grating, almost disyllabic "ear'rink!" or "ar'rrenk!", delivered on a level tone, or with the second half descending and lower in pitch. It is often described as "kerrick" or "kirrink" and is audible from some distance. The species has a limited variety of other calls, all of them harsh, such as a dry chattering "ih'ih'ih'ih", a short sharp "ik'ik", and some short growling "aekh! aekh!" notes, as well as a vowel-less growling "krrr'rrrgh". They also give a higher-pitched trilling "srrreee" or "rrrrr'i'i'i'i", and juveniles are vocal when following adults, giving a high plaintive "psee-psee".

Common Tern
Sterna hirundo

LENGTH: 31–35cm (inc. tail of up to 20cm)

WINGSPAN: 75–85cm

🔊 **CALL:** "keeee-yaaa"

⬤ **TRACK:** 1:71

IDENTIFICATION

A slender and graceful bird, with a black-tipped orange-red bill and red legs, long wings and a deeply forked tail with extended outer tail-feathers forming long streamers. The cap and nape are black, the upperparts pearly grey. Very similar to Arctic Tern, but dark-tipped bill and longer legs help distinguish it, as does the subtle wing pattern. It shows a smoky trailing edge to the outer primaries that extends inwards along the middle (fourth–sixth) primary feathers to form a dusky wedge, contrasting with translucent inner primaries. This feature is less obvious in fresher spring plumage.

HABITAT

When breeding, it uses the widest range of habitats – both coastal and inland – of all our terns. Prefers safe nesting sites out of reach of predators, such as inshore islands and islets, lagoons, quiet beaches, shingle and sand spits, dunes and saltmarshes, above the reach of the highest tides. Inland it can be found along slow-flowing rivers, gravel pits, lakes and marshes, nesting on islands and gravel banks and occasionally on manmade 'tern rafts'. Outside the breeding season it can be found widely as a migrant in coastal and freshwater habitats, spending the winter off the coasts of Africa.

CALL/SONG

Vocal and noisy, particularly in the breeding season, it gives a variety of harsh screeching and shrill calls that are lower in pitch than Arctic Tern, such as a short sharp "kit", often repeated in a series of quarrelling notes such as "ik'ik'ik'ik" or "kt'kt'kt'kt'kt". A downwards-inflected mono-syllabic or disyllabic call is commonly given, such as "keeee-yaaa" or "eee-arrr", and this is often combined with other calls like "kit-kit-kit keee-yaaa" and "i'i'i'eeeeyah". Longer series of calls are also given, such as "kirri-kirri-kirri-kirri" or "irri'irri'irri'irri", "ea'i'ea'i'ea'i'ea'i", and a harsher, scolding "krrrr'krrr'krrrr'krrr". Juveniles following their parents call with a shrill "keee".

ADULT
SUMMER
PLUMAGE

Arctic Tern
Sterna paradisaea

LENGTH: 33–38cm (inc. tail of up to 20cm)

WINGSPAN: 75–85cm

🔊 **CALL:** "keeee'rr"

⏺ **TRACK:** 1:72

CALL/SONG

A similar range of notes to Common Tern, but noticeably different, being higher pitched, shrill rather than harsh, and with a drier quality. Very vocal and noisy around the breeding grounds, a commonly heard call is a sharp "kik", often repeated. It also gives a high-pitched piping "ki'ki'ki'ki'ki" or "i'i'i'i'i'i'i", and a longer cry similar to that of Common Tern but harder and drier with the emphasis on the first syllable, as in "wheeer'i", "keeee'rr" or "krri-errrrr". Variants include "eeeerr'eeeeerr", a harsh "eeerri'eeerri" and a scolding "i'i'i'i'i'irrr". Also makes a hard dry "kt'kt'kt'kt" and a high whistled "peee-peee-peee". Juveniles also make a high, plaintive "peee".

IDENTIFICATION

Essentially similar to Common Tern, but smaller bodied and longer tailed, and is 15–20 per cent lighter than that species. It is short-legged and short-necked, the short bill is blood-red, and the tail extends beyond the wingtips at rest. In flight the upperwing shows cleaner-looking primaries, with a narrow, dusky trailing edge to the outer primaries, and the underwing shows a neat, narrow black trailing edge to the outer primaries. The underparts are washed grey, contrasting subtly with the white cheeks and chin.

HABITAT

A summer visitor to higher latitudes than any other of our terns, it typically nests colonially and in the north of its range these colonies can be very large. Almost always found nesting close to the coast, on inshore islets and islands, shingle beaches, rocky shores, pastures, sedge moor and coastal meadows. In northern Scandinavia, however, it also nests far inland along rivers on islands and banks. Outside the breeding season it can be found migrating along the coasts of our region, occasionally visiting inland water bodies when weather conditions funnel migrants overland. It has possibly the longest migration of any bird, wintering in Antarctica.

ADULT SUMMER PLUMAGE

Puffin
Fratercula arctica

LENGTH: 26–29cm

WINGSPAN: 47–63cm

🔊 **CALL:** "owrrr aarrrr – hwa hwa hwa hwa"

⏺ **TRACK:** 1:73

ADULT
SUMMER
PLUMAGE

IDENTIFICATION

The word 'comical' springs to mind when describing this handsome bird. A dumpy, large-headed auk, in summer it has a huge parrot-like bill that is deep but narrow, patterned with vertical bands of yellow, blue and red. It shows a large, pale grey face and cheek with a broad black collar around the throat. In winter the bill sheds its outer layer, so adults look smaller-billed and duller at this season. Young birds (which leave the nest alone, and head out to sea for 4–5 years!) show a much smaller bill.

HABITAT

A true seabird, only ever visiting land and inshore waters during the breeding season and staying well offshore in the Atlantic for the rest of the year. It nests in large colonies, mainly around the Atlantic coasts, with some colonies in the English Channel and on North Sea coasts, and favours small islets, rocky islands, and either steep or gentle grassy cliffs where it can excavate nest burrows in the soil. It will exploit burrows ready-made by rabbits or Manx Shearwaters, and further north in its range it is found in rockier cliff habitat, nesting in cavities in cliffs or scree, especially where frost prevents excavation.

CALL/SONG

Not particularly vocal, and usually at sea and therefore out of earshot outside the breeding season. However, on its breeding grounds it gives some curious and endearing vocalizations that warrant its inclusion here. Typically calling from its nest burrow, it gives a low nasal growl, rising on the first syllable, descending on the second, and followed by three or four guffawing notes that descend in pitch and tail off, to sound like "owrrr aarrrr-hwa hwa hwa hwa" or "whorrr-aaarrr wah-wah wah wah", the first part of the call lasting 2–2.5 seconds, the whole call lasting about 4.5 seconds.

ADULT SUMMER
PLUMAGE

IDENTIFICATION

Superficially similar to Rock Dove or a small Woodpigeon, it is dumpy, compact and shorter-tailed. The plumage overall is a uniform grey-blue, darker and bluer than similar species, with no white rump or wingbar but with a black trailing edge and leading edge to the primaries, which give a black frame to the bluish wings. It has a broad black tail band, a vinaceous wash to the breast and a metallic flash on its neck of shimmering green and lilac.

HABITAT

A rather shy and discreet bird, favouring open deciduous woodland and forest edge, large parklands and mature hedgerows, occupying the narrow interface between woodland and open country – it is most frequently seen around arable land. It is dependent on finding suitable nest holes and hollows in large old trees such as oaks, but also requires access to feeding areas in fields rich in weeds and seed crops, open bare ground where it can feed and with drinking water nearby. It will nest locally in rock crevices or in buildings when suitable trees are absent.

CALL/SONG

The most frequently heard call is the advertising call, a deep two-note sound "ooo-wuhh, ooo-wuhh, ooo-wuhh…", the first syllable longer and higher pitched, the second lower and sounding as though the note is being swallowed, repeated eight or nine times in a series. This is often heard in spring coming from large woodland trees, but can be easily overlooked. Another similar call is given by the

Stock Dove
Columba oenas

LENGTH: 32–34cm

WINGSPAN: 63–69cm

🔊 **CALL:** "ooo-wuhh"

⏺ **TRACK:** 1:74

male in display to the female, a more drawn-out and low-pitched "uuh'whurrr uuh'whurrr". In his display flight the male flies horizontally with slow, deep wingbeats, clapping the wingtips over his back, followed by a glide.

Woodpigeon
Columba palumbus

LENGTH: 40–42cm

WINGSPAN: 75–80cm

CALL: "wu-WHOOR-ooh, wor-hoo"

TRACK: 1:75

IDENTIFICATION

The largest of our pigeons, a very plump and heavy bird with a small head and medium-long tail. It is light blue-grey all over, with a prominent white patch on the side of the neck and a prominent white transverse bar on the upperwing. The outer halves of the wings are black, and it has a greyish-white sub-terminal tail band, and a broad black terminal tail band. The deep chest is washed purplish-pink.

HABITAT

Very common and even abundant in many places, found in parks, gardens and urban areas, forests, small scattered or fragmented woodlands, and particularly in agricultural areas and fields, where they often feed in large flocks. British birds are resident, but many immigrants arrive for the winter from northern and eastern parts of Europe, and can be seen in large numbers at migration watchpoints.

CALL/SONG

The commonly heard song or advertising call, given from early spring through to autumn, is a deep (between 450 and 500Hz) five-syllable "wooh-oooo, wor-ooh, woh-WHOOR-ooh, wor-hoo, woh-WHOOR-ooh, wor-hoo, wu-WHOOR-ooh, wor-hoo", repeated three to five times and often finished with a short upward inflected "whu!". Another call is given by the male in a bowing display towards the female, a low, growling "whu'- oorr" repeated at intervals. His display flight consists of a short steep climb, at the apex of which he delivers several loud wing claps, before gliding back down. When disturbed, birds will make a lot of wing clapping and clattering noises on take off, which functions as an alarm call.

Collared Dove
Streptopelia decaocto

LENGTH: 31–33cm

WINGSPAN: 47–55cm

CALL: "Ooh'OOO-oo"

TRACK: 1:76

IDENTIFICATION

A medium-sized pigeon, much more slender and elegant than the Woodpigeon, and weighing just 40 per cent of the most well fed of that species. Overall it is a pallid greyish-buff mushroom colour, with a browner cast to the back and wings. It has an obvious black half-collar, a beady eye, grey flight feathers and a pale blue-grey panel on the greater coverts. The tail is quite long with a broad white terminal band on all but the central feathers.

HABITAT

In western Europe and, indeed, throughout much of its wider range, it is a common bird of suburban areas, found in gardens, parks, churchyards and orchards. It also occurs around farmyards, particularly where there is spilt grain, and wherever there are a few dense trees together with numerous perches such as telephone poles and wires. During the last century it underwent a remarkable expansion of its range in Europe, where the population spread north-westwards from the Balkans after the 1930s, first colonizing Britain in 1955. In the core of its range in India it is a bird of drier habitats, found even in semi-desert.

CALL/SONG

Although very vocal, and singing throughout much of the year, its range is limited. The commonly heard advertising call is a trisyllabic hollow cooing, with the first syllable being a little higher in pitch and somewhat more emphatic; the second syllable also emphatic and the longest of the three notes in duration; the third syllable shorter and rather 'swallowed', such as "Ooh'OOO-oo Ooh'OOO-oo Ooh'OOO-oo…". It has one other commonly heard call given in excitement, in flight and upon alighting – a rather thin nasal "eerrrrr" or "rrrrrehh". It also produces noisy wing flaps when flushed.

Turtle Dove
Streptopelia turtur

LENGTH: 26–28cm

WINGSPAN: 47–53cm

CALL: "crrrrrr 'orrr 'orrr"

TRACK: 1:77

IDENTIFICATION

A slim dove with fairly long, pointed wings and a swift, dashing flight. The head and underparts are pale pinky-grey, and it has a bold pattern on the neck side comprising five bluish-white bars interspersed with four black ones, although these may vary. The most obvious plumage feature is the bright orange-rufous black-centred feathers on the mantle and lesser coverts, with a pale grey-blue panel on the greater coverts. The tail is boldly marked, with a white terminal band, a black sub-terminal band on the upperside and more extensive black on the underside. It has a patch of bare dark red skin surrounding the eye.

HABITAT

A summer visitor that spends the winter in sub-Saharan Africa. It favours dry, sunny and sheltered lowlands, breeding in open deciduous woodlands with rich undergrowth, open country with mature hedges and scattered trees, copses and forest edge, commonly in cultivated areas with dry open patches. It generally avoids human habitation. Much decreased in Britain since the 1980s, and heavily hunted while on passage through Mediterranean countries. Generally shy in its habits.

CALL/SONG

The song is one of the evocative sounds of a summer's day in the countryside, and traditionally described as a "tur-tur", as per the bird's scientific name. It is a deep, hard purring sound, between 570–620Hz, typically in three-syllable phrases (although often just two syllables), and repeated for 3–12 phrases at a time. The longer first syllable rises slightly, the others are level, such as "crrrrrr 'orrr 'orrr', crrrrrr 'orrr 'orrr', crrrrrr 'orrr 'orrr', crrrrr 'orrr 'orrr", or "rrrrrr-rrrr-rrr", etc. It can also give a faster and more hurried version of this song, delivered by the male directly towards the female in a bobbing display. It also has a short popping call, given in excitement.

MALE

Cuckoo
Cuculus canorus

LENGTH: 32–34cm

WINGSPAN: 55–60cm

🔊 **CALL:** "HAK-koo HAK-koo"

⬤ **TRACK:** 1:78

IDENTIFICATION

A slim, rakish bird with a superficial similarity to a small falcon, with pointed wings and a long rounded tail. However, it has a distinctive silhouette in flight as it beats its wings rapidly below the body without gliding at all. When perched and calling, it typically droops the long wingtips below the body. It has a small rounded head and a small thin bill, and is uniformly grey on the head, breast and upperparts, and white on the belly with regular fine black bands. Rufous, or 'hepatic', morphs – occurring only in the female – are rusty-red barred with black and with a white belly barred with black.

HABITAT

Found in a very wide range of habitats, typically in wooded areas, scrub, open country with hedges and scattered trees, reedbeds and wetland margins. All it requires are song perches and any of the 100 different possible host species that have been recorded as being 'nest-parasitized'.

CALL/SONG

The song is widely recognized and gives the bird its name in many languages. Given by the male in the breeding season, from a perch and also in flight to advertise his occupancy of territory, it is a disyllabic "HAK-koo HAK-koo HAK-koo…" the first syllable being higher pitched than the second. This is repeated in long sequences, sometimes at night, and in Britain is typically heard from the birds' arrival in April until June. A variant is also sung, in which the first syllable is repeated two or three times, as in "hak-hak-hak-koo", and it is not uncommon to hear a songster with what sounds like a sore throat, emitting a strangled croak instead of the full note. Females have a bright liquid bubbling call, not dissimilar to the Little Grebe's call and lasting for a couple of seconds. Another call is a harsh "gowk", often repeated, and juveniles can be noisy with a piercing "chiz-chiz-chiz".

HEPATIC FEMALE

Barn Owl
Tyto alba

LENGTH: 33–35cm

WINGSPAN: 85–93cm

🔊 **CALL:** "ekhhhhrrrrrr!"

⏺ **TRACK:** 1:79

IDENTIFICATION

A medium-sized owl with a slim body, long broad wings and long legs, which are often dangled beneath. The heart-shaped facial disc is white, and the eyes are black. The underparts and underwing are pure white, the upperwing and remainder of the upperparts are marbled pale grey on pale yellow-buff. It has an upright stance when perched. In flight it appears ghostly and can often be seen hunting in a slow and measured fashion, low over the ground, hovering briefly before dropping onto prey.

HABITAT

It has a huge worldwide range, and in Britain is localized but not uncommon. It favours open country with scattered trees, farmland mixed with small woods, hedges, scrub, margins of wetlands and areas with rough grass and herbage cover that provide a ready supply of mice and other prey.

HUNTING FLIGHT

As the name suggests, it nests in barns, as well as haystacks, roofs, old buildings, undisturbed outhouses, ruins, cliffs and quarries, often using nest boxes placed within buildings. It also nests in old or dead trees with large cavities.

CALL/SONG

It has a variety of unique screeching and rasping sounds which can sound eerie and perturbing when heard for the first time. The typical call, given by the female, is a rising and high-pitched rasp "ekhhhhrrrrrr!" or a higher-pitched "iiiiieeeeeee". Another similar call is a "ssschhhhhhhhh", not unlike steam being forced out of a small aperture. The advertising call or song of the male, often given in flight, is a little more rolling, with a liquid gargling quality "iiirrrrrrr"r'r'r'r'r!". Young birds in the nest can be quite noisy, making snoring and vowel-less rasping 'ghosts in the attic'-type noises, such as "hhhkhkhkhkh…".

Eagle Owl
Bubo bubo

LENGTH: 60–75cm

WINGSPAN: 160–188cm

🔊 **CALL:** "OOh'oh"

⏺ **TRACK:** 1:80

IDENTIFICATION

A massive owl, weighing up to 4kg. It has long, prominent ear tufts, orange eyes, a large, powerful bill and a rather plain facial disc. The upperparts are tawny or greyish-brown, boldly patterned with black centres to the feathers, and the underparts are buff with heavy black streaks on the breast that fade into narrow streaks on the belly. Flies with powerful wingbeats interspersed with glides, looking like a large raptor with a huge head.

HABITAT

A resident species, found at low densities in mountains, forest and wilderness areas across a wide spread of latitudes. It favours broken terrain with rocky areas, cliffs, quarries, ravines, open wooded areas, mature coniferous forest, scrub, grassy country and tracts of semi-desert with rocky outcrops; it may also be found on the margins of urban areas at rubbish dumps or even on large buildings such as football stadiums! Although probably not native to Britain, introduced or escaped birds started breeding in the wild from around 1996 onwards, often with devastating consequences for the local wildlife!

CALL/SONG

The advertising and territorial call given by the male is a deep powerful "OOh'oh" or "OO'o-oo", with the stress on the first syllable, rising slightly, audible at great range and repeated every 8–12 seconds. It is variable in pitch. The female gives a hoarser, less audible and higher-pitched version, which is also used territorially. When agitated and excited they make a rapid gibbon-like "ou'ou'ou'ou'ouh", with a similar hollow-sounding tone. Other calls are a rather hoarse and screeching "aerrh!" or "rhaeh!", given by the female, and a harsh Heron-like barking "kwa-kwa-kwa!" alarm call. Young birds call with a rasping and slightly ascending "hrrrkh".

Little Owl
Athene noctua

LENGTH: 21–23cm

WINGSPAN: 54–58cm

🔊 **CALL:** "keiw-ho!"

⏺ **TRACK:** 1:81

IDENTIFICATION

A small and tubby owl, with a broad, rounded head and longish legs. It is mid-brown all over, with whitish underparts heavily streaked brown, white spotted upperparts and long pale eyebrows that give it a frowning expression. The eyes are yellow, and it lacks the clearly defined facial disc present in other owl species. Often bobs excitedly, and the flight is bounding like that of a woodpecker.

HABITAT

Introduced into Britain from continental Europe in the late nineteenth century, it favours open country and farmland with scattered trees, quarries, hedges, copses, orchards and parkland, especially where old trees or farm buildings are available to provide roosting and nesting cavities, plus plenty of perching posts. It can also be found in marginal habitats such as cliffs, moorland and waste ground, but avoids dense vegetation and wet areas, and has a liking for semi-arid habitats, which are commonly used further east and south in its range. More terrestrial than other owls, and often encountered during the day.

CALL/SONG

Quite vocal at dusk, when it uses a shrill, disyllabic, sharply descending contact call, "ii!'poh" or "keiw-ho!", with a higher first syllable and a lower-pitched second syllable, vaguely similar to a shortened Curlew call. The advertising call of the male is a clear whistling and rather mournful hoot, again a disyllabic sound but with the second syllable rising and higher pitched than the longer first syllable, such as "U'aaaoo-uh!" or "aaaaa-uh!", repeated every 5–10 seconds. The female gives a version of this call which is flatter and less inflected, such as "Aooo-oo". Other calls are an emphatic, forced-sounding "wheow!" or "wheee'u", a wheezy "thup thup", and an alarm call of repeated sharp wheezy notes, "shi'shi'shi'shi'shi'shi" or "ik'ik'ik'ik…".

JUVENILE

Tawny Owl
Strix aluco

LENGTH: 37–39cm

WINGSPAN: 94–104cm

CALL: "ke'vick"

TRACK: 1:82

IDENTIFICATION

A medium-sized broad-winged owl with a dumpy, hunched shape and large rounded head. It is brown all over, mottled and variegated with darker markings and with paler brown-streaked underparts. It shows two obvious pale stripes on the crown and some pale spotting on the scapulars and covert tips. The large facial disc is plain brown with a narrow blackish rim, and the large eyes are black. It occurs in both grey and rufous phases, the latter being commonest in Britain.

HABITAT

Essentially a woodland bird, but can be found wherever large old oaks and other mature broad-leaved trees occur, such as parks, gardens, churchyards and wooded farmland, as well as in mixed woodland and mature coniferous forest. It is the most familiar and widespread owl in our region, even penetrating urban areas if habitat is available.

CALL/SONG

The song or advertising call is a series of hollow-sounding hooting notes, mistakenly described by the layman as "too'whit-too'woo". Sung by the male, the initial note is a strong hoot, followed by a pause of 2–4 seconds, then a short introductory hoot swiftly followed by a shivering sequence of rapid 'hoo-ing', with a longer final hoot being comparable in strength to the first, as in "hoooooo……..hu'- hu'hu'hu'hu' hoooooh!" or

"hwaooow……..hw'- hwa'ow'ow'- oooow". The female sometimes gives a shorter, simpler hooting in a similar pattern, and both sexes give a loud sharp contact call "ke'vick" or "ae'wick", rising quite sharply on the second note. A variant of this is sometimes repeated sharply in alarm as "kvik kvik kvik". A rarely heard bubbling trill is also given by both sexes during courtship, quite similar to the call of Tengmalm's Owl but audible only at close range. Juvenile birds make a "psee'hip" call.

ADULT

Long-eared Owl
Asio otus

LENGTH: 35–37cm

WINGSPAN: 90–100cm

🔊 **CALL:** "whooo!"

⏺ **TRACK:** 1:83

and the feathering around the bill is also white. The upperparts are brown marked with black with a line of pale spots on the scapulars, and the underparts are buffy, patterned with black arrowhead streaks. The wings are long, with a prominent orange-buff patch on the base of the primaries.

HABITAT

A forest owl, favouring both deciduous and coniferous woodland with adjoining open areas required for hunting. It can be found in farmland with scattered woods, copses, hedges, scrub, parks and plantations. It uses an old stick nest of a crow or an old squirrel's drey, typically in dense vegetation but sometimes on the ground. It disperses more widely in winter, and migrants can be found in coastal scrub or in open areas such as dunes. Communal roosts are formed in winter, usually in a dense impenetrable thicket.

CALL/SONG

Not particularly vocal. The song or advertising call of the male is a simple, deep muffled "whooo!", repeated several times at intervals of 2.5 seconds, not particularly loud but audible from a long distance. The female gives an unusual nasal sneezing "hhhhee!", sometimes in duet with the hooting of the male. Both sexes can give a more barking alarm call "hwik" and "hwak'HWAK". Another far-carrying call that is regularly encountered is the 'rusty gate' call of begging juveniles, a disyllabic call descending on the second syllable "wiz'zee" or "eee'iiii".

IDENTIFICATION

A medium-sized owl with long, prominent ear tufts that are held erect when roosting, in alarm or in courtship. The face is strongly marked and predominantly plain rufous, with a dark area below, above and around the orange eyes, giving it a 'sad clown' effect. The rim of the forehead feathering above the bill is whitish, forming bold vertical lines,

Tengmalm's Owl
Aegolius funereus

LENGTH: 22–26cm

WINGSPAN: 54–62cm

🔊 **CALL:** "op'up'up'up'up'up'up'up'"

⏺ **TRACK:** 1:84

CALL/SONG

The advertising call of the male is a repetitive short deep hoot, audible up to 2km range, "op'up'up'up'up'up'up'up'…", sung in the run-up to the breeding season from January to April, although unmated birds can call into July. It is usually heard at night but occasionally also during the day. The call typically lasts for just 6–8 syllables, but can be much longer depending on the bird's state of excitement, and rises and falls in pitch through the course of the whole sequence. The most frequently heard call is a short "chi-ak" and a yelping "ku'waik", not unlike that of the Tawny Owl, plus a softer "awr'ehh". The young call with a short, rasping "pjjeh".

YOUNG AT NEST-HOLE

IDENTIFICATION

A small owl, slightly larger than the Little Owl, and with a large rectangular head. It has a striking face, with a large whitish-grey facial disc ringed with a black border, large yellow eyes and a distinctively startled or surprised expression. The upperparts are dull brown with a profusion of whitish spots, with finer spotting on the crown and whitish underparts with warm vinous-brown blotches arranged in stripes.

HABITAT

A very rare vagrant in Britain, but there are small and discreet populations in mountainous forested areas in many European countries. It is most frequently found in the boreal forests of Scandinavia and Russia, and these northern populations occasionally irrupt southwards after a good vole year. Found in mature coniferous forest with small clearings and bogs, particularly in spruce, it is rather dependent on Black Woodpecker holes for nesting, although it can be found in plantations and secondary woodland where nest boxes are provided.

Nightjar
Caprimulgus europaeus

LENGTH: 26–28cm

WINGSPAN: 57–64cm

CALL: "koo'ik"

TRACK: 1:85

FEMALE

IDENTIFICATION

A superbly camouflaged and cryptically plumaged bird, very hard to find in the daytime, although in summer birds will emerge from roosts before it is completely dark. The plumage is a blend of greys, browns and blacks, so that when roosting it looks just like a branch. The male has very bold white spots near the tips of the primaries and big square white corners to the long tail, features absent in the more uniform female. In flight it sails along buoyantly, showing long narrow wings and tail, and catching insects on the wing with sharply erratic movements.

HABITAT

A summer visitor to our region from Africa, it can be found around woodland but avoids densely forested country, favouring areas with clearings, glades, young conifer plantations, heaths, moorland, forest edge and adjoining open country. It has a preference for sandy soils and bare ground. Roosts on the ground, on a log or on a branch, and will typically sing from a raised perch.

CALL/SONG

The song of the male is a haunting churring, resembling a distant two-stroke motor or a very butch Mole Cricket, sung at night, pre-dawn, and often at dusk when birds emerge from their roost. It can continue unbroken for several minutes, interspersed with short 'gear changes' of lower-pitched churrs, as in "r'r'r'r'r'r'r'r'r'r'orrr"r'r'r'r'r' r'r'r'orrrr"r'r'r'r'r'r'..." etc. It may end the churring sequence by petering out into a descending "kwhirr-kwhirr-kwhirr'r'r'r'r'r'r'..." or continue by rumbling along in a lower-pitched, quieter 'half-churr'. Between churring bouts, it takes to the wing and often makes a loud wing clap, a slapping 'bapp bapp' sound. The call note frequently given in flight by both sexes is a frog-like "koo'ik" or "oo-whick". A shorter, rather barking "kwuk!" call is given in alarm when a nest is approached.

MALE

IDENTIFICATION

A remarkably well-adapted bird, with an almost entirely aerial life. It is uniformly dark brown with a whitish throat, although often appears black at long range or in poor light. It has a slender cigar-like body with a short forked tail, a short rounded head and very long and narrow sickle-shaped wings that are almost entirely 'hand', the 'elbow' or carpal joint lying very close to the body. They fly strongly, the narrow wings appearing to flicker in rapid flight, although for most of the time they glide or soar, even sleeping on the wing, which they achieve by shutting down the brain one hemisphere at a time.

HABITAT

Found over virtually all and every habitat, the choice dictated only by the abundance of flying insects. Swifts can often be seen feeding low over water bodies in poor weather, conditions in which aquatic insects are more likely to emerge than terrestrial ones. Large weather systems are avoided, the swifts leaving the area completely, but in fine weather they use all available airspace. Formerly adapted to nesting in crevices in cliffs or even in trees, in modern times they nest in urban areas, favouring older houses and churches and using roof eaves, wall cavities and any available crack or crevice in a building.

Swift
Apus apus

LENGTH: 16–17cm

WINGSPAN: 42–48cm

CALL: "ssrrriiii…"

TRACK: 1:86

CALL/SONG

During the breeding season they are quite vocal, particularly in the evenings when nesting birds will perform a group screaming display, racing around their loose colony in a fast-moving flock, sometimes joined by other birds calling from within their nests. Non-breeders will also do this when gathering prior to ascending to higher altitudes for aerial roosting. The calls are high-pitched shrill trilling sounds, varying in pitch and tempo, such as "rrrheeeiiii…", "ssrrriiii…", "zrrreeee…" or "iiiiirrrrreeeeee…", sometimes begun more slowly with hoarse stuttering sounds.

Kingfisher
Alcedo atthis

LENGTH: 16–17cm

WINGSPAN: 24–26cm

🔊 **CALL:** "zii!'eeeee!"

⏺ **TRACK:** 1:87

MALE

IDENTIFICATION

A small, dumpy bird with a short tail, short legs, a large head and a long powerful bill. Beautifully coloured, with a bright, pale blue back and uppertail that catch the attention when in flight, and a darker turquoise blue – which appears greenish in certain lights – on the crown, nape, wings and scapulars. The underparts are rufous-orange, as is the cheek, and the throat is white, with a white patch also on the neck to the rear of the cheek. Sits motionless while searching for fish, otherwise usually seen in fast direct flight low over the surface of the water.

DIVING IN FLIGHT

HABITAT

It nests in a long burrow in a sandy bank, ideally along a slow-flowing fish-rich river or stream, with some trees or bushy margins to provide cover and fishing perches. Also found in other freshwater habitats, such as canals, lakes, reservoirs, dykes, ditches and fishponds, and outside the breeding season can sometimes be found in marine habitats, such as lagoons, sheltered rocky coasts and estuaries.

CALL/SONG

As is so often the case with brightly coloured birds, the calls are simple and uncomplicated. The commonly heard call is a sharp, high-pitched and penetrating whistle, a "tszeeee!" or "peeeep", extended into a repeated disyllabic "ti-peeee ti-peeee ti-peeee" or "zii!'eeeee! zii!'eeeee!", often given in flight. This call is frequently the first or only indication of the presence of the species as it zips past in a high-speed blur of blue. It also gives a softer and more conversational "pee-pee-pee". In spring it is occasionally heard to give a sweet and varied song of trilling whistles, and sometimes a rich warble, and it will engage in noisy chases during courtship.

IDENTIFICATION

An unmistakable bird, rather like a butterfly in flight when it shows its startling pattern of large white spots and bands of white on black wings. The tail is black with a broad white band. The head, neck and breast are pinky-buff, the belly white. The bill is rather long, slender and slightly decurved. It has long pinky-buff feathers on the crest, which are broadly tipped with black, which usually lie flat to the head, but are briefly raised on alighting.

HABITAT

A scarce visitor to Britain, typically as a spring overshoot to southern counties from continental Europe. It is found in flat, undulating or gently hilly open country with scattered trees and bushes, farmland, orchards, vineyards, meadows, clearings and forest edge, as well as on treeless plains where gullies and banks can provide nesting cavities. It spends much of its time feeding on the ground, requiring a short sward of vegetation and open bare ground, and is usually found in rather dry areas. Nest sites are usually in a tree, old building, stone wall or nest box.

Hoopoe
Upupa epops

LENGTH: 26–28cm

WINGSPAN: 42–46cm

🔊 **CALL:** "wohp-wohp-wohp"

⏺ **TRACK:** 1:88

CALL/SONG

The eponymous call of this lovely bird is the song of the male, a trisyllabic hollow-sounding "wohp-wohp-wohp", "oop-oop-oop" or "woud' woud'woud!", somewhat like blowing across the top of a bottle. Repeated frequently and persistently, it sounds weak when close by, but carries for quite a distance. It is rarely heard outside the breeding season. Other calls are rather harsh and uncomplicated, with a scolding "hwkhhhrrr" given in alarm, and a less anxious-sounding and lower-pitched "khwrrrr", given in various contexts such as when attending the young or in conversation with a mate. Young in the nest make a high-pitched "ssi, ssi, ssi, sssi".

Wryneck
Jynx torquilla

LENGTH: 16–18cm

WINGSPAN: 25–27cm

🔊 **CALL:** "kew'kew'kew'kew'kew'kew'"

⏺ **TRACK:** 1:89

IDENTIFICATION

An atypical woodpecker, small and slim with the appearance of a passerine. It is intricately patterned with a complex array of barring, mottling and speckling. The upperparts have a soft grey ground colour, patterned with blackish stripes on the crown, through the eye and onto the neck sides, a larger patch on the back, and a blackish line along the scapulars. The brown wings are subtly marked. The underparts are buffish scalloped black, richer on the throat and whiter on the belly. The tail is rather long and grey, with faint black cross-bars.

HABITAT

Formerly breeding quite widely in England and Wales, it had become extinct by the 1970s although occasional breeding has occurred in Scotland since then . It remains widespread in Europe. Most likely to be encountered in Britain as an autumn migrant on the east coast during easterly winds, when it can be found in scrub and bushes. Its breeding habitat is open woodland, orchards, parks, gardens, scrubby pastures and forest edge, with a preference for deciduous trees. It does not excavate its own nest hole, so breeding is dictated by the availability of holes and also by open bare ground, where its favourite food of ants is available.

CALL/SONG

The advertising call is given by both sexes, occasionally in duet, and only during the breeding season. It is a rather shrill and repeated "kew'ke w'kew'kew'kew'kew'kew'...", with a slight rise and fall in tone over the whole sequence. The "kew" note is typically repeated 12–15 times, but regularly up to 30 times at a rate of 6 notes per second. It is most similar to the call of a Hobby, and also resembles that of Lesser Spotted Woodpecker, although stronger and more metallic sounding. It gives hard "tuck" notes in alarm, typically when close to the nest, and a hissing sound when alarmed at the nest itself.

Black Woodpecker
Dryocopus martius

LENGTH: 45–47cm

WINGSPAN: 64–68cm

🔊 **CALL:** "khxlooo"

⏺ **TRACK:** 1:90

CALL/SONG

Vocal and loud throughout the year, with a variety of different calls. The call usually given in flight or alarm is a mechanical-sounding and guttural "krrr h'krrrh'krrrh'krrrh'krrrh…". While perched it gives an often repeated, loud clear "kluuue", which on closer analysis is a rather disyllabic sound with a swallowed short first syllable, such as "khxlooo". The advertising call, analogous to the "yaffle" of the Green Woodpecker, is a rather long "ee'qwe 'qwe'qwe'qwe'qwe'qwe'qwe…", rising in pitch and tempo. It also gives another disyllabic call, a "ke'viou ke'viou" or "ih'kvui, ih'kvui", again with a swallowed first syllable. It has the loudest and longest drum of any of our woodpeckers, typically lasting 2.25 seconds and with a very fast rate of 16–18 'knocks' per second. It also uses loud tapping and knocking sounds as contact calls.

IDENTIFICATION

Unmistakable. A crow-sized woodpecker with a direct if flappy and rather clumsy-looking flight. All black, with a powerful ivory-coloured bill. The male has an entirely red crown, while in the female red is restricted to the hind crown. The eye is white with a boldly staring effect. Quite shy and unobtrusive despite its size, but it is inquisitive and responds to imitations of its call.

HABITAT

Although never reliably recorded in Britain, it is found just a short ferry ride away on the near coast of Europe. It favours mature coniferous and mixed forest, but also occurs in deciduous forest such as beech, up to 2000m on occasion, and requires a large breeding territory. It can range more widely in winter, visiting isolated woods and secondary stands. Although expanding in the north-west of its range, on the whole it is sedentary.

Grey-headed Woodpecker
Picus canus

LENGTH: 25–26cm

WINGSPAN: 38–40cm

🔊 **CALL:** "huw'huw'huw-huw-huw"

⏺ **TRACK:** 1:91

MALE

IDENTIFICATION

Similar to the Green Woodpecker, but smaller, slimmer and longer tailed. The bill is slimmer and shorter, and the head pattern is quite different, giving it a unique expression. The head is a clean grey, with an orangey-brown eye, a restricted black patch on the lores and a narrow black malar stripe. Only the male has red on the head, confined to the forecrown. The upperparts are a cold green, and the slightly brighter rump is less contrasting than on Green Woodpecker. The underparts are pale grey-green and unmarked. Generally shyer than the Green, spending less time on the ground.

HABITAT

Never recorded in Britain, it is resident in parts of Scandinavia and central France eastwards. It is found in subtly different habitat from that of the Green Woodpecker, extending more into upland areas. It occurs in mature deciduous forest, open woodland with beech, oak and hornbeam, and locally in mixed coniferous forest. It favours forest edge, riverine, swampy and marshy woods, parklands with mature trees, and occasionally gardens.

CALL/SONG

The advertising song is similar to that of the Green, but is slower, more fluty and drawn out, typically lasting for 4–9 notes, with 3.5–4 notes per second. The call decelerates and drops in pitch over the sequence, such as "huw!'huw!'huw-huw-huuw…" or "hi'hi'hi'hii hii hiou", often extended to more than 10 notes at an even slower rate and fading away. The Green's 'yaffle' differs in that it accelerates slightly. Short calls given while agitated are a short "jhk" or "kik", and a Green Woodpecker-like "kya'kya'kya'kyak", given both in flight and when perched.

FEMALE

FEMALE

Green Woodpecker
Picus viridis

LENGTH: 31–33cm

WINGSPAN: 40–42cm

🔊 **CALL:** "hwa'hwa'hwa'hwa'hwa'hwa..."

⚫ **TRACK:** 1:92

IDENTIFICATION

A large woodpecker, with green upperparts that are yellower on the rump, which shows clearly in the deeply undulating flight. The underparts are pale greenish-grey, and it has a long, powerful horn-coloured bill. The head and face are boldly marked, with a red crown that extends to the nape. The face is black, with a staring white eye, and a short black moustache which is centred with red in the male, but is all black in the female.

HABITAT

A familiar and common bird, resident across our region. It avoids dense forest and is found in open broad-leaved woodlands with clearings, forest edge, large gardens, parkland, orchards, hedges with mature trees, farmland, pastures, rough grassland and heaths with scattered trees. Often encountered in areas with open ground and grassy areas such as golf courses, it spends much of its time on the ground. Turf-dwelling ants are a favourite food, and it has a very long tongue with which to lick them up.

CALL/SONG

The advertising call of the male, usually sung from high in a large tree, is a far-carrying, and slightly accelerating laughing series of notes, "hwa'hwa'hwa'hwa'hwa'hwa...", colloquially described as 'yaffling'. It typically lasts for 1–3 seconds, dropping in pitch towards the end of the call, with a rate of about 6 'yaffs' per second. The female gives a shorter, flatter 'yaffle', not dissimilar to the call of the Whimbrel. In flight both sexes give a loud, chuckling and oft-repeated call of 3–4 syllables, such as "chyuk'chyuk'chyuk'chyuk" or "kye'kye'kye", also expressed when perched as an alarm or excitement call. The drum is rarely heard, and said to be fairly quiet and last 1.5 seconds.

MALE

Great Spotted Woodpecker
Dendrocopos major

LENGTH: 22–23cm
WINGSPAN: 34–39cm
CALL: "kik"
TRACK: 1:93

IDENTIFICATION

A familiar bird across most of our region. The upperparts are black, patterned with white, two large oval white patches on the scapulars being the boldest feature. The flight feathers are banded with white transverse bars, and the short stiff tail is black, the outer feathers white barred with black. It has a black nape and crown, with a large white cheek patch enclosed by a black 'bridle' that loops from the bill to the rear of the cheek, plus a smaller white patch set within the black on the sides of the neck. The undertail coverts are crimson, and the remaining underparts are buffish-white. In the male, there is a distinct patch of red on the nape, lacking in the female.

MALE

FEMALE
FEEDING

HABITAT

A resident, and the commonest of its family in northern and western Europe. It is found in all types of forest, both deciduous and coniferous, plus mature hedges, large gardens, parkland and smaller wooded patches. More northerly populations may disperse southwards when cone crops fail, and migrants can appear in various coastal habitats and even on treeless islands.

CALL/SONG

Attention is usually drawn by its call, as it shins up a tree trunk or flies in strongly undulating flight from one patch of trees to the next, uttering a loud "pick!" or "kik", usually uttered singly. When agitated it gives a series of rapidly repeated excited calls, accelerating into a hard rattling trill on occasions. It also has a softer "tchick". In spring it frequently 'drums', a resonant mechanical raining of blows on a suitably dry branch, often at the very top of a tree. The drum typically lasts for between 0.5 and 0.7 of a second, and includes 12–14 'knocks'. Both sexes drum, usually between February and May, with females drumming in the earlier part of this period.

IDENTIFICATION

Much the smallest of our woodpeckers, a real midget with a short stubby bill and small rounded head, and at 17–25g is just 25 per cent of the weight of the Great Spotted. The underparts are whitish without red on the vent, and with a prominent black submoustachial stripe from the bill that flares on the neck side and disperses downwards into streaks on the flanks. Upperparts are black, cross-barred with white bands from mantle to flight feathers. The male has a red crown, lacking in the female which has a buffy-white patch restricted to the forecrown.

HABITAT

Resident in our region, although it is rather unobtrusive and easily overlooked, and has much declined in England in recent years. It can be found in broad-leaved and mixed woodlands, favouring parks, large gardens, orchards, copses, groves and alder trees along river valleys, ranging into more marginal habitats in winter. Feeds on insects by gleaning along trunks, small branches and twigs, also known to 'flycatch', and usually requires a good supply of decaying wood.

Lesser Spotted Woodpecker
Dendrocopos minor

LENGTH: 14–15cm

WINGSPAN: 25–27cm

CALL: "e-pee'pee'pee'peee'pee'pee'pee"

TRACK: 1:94

FEMALE

MALE

CALL/SONG

The short "chick" call is similar to and confusable with that of the Great Spotted, yet is weaker, higher-pitched and less far-carrying. The advertising call is a long, fast series of rather shrill piping notes, "e-pee'pee'pee'peee'pee'pee'pee" or "qwi'qwi'qwi'qwi'qwi …", sometimes trailing away at the end. It is rather similar to the calls of Wryneck and Kestrel. This call is primarily used in the breeding season, but may be heard at other times, as is the drumming, which is used as a territorial 'call'. It drums faster, longer and more evenly than the Great Spotted, lacking the 'drum roll', and lasting up to 1.75 seconds at a rate of 18–19 'hits' per second.

Woodlark
Lullula arborea

LENGTH: 14–15cm

WINGSPAN: 30–36cm

CALL: "dudlooee"

TRACK: 1:95

IDENTIFICATION

Smaller and slimmer than the Skylark, with a distinctively short-tailed appearance in flight. It lacks any white on the trailing edge of the wing, but has a broad pale bar on the tips of the primary coverts. The tail feathers are white-tipped, forming a transverse bar. The upperparts are neatly and boldly streaked black on a warm brown ground colour, the head is boldly patterned with a long, whitish supercilium that joins at the rear of the crown, the cheeks are rufous-brown with a dark surround and the bill is rather slender. The chest is warm buff with clear black streaks forming a breast band, and the remainder of the underparts are white.

HABITAT

Occupies quite a variety of habitats across Europe, but seems to require a mosaic of short grass for feeding, longer vegetation such as heather for nesting, with scattered bushes and small trees for perches and song posts. It can be found on sandy or well-drained soils, in clearings in open pine or broadleaved forest, young plantations, heaths, moors, parkland, weedy derelict fields, partly scrubby mountainsides, forest edge, burnt areas, dunes and cork oak *dehesas*. In winter it ranges more widely and can be found in stubble fields, although it is less gregarious than other lark species.

CALL/SONG

One of the most beautiful and enchanting songs, delivered from the ground, a prominent perch or in a song flight. The song is clearly broken into phrases, each lasting 1.5–4 seconds with clear pauses between of 1–2 seconds, and introduced by two or three slower hesitant notes followed by a descending cadence of several varying fluty notes, such as "dlui-dlui' dlui'dlui'dlui'dlui", "tit'tit'tit'toodle 'toodle'toodle", "chi'chi-tuue'tuue'tuue'tuue'tuue", etc. The call note, given as an alarm or contact note, is a one- to three-syllable "tid'loo-eet", "dudlooee" and "dlewee-dlewee".

Skylark
Alauda arvensis

LENGTH: 17–18cm

WINGSPAN: 30–36cm

🔊 **CALL:** "churrrrip"

⏺ **TRACK:** 1:96

IDENTIFICATION

The commonest lark in our region. It is rather robust, with a stubby half-crest, rather broad wings with a whitish trailing edge, white outer tail feathers and a distinctively hesitant and fluttering flight action, with much hovering and dithering in the air. The plumage is unspectacular, with the upperparts streaked blackish on buffy-brown, the crown finely streaked black, and the face pale with a whitish supercilium, lores and eyering. The underparts are whitish, with clear blackish streaking on the upper breast forming an obvious breast band.

HABITAT

A bird of open country, farmland and steppe, frequently found in cultivated fields. It favours grasslands, coastal meadows, dunes, pastures, heaths, heather moors and grassy hilltops. It requires some open flat areas, and can be found in low stature crops and herbage, as well as in taller crops so long as open ground is available nearby. Western European birds are generally resident, their numbers supplemented in winter by migrant birds from further north and east, which can form large flocks. Migrating birds are easily located by call as they pass overhead.

CALL/SONG

The song is a familiar sound, a melodious collection of sweet chirruping and whistling phrases with a hypnotic cyclical quality. Typically it is sung without breaks for 1–5 minutes, occasionally for longer, and usually commencing from take-off as the bird ascends into its song flight, which takes it high into the sky. It sings freely from the ground also, although with a less exuberant version. The song sometimes includes mimicry of other species. The calls are frequently heard, and include a variable but bright-sounding dry rolling chirrup, such as "prrr'id", "churrrrip", "prrr'i'i'ew", "pruurt", "pree'eep" and "rreep'chechew", often sounding rather slurred.

Shore Lark
Eremophila alpestris

LENGTH: 14–17cm

WINGSPAN: 30–35cm

CALL: "thissip"

TRACK: 1:97

FEEDING PARTY ON SALTMARSH

IDENTIFICATION

An attractive lark, unique in our region in having a yellow face, throat and eyebrows, with a bold black 'comma' on the fore part of the cheek and extending through the eye, lores and over the bill. It has a black bar across the crown, with elongated feathers at the sides forming narrow black horns, prominent when held erect but often hard to see. They are most obvious on a male in spring plumage; immature birds lack these horns and they are more reduced in the female. The underparts are white with a pinky-brown wash on the flanks, the upperparts are pinky-brown lightly streaked with brown. When seen from below, the tail feathers are black. The race found in our region is *flava,* and many other races occur around the Holarctic.

HABITAT

Unlike other lark species, it breeds at high altitude or high latitude, above the tree line on barren dry mountain tops, high fells, alpine moors and on dry tundra down to sea level in the Arctic zone. In winter, when it is most likely to be seen along the east coasts of Britain, it favours sandy beaches with emergent vegetation, dunes, saltmarshes, stubble fields and coastal meadows with a short sward.

CALL/SONG

It has a rather mournful little song, delivered in short phrases with a bright tinkling quality reminiscent of the songs of both Snow and Lapland Buntings. The song phrase starts a little hesitantly and discordantly, accelerating and rising towards the end before finishing with a short jangle. It lasts on average about 1.5 seconds and comprises 9–10 notes or groups of notes, such as "tu dit ee'tee'hlee'dli'dleedl'tee'eh". It is not noticeably loud or far-carrying, and is delivered either from the ground or in a high song flight. The call notes are rather soft and thin, variants including "thissip", "tseep", "tsee-sirrp", "hee-du" and "hee-eedu".

Sand Martin
Riparia riparia

LENGTH: 12–13cm

WINGSPAN: 26–29cm

🔊 **CALL:** "tschrr"

⏺ **TRACK:** 1:98

CALL/SONG

The call is a distinctive dry rattling trill, fairly high-pitched and with a harsh quality. The short call is a monosyllabic vowel-less "tschrr" or "trrrkhr", similar to the call of the Lesser Short-toed Lark. When numerous birds are present, such as at a colony, the call becomes a continuous excited chirruping, and a high-pitched "tscheeer!" or "schweer!" is given in alarm when aerial predators are spotted. The song is poorly developed and similar in quality to the call, a simple dry rolling, trilling and chirruping twitter but delivered in a longer accelerating sequence, although it can be hard to discern from the sound of an excited group.

IDENTIFICATION

The smallest swallow in our region. A slim and delicate bird, with a fast flickering flight with the wings angled close to the body, and not usually gliding like some of its relatives. The upperparts are a uniform earth-brown, the underparts white, and it has a diagnostic clear brown band across the upper breast, enclosing the white throat which extends in a half-collar at the neck sides.

HABITAT

A summer visitor to our region from Africa, its habitat choices are strongly linked to available nesting sites. Nests are made in vertically faced sandy banks along a river or sea cliff or in a quarry or sand pit, with tunnels excavated into the bank to a depth of more than 60cm. Favoured habitats include river valleys, gravel pits, lakes and coastal areas. They feed on aerial insects and can therefore be encountered over any area that provides good feeding, and frequently over water. At migration periods they can form large roosts in reedbeds.

GROUP AT COLONY

Swallow
Hirundo rustica

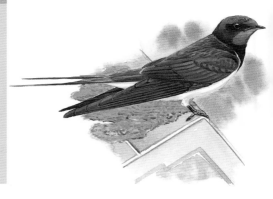

LENGTH: 17–19cm (inc. tail streamers of up to 6.5cm)

WINGSPAN: 32–34.5cm

◀)) **CALL:** "vhit vhit vhit"

● **TRACK:** 1:99a

IDENTIFICATION

The classic harbinger of summer, an elegant streamlined bird with a deeply forked tail that carries narrow elongated streamers on the outer tail feathers. The upperparts are a glossy midnight blue, with a deep red forehead and throat, a dark blue breast band and buffish-cream underparts. Immature birds have short tail streamers and a dingy buff throat. When spread, the tail shows white spots on the feather webs. The flight is light and graceful, with rapid swoops after insects.

HABITAT

A summer visitor to our shores from Africa. As an aerial feeder dependent on flying insects, it can exploit a very wide range of habitats provided that food is plentiful. It tends to avoid densely forested and mountainous areas, but otherwise can be found in all types of open country, although most commonly in farmland and villages where grazing animals are present. It can be seen feeding low over meadows and pastures and also over freshwater bodies, marshes and other wetlands. It is also dependent on suitable nesting places, favouring partly open farm buildings, barns, outhouses, stables and other similar structures.

CALL/SONG

The song is a melodious twittering and spluttering, periodically interspersed with a strangled croak followed by a trilling rattle, and can be sung persistently either in flight or from a perch such as a wire. Sub-song or short twittering phrases are frequently heard, such as "wttwtitwttwwtit". It has a variety of calls, such as a commonly heard "vhit!", often repeated as "vhit vhit vhit", and a sharp, higher-pitched, slightly ascending "vheet! vheet!" or "plee-vhink" as an alarm call in response to aerial predators. Other variations are a conversational "tit'tich'iwitt" and "wtwittit", a quick "thwitt" and a sharp "tjjup!".

House Martin
Delichon urbicum

LENGTH: 13–15cm

WINGSPAN: 26–29cm

🔊 **CALL:** "jijitt"

⏺ **TRACK:** 1:99b

CALL/SONG

The commonly heard note is the contact call, a short dry stony rattle with a bright quality, as in "prrrt", either monosyllabic or often repeated two or three times in rapid succession, such as "jijitt", "prrrr-tit" and "jrrrr-tit'it". It also gives a shrill descending "schreeeo" as an anxiety call, often in response to aerial predators. All of these calls are typically heard from flying birds. The song is made up of several call notes run together, plus a throaty rapid warbling without any structured phrases, a rambling chuntering that is sung usually when close to the breeding area or at the nest itself.

IDENTIFICATION

A dumpy and compact swallow, and simply patterned. It has blue-black upperparts, cap and tail, with a large white rump as its most distinctive feature. The underparts are white, including the underwing coverts and the feathered feet, and the tail is rather short but with a prominent fork. The flight action is rather different from the other swallows in our region, being slower with much gliding on straight wings, often in long lazy arcs.

HABITAT

A summer visitor from Africa. Originally a cliff-nester (still the case in some parts of its range), it is now more commonly found around towns and villages where it nests in closed mud-built structures, typically located under the eaves of houses. Bridges and other man-made structures are also used, and as a consequence it can be quite confiding with humans. It requires a good supply of mud with which to build its cup-shaped nest, and breeding sites therefore usually reflect the proximity of a nearby source. It avoids densely forested areas, and often feeds high in the air with Swifts. It is less tied to water than some of its relatives.

Tree Pipit
Anthus trivialis

LENGTH: 15cm

WINGSPAN: 25–27cm

CALL: "bzzzt"

TRACK: 2:1

IDENTIFICATION

A subtly different bird to the Meadow Pipit, with a stronger bill, a bolder pale supercilium, a broader and paler submoustachial stripe, and a hint of a dark eyestripe that bisects the orbital eyering. It also shows a small pale spot on the rear of the ear coverts. The streaked mantle is subtly less contrasting, the breast is buff and contrasts with a whiter belly, the breast markings are neat and extend onto the flanks only as very fine and narrow streaks. The legs are brighter pink. The call is the surest way to identify this species, coupled with its habit of perching in trees.

HABITAT

A summer visitor, favouring open woodland, old oak and birchwoods, young conifer plantations, parkland, heaths, commons, scrubby downs, grassland with scattered trees, up to the tree line in mountains but avoiding areas that are too open or too dense. Migrants can be found in a wider range of habitats, typically with trees and scrub, or flying over open country, when they can be identified by their call.

CALL/SONG

The call is distinctly different from that of the Meadow, being stronger, louder and audible from further away, a buzzing and slightly descending "bzzzt", "teezz" or "sbihz". The anxiety call, given on the breeding grounds, is a short alert "chitp". The song is long sequence of fluty whistles, louder and sweeter than closely related species and delivered from a treetop or similar perch, or in a parachuting song flight. It comprises four or more segments of calls delivered at different tempos, including clear trills, such as "che'che'che chi'di chi'di chi'di chi'di chi'di chyew chyew chyew chyew chyew ti'ti'ti'ti'ti' trrrrrrrrrr seeeoo", with many variations, even from the same songster.

Meadow Pipit
Anthus pratensis

LENGTH: 14.5–15.5cm

WINGSPAN: 22–25cm

🔊 **CALL:** "tssit'ssit'ssit"

⏺ **TRACK:** 2:2

IDENTIFICATION

Perhaps the archetypal little brown bird, with few features to distinguish it! It is olive-brown on the upperparts, well streaked with black on the mantle, plain on the rump, with bold white outer tail feathers. The brown crown is streaked black, the bill is slender with a mostly yellowish lower mandible, and the face is pale, with pale lores and a short diffuse pale eyebrow. The underparts are whitish to pale buff, with a bold malar stripe, clear black spots and streaks on the breast extending down on to the flanks. The legs are pinkish.

HABITAT

It favours open country, breeding in grassland, moorland (where often abundant), meadows, coastal pastures, saltmarshes, heaths and young plantations. Outside the breeding season it ranges more widely into virtually any open country, such as farmland, wetlands and beaches. Birds that breed at higher elevations descend in winter, and populations in temperate western Europe are usually resident, their numbers supplemented in winter by birds arriving from areas to the north and east, where they tend to be migratory.

CALL/SONG

The commonly heard call, frequently uttered on take-off, is a thin "tssit'ssit'ssit", typically repeated in triplets although also often singly, sometimes with a variation, as in "weesp". A more abbreviated "ssit" or "chip" note is also used, and the anxiety call used frequently near the nest is a rapid, clipped "tse'tut". The song is brighter and more bubbling than that of the Rock Pipit, quickly accelerating with more variety in tone and with more rattling trills thrown in, such as "tsilp tsilp tsilp tsilp'tsilp'tsilp'tsilp'tsilp'tttrrrrrrr bl'bl'bl' bl'bl'bli'bli'bli'bli", often with a few buoyant "bing bing bing" notes added. The pitch and harshness vary between songsters. The full song is only delivered in a parachuting display flight, but birds frequently sing from the ground with a shorter and simpler version of repeated introductory notes.

DISPLAY
FLIGHT

Rock Pipit
Anthus petrosus

LENGTH: 16–17cm
WINGSPAN: 23–28cm
CALL: "wheesp"
TRACK: 2:3

IDENTIFICATION

Larger than the Meadow Pipit, which is the most likely candidate for confusion. Robust and fairly long-tailed, with an overall dingy appearance that helps it merge with its favoured rocky habitat. The legs are dark, as is the slender bill. The upperparts are grey-brown, with darker smudgy lines on the mantle, and the whitish tips to the wing coverts form wingbars. The head lacks a prominent supercilium, and the face is dominated by a narrow white orbital eye-ring and a well-defined blackish malar stripe. The tail is quite long and full, with pale smoky-grey outer tail feathers. The underparts are dingy buff with bold smudgy dark streaks on the breast extending down to the rear flanks.

HABITAT

Strongly tied to the coast and rarely found away from it, favouring cliffs, islands, rocky gullies and beaches, usually in somewhat sheltered places although not averse to wind and spray. In winter it ranges more freely, onto estuaries, saltmarshes and beaches, with northern European birds spending the winter in western Europe alongside the resident population.

CALL/SONG

The call is a rather explosive, slightly rising "wheesp" or "phisst", with a shriller quality than the Meadow Pipit, and usually given singly. Other calls are a fuller, flatter "chilp", given when slightly anxious, shortening to a "stip" or "tsutt" but also extended into a dry stuttering "trr'r'r'r'rrrt". The song is similar to that of the Meadow, but somewhat more musical and metallic, with a stronger terminal trill, and is also delivered in an ascending song flight with a parachuting descent to the ground on rigid wings as it sings the final phrases. The song phrase begins by rising and accelerating, then descending in tone near the end, as in "fss'p-fss'p-fss'p'sillp sillp sillp sillp sillp sillp sllp'sllp'slp'slp'slp'sip 'sip – che'che'che'che'chu'chu'chu'chu du du trrrr'r'r'r'r'r".

FEMALE

Yellow Wagtail
Motacilla flava

LENGTH: 15–17cm

WINGSPAN: 23–27cm

CALL: "fsseep"

TRACK: 2:4

IDENTIFICATION

Two forms occur within our region, the 'Yellow' Wagtail *M. flava flavissima*, which breeds in Britain and in adjacent Europe, and the 'Blue-headed' Wagtail *M. flava flava*, which occurs across most of Europe. Both forms share many features, being rich yellow from chin to vent, with a long white-edged tail, green upperparts and wing feathers patterned with darker centres and pale fringes. The male *flavissima* has a greyish-green crown and eyestripe, the yellow of the underparts extending onto the face, supercilium and forehead, while the male *flava* has a blue-grey crown, cheek and nape, with a white supercilium. Females are paler, washed primrose-yellow below, whiter on the throat and with duller pale grey-brown heads.

MALE

HABITAT

A summer visitor from Africa, it breeds in damp, grassy habitats and the margins of wetlands, such as saltmarshes, pastures, water meadows, marshes, lakes, riversides, fens, peat bogs and sewage farms, as well as in crops where wet or marshy areas occur nearby. It is often seen in close association with livestock, feeding around their feet on the insects that are disturbed. On migration it can be found in similar habitats, often on pastures, golf courses and other short-cropped grassy areas. The form *M. flava flavissima* has decreased considerably in Britain in recent years.

CALL/SONG

The typical call, frequently given in flight, is a liquid, often plaintive "fsseep", "fsss'up", "wzeeer" or "wee'ssep", often with two components audible although not quite disyllabic, descending towards the end of the note. It also gives a single shorter "tseh" and an anxious Chaffinch-like "chiwaink". The song is very simple, an undeveloped couple of rasping buzzy notes such as "zeeri'ziip", "zeeer'p" or "wzzzeer-zeup", sometimes with a phrase of twittering notes, and delivered from the top of a large plant, fence post or bush, and sometimes in a song flight of languid undulations.

Grey Wagtail
Motacilla cinerea

LENGTH: 17–20cm

WINGSPAN: 25–27cm

CALL: "dji'dih"

TRACK: 2:5

IDENTIFICATION

An elegant and attractive bird, with a very long white-edged tail which is pumped continuously, rocking the whole rear of the bird. In all plumages it shows a bright yellow vent and brownish-pink legs. The head and mantle are pure grey, the wings blackish with white edges to the long tertial feathers. In summer the male has a rich yellow on the breast, and a bright white supercilium and submoustachial stripe and a black throat. The female typically has a white or dingy greyish throat, a buff supercilium and paler yellow underparts. In winter both sexes show a white throat, and the underparts are pale whitish-yellow.

HABITAT

More closely tied to water than its relatives, it breeds along fast-flowing streams and rivers, canals, lakesides and some larger slower rivers, which can provide perches on rocks, shingle, weirs and locks, plus cavities for nests in walls, roofs, rocks and culverts, with trees and bushes alongside. Commonly found on upland and mountain streams, and outside the breeding season it ranges more widely into lowland areas, also occurring on estuaries, coasts and sewage farms. It also appears in towns and cities, often using the flat roofs of tall buildings where rainwater collects.

CALL/SONG

The vocalizations are high pitched, as is typical for birds living around rivers, which produce a lot of low-frequency noise. The typical call is a disyllabic "dji'dih" or "chiddih", also uttered singly as "djitd" and often heard in flight. The anxiety call when near the nest is a rising "sweee" or "chwea". There is also a three- or four-syllable penetrating high-pitched call, "tsi'tsi'tsi'tsi". The song is a bright, high-pitched tinkling series of varying phrases of notes, not unlike a shorter, more rapid version of the Tree Pipit song, such as "di di ti'ti'ti chichichi chew trrrrrrr pink pink pink see-chew". Another phrase, sometimes intro-duced or sung singly, is a simple "si'si'si see-chew".

MALE SUMMER
PLUMAGE

MALE WHITE
WAGTAIL (*M. A.
ALBA*) SUMMER
PLUMAGE

Pied/White Wagtail
Motacilla alba

LENGTH: 16.5–19cm

WINGSPAN: 25–30cm

🔊 **CALL:** "chissick"

⏺ **TRACK:** 2:6

IDENTIFICATION

Two forms of this bird occur in our region, the Pied Wagtail *M. alba yarrelli* in Britain and along the Channel coasts, and the White Wagtail *M. alba alba* across Europe. Birds are semi-resident in western Europe, while elsewhere they are summer visitors. The Pied Wagtail is black on the back in the male, dark grey in the female, with little or no contrast between back and head pattern, plus a blackish rump. The White Wagtail has an ash-grey mantle with a sharp border to the black nape, more diffuse in the female. In winter both forms lose the black throat.

HABITAT

Found in a wide range of open habitats, typically close to wet areas such as lakes, rivers, streams, gravel pits, estuaries and coasts, and also in open areas such as farmland, fields, pastures, parks, gardens, airfields, golf courses and along roads, ideally where water is present but most importantly having flat open areas in which it can see and run. It is also regularly found in towns and villages, around buildings with suitable surrounding habitat. It often forms communal roosts in urban areas in winter, on large city buildings such as office blocks, hospitals and supermarkets, on window ledges, rooftops or in adjacent trees.

MALE PIED WAGTAIL
(*M. A. YARRELLI*)
SUMMER PLUMAGE

CALL/SONG

Commonly heard calls include an emphatic high-pitched disyllabic "chissick", sometimes uttered as a single syllable "chitt" or "tschick", and also the flight call, which is a thinner-sounding and more liquid "tsli-wee", "tslee-vit" or a trisyllabic "tslee-li-vit". Another call is a more slurred and slightly descending "tzwerr'p". The song, given at a fast tempo when in a state of excitement, such as display or alarm, is a very rapid sequence of call notes run together in varying pitches, with harder single-syllable notes dominating the structure and interspersed with higher liquid notes. It also gives a more languid song, a series of twittering notes interspersed with pauses.

Waxwing
Bombycilla garrulus

LENGTH: 18–21cm

WINGSPAN: 32–35cm

🔊 **CALL:** "ssrrrrrrrrrr"

⬤ **TRACK:** 2:7

IDENTIFICATION

A gorgeous bird, roughly the size of a Starling although plumper, thicker-necked and more compact. The plumage overall is a pinky grey-brown, with a greyer rump and chestnut vent, and a band of yellow on the tail tip, broadest on the male. It has a distinctive soft crest, a black patch on the lores extending behind the eye, a white spot at the bill base and a black throat. The wings of the male are strikingly patterned with white bands on the primary covert and secondary tips, the latter having little red waxy appendages that give the bird its name. The primaries have sharp white crescents on the very tips, and yellow tips on the outer webs forming a bold yellow line on the closed wing. These features are duller and reduced on the female.

HABITAT

A winter visitor to Britain and irregular in occurrence, some years seeing large invasions but other years very few. Typically in flocks, they can be found wherever their favourite winter diet of berries is available, favouring Rowan and other *Sorbus* species plus a variety of introduced berry-bearing trees and bushes. They can appear in hedgerows, parks, gardens and street trees. In summer they breed in boreal mature coniferous forest rich in *Usnea* lichen, feeding on insects and often engaging in flycatching sallies from the tops of tall trees.

CALL/SONG

The call is a distinctive silvery trilling "srrrrrrrrr", often given in half-second bursts although frequently for longer, at a rate of about 22 notes per second. Most regularly encountered in our region in winter flocks, this trilling can be continuous when many birds are calling and is given most emphatically just prior to flight. The song is a slow and halting combination of trilling phrases and harsh raucous sounds, such as "srrrrrrr sirrrrrr chark chark chi-chark srrrrrrr srrrrrrr", etc.

Dipper
Cinclus cinclus

LENGTH: 17–20cm

WINGSPAN: 26–30cm

CALL: "djih!"

TRACK: 2:8

IDENTIFICATION

A Starling-sized bird, very rotund and chunky, and closely tied to its aquatic habitat. It is cold brown on the upperparts, and a warmer rusty-brown on the head. The single most obvious feature is the large pure white bib, which extends from chin to mid-breast, often appearing as broad as it is deep due to the girth of the bird. The short tail is often held half-cocked. British birds are rusty-brown on the lower breast and belly, while nominate continental birds (the 'Black-bellied' Dipper) are brownish-black below. Typically encountered as it sits, bobbing and winking its white eyelids, on a mid-stream rock from which it dives underwater and swims, often surfacing with wings spread. Flies fast and direct like a fat brown bullet.

HABITAT

Found along watercourses in upland and mountainous areas and also down to sea level, favouring shallow but fast-flowing streams and rivers where ample mid-stream perches such as rocks are available, especially where bordered by trees. It makes a domed mossy nest in a cavity in an undisturbed wall, bank or bridge, often overhanging the water and even behind waterfalls. It can also be found occasionally on slower-flowing rivers with weirs. Although primarily a resident species, continental birds regularly disperse in the winter months and occasionally reach southern and eastern England.

CALL/SONG

The call is a sharp note that is audible above the noise of roaring rivers, a curious and penetrating "djih!", also rendered as "stretts" or "zitt" and given often in flight. Both sexes sing, a rather understated medley of warbles and high hard notes, not unlike the sub-song of an immature Blackbird. The female's version is less melodious, sounding more disconnected and scratchy.

Wren
Troglodytes troglodytes

LENGTH: 9–10cm

WINGSPAN: 13–17cm

CALL: "tchek"

TRACK: 2:9

IDENTIFICATION

A tiny brown bird, with the distinctive habit of cocking its tail up and over its back. Often found skulking in dense undergrowth, restlessly foraging close to the ground or flying between cover like a brown bee. The upperparts and head are a warm reddish-brown and the short wings are finely vermiculated and barred. The underparts are paler and mottled on the flanks, and it has a slender bill and a long pale creamy supercilium.

HABITAT

A widespread and common bird throughout our region, particularly in woodland with dense undergrowth, as well as in scrub, hedges, gardens, parks, moorland where bracken-filled gullies offer shelter, sea cliffs and other rocky places with crevices. Occurs up to the tree line in some parts of its range. Resident in Britain, but birds in northern Europe move south in winter.

CALL/SONG

Very vocal, typical call notes are a hard "tchek" or "chudt", often extended into "tchek'eck'eck". It also gives a low rattling churr. When anxious, near the nest or young or in response to danger such as a cat, it gives a higher-pitched hard rattle not unlike someone sucking on the corner of their mouth to produce a rasping sound, such as "tr'tr'tr'tr'tr'tr'tr". The song is remarkably loud and shrill for such a tiny bird, and is a very rapid series of well-structured piercing notes, usually including or ending with a loud trill. It usually lasts for 4–7 seconds, during which time it produces about 6–8 notes per second, such as "see'se'seo w'see'seee'ch'ch'ch'ch'ch'see'suwi'suwi'see'su'e e'trrrrrrrrrr chu'chu'see!".

IDENTIFICATION

A demure little bird, skulking and frequently unobtrusive, usually seen shuffling mouse-like on the ground. It is brown and grey, the warm brown mantle clearly streaked with black, and the underparts are dull grey-brown with mottled brown streaks along the flanks. The head, neck, throat and breast are a clean lead-grey, with brown cheeks and a darker mottled crown. The bill is thin, black and warbler-like.

HABITAT

A familiar resident 'pioneer' garden bird in Britain, which can be found anywhere with dense scrubby undergrowth. It is commonly encountered in gardens, parks, churchyards, open mixed woodland, farms, scrub, hedges, young conifer plantations and heaths, as well as on overgrown rough ground in urban areas such as railway embankments, especially where these are a little damp. It is attached to spruce forest in northern parts of its range, where it is usually just a summer visitor.

CALL/SONG

The common call is a rather coarse, high-pitched "tiih", often repeated a number of times and given both as a contact call and an alarm. It also gives a thinner, less coarse "seep" and a shivering "itititi", the latter typically given outside the breeding season and rather like the alarm call, but more silvery in quality. The song is a high-pitched scratchy little ditty, fairly rapid and expressed on a level tone without trills or flourishes, confusable with the Wren's song but slower and much less emphatic, lasting 1.5–3 seconds but also in longer

Dunnock
Prunella modularis

LENGTH: 13–14.5cm
WINGSPAN: 19–21cm
🔊 **CALL:** "tiih"
⏺ **TRACK:** 2:10

phrases. It is rather regular and unvarying, such as "s s'tsi'ti'si'ti'teew'ti'ti'deuw'tii'si'si'ti".

Robin
Erithacus rubecula

LENGTH: 12.5–14cm

WINGSPAN: 20–22cm

🔊 **CALL:** "tic-tic'tic"

⏺ **TRACK:** 2:11

IDENTIFICATION

A familiar bird to many, this is a delicate but plump bird, with brown upperparts and crown, a narrow buff wingbar, and a large orange-red breast extending across the face and over the bill, rimmed with a blue-grey border. The underparts are whitish with a brown wash on the flanks. A ground feeder, it hops along and pauses watchfully, with flicks of the wings and tail. It is famously aggressive and territorial towards other members of its species.

HABITAT

Essentially a forest bird, found in shady woodland with undergrowth and commonly in gardens, parks and other managed places offering dense cover. In Britain it is common and notably confiding, but elsewhere in northern Europe it frequents coniferous forest, is migratory, and much more retiring.

CALL/SONG

Quite vocal. A commonly heard call is a territorial note "tic", usually repeated as "tic-tic'tic", "pt-pt'pt", or often as "tikatik-tik", and often likened to the sound of an old-fashioned watch being wound up. It has a thin sharp "tseeeh", used in alarm. The song is heard throughout much of the year and frequently in autumn and winter, when resident local birds react territorially to the arrival of wintering birds from the continent. It is a languid, melodic sequence of clear fluty whistles and rippling notes, switching between high and low frequencies and interspersed with pauses. The song is very variable, typically commencing with a few thin high notes, then dropping into lower richer notes before speeding up into a warbling trill, and frequently including a "dee-diddlee'dee" phrase. It can sing at length, but phrases typically last for 2–3 seconds, with measured pauses between.

Thrush Nightingale
Luscinia luscinia

LENGTH: 15–17cm

WINGSPAN: 24–26.5cm

🔊 **CALL:** "eep"

⏺ **TRACK:** 2:12

IDENTIFICATION

Similar to and confusable with the Nightingale, it is a duller, cold earth-brown on the head and upperparts. The tail is more chestnut and of a deeper red tone, and although less bright than the corresponding parts of the Nightingale, this creates a noticeable contrast, particularly in flight. The underparts are drabber, with mottlings of grey-brown, forming clear malar stripes and extending into a dingy but noticeable breast band that contrasts with the white throat. It is lightly mottled on whitish flanks, and the undertail coverts can show small dark spots on the sides.

HABITAT

Only a rare vagrant to Britain, but a summer visitor to southern Scandinavia and the Baltic region, where it replaces the Nightingale. It favours similar habitats of dense, shady, scrubby undergrowth in broad-leaved woodland, hazel stands and waterside scrub, as well as parks and gardens with components of damp or swampy ground with rich leaf litter and humus. Feeds on the ground and often prefers to run rather than fly.

CALL/SONG

Some of its calls are similar to those of the Nightingale, such as a flat Chiffchaff-like whistle "eep" or "whit", a hard croaking churr "khrrrrrrr", sometimes delivered together as "eeeep-khrrrrrr", and a short deep "chuk". The song is also similar to the Nightingale, but is louder and less sweet, with more deeper and lower frequency segments. It is delivered at a rather slower pace, and consequently phrases tend to be longer, typically lasting 4–6 seconds. It includes popping, tongue-clicking, glottal stops and harder rattles, and is highly variable, going something like "chow chow chiwerh' o chiwerh' o chiwerh' o chii'oh chii'oh chii'oh gkrgkrgkrgkrgkrgkr kh'kh'kh'kh'kh'kh'kh' shi" or "hwe cho hwe cho krrrre'i krrrre'i krrrre'i pocpocpoc chauw tsrit tsrit tsrit kna'kna'kna'kna chichichichi-si".

Nightingale
Luscinia megarhychos

LENGTH: 15–16.5cm

WINGSPAN: 23–26cm

CALL: "hweet"

TRACK: 2:13

HABITAT

A summer visitor from Africa, although much decreased in Britain. It favours dense undergrowth, often within broad-leaved woodland and frequently in damp and swampy areas. It can be found in more open woodland with clear ground beneath, or in dense scrub, hedges, gardens, orchards and riverine thickets. Migrants can be found in a wider range of habitats, but usually stay hidden in dense cover.

CALL/SONG

Famous as a songster, it vigorously delivers its loud, rich song at any time of day or night, typically from dense cover, although in some areas – such as around the Mediterranean – it sits out in the open and will even sing from wires! The song bursts typically last for 2–4 seconds and can be very varied, but usually include a series of components including drawn-out low whistles, hard trills, hard "choc-choc-choc" and "jug jug jug" notes and crescendos, and with a little flourish at the end of the phrase, such as "oooo oooo oooo chew'chew'chew titi'churr chi'ur'chih! weeee-weeer-weeer urrr'r'r'r'r chyu'chyu'chyu'chit! whichoo'wichee kr'r'r'r'r'r'r weechup!" and so on. It has various calls, such a guttural frog-like croaking "krrrrrrrr", a low "tuc-tuc", a clear Chiffchaff-like "hweet" or "uiihp", and a rather feeble plaintive "eeeep", frequently repeated.

IDENTIFICATION

A remarkably plain-looking bird considering that its song is so exotic and rich. It is warm brown above, with a rather long and broad tail that is often cocked, and both the tail and rump are a richer rusty-red than the remaining upperparts. The underparts are whitish with a sandy wash across the breast and down the flanks, and the crown and cheeks are warm brown. The face is very plain and has an open, gentle expression, enhanced by a narrow pale eyering; there is a grey wash to the supercilium and on the neck sides. When not sitting low in a bush it feeds on the ground, hopping with wings drooped and tail raised.

MALE

Bluethroat
Luscinia svecica

LENGTH: 13–14cm

WINGSPAN: 20–22.5cm

🔊 **CALL:** "thuck"

⏺ **TRACK:** 2:14

a swampy component. It winters in north-east Africa, India and south-east Asia.

IDENTIFICATION

Similar in shape to the Robin, but slimmer and longer legged. On the ground it hops and runs well, with the tail cocked and a noticeably erect carriage. The male is unmistakable, with a bright blue throat and chest, ringed on the lower edge with a black band, a narrow whitish band and a broad rusty-reddish band above the belly. Most populations have a large red throat spot, although this spot is white in the race *cyanecula* or 'White-spotted' Bluethroat, which breeds from eastern France to Russia. It has a long broad whitish supercilium, a whitish belly and cold brown upper-parts. The tail is diagnostic, being blackish-brown with a chestnut basal half which shows as side panels when fanned or as the bird flies low over the ground. Females and immatures lack the full blue throat to varying degrees, the least well-marked birds showing just a buffy white throat ringed by a greyish-brown gorget.

HABITAT

A scarce migrant in Britain, the breeding range stretching in separated blocks from Spain and France to eastern Europe and Scandinavia. It favours scrub and bushy thickets, wooded clearings, open boggy willow and birch forest, thick stands of herbage, fens, reedbeds and riverine woodland, nearly always with

CALL/SONG

It has various little chat-like calls, a throaty swallowed "thuck", a churring "trrrk", a high-pitched "tzii", and an anxious descending "zree'ze'ze'ze'ze", heard sometimes on the wintering grounds. The song has similarities with the Nightingale's, but is busier and more highly pitched, with squeaky and buzzy elements, throat clicks and squelching sounds. It is incredibly varied, including much mimicry of other species, with particular groups of notes usually repeated twice, and is often sung continuously rather than in set phrases, such as "suchee sichoo chk'chk'chk, eeh-di'didi'choo, eeh'di'didi'choo, kik'wheeee, kik'wheeee, trac trac trac, fzzzrrrt fzzzrrrt, it'titi'titi'ti, trrrr trrrrr…" etc.

FEMALE

Black Redstart
Phoenicurus ochruros

LENGTH: 14.5cm

WINGSPAN: 23–26cm

CALL: "iisp-teck'teck teck"

TRACK: 2:15

FEMALE

IDENTIFICATION

Similar in size and shape to the Redstart, also perching upright and shivering its rusty-red tail. The male is charcoal-grey, with blacker face and underparts, and with a prominent white wing-patch on the secondaries, visible on the closed wing. The female is sooty grey-brown above and below, with a less obvious pale eyering than Redstart. In fresh plumage it shows fine silvery edges to the wing feathers.

MALE

HABITAT

A rare and localized breeder in Britain, but not uncommon on the continent. Resident in the more temperate parts of western Europe, it is otherwise a summer migrant and winters mainly around the Mediterranean. It is found from uplands to lowland towns and cities, favouring rocky and craggy terrain with bushes, industrial areas, chimneys, church towers and marginal urban areas with rank weedy growths, where it nests in a crevice or cavity in rocks, walls, roofs etc.

CALL/SONG

The calls follow a similar pattern to those of its close relative, but it has a higher-pitched "seep" or "iisp" than the Redstart and also a harder and 'stonier' "teck'teck'teck'teck". The calls are often combined into a "iisp'teck'teck'teck" when the bird is more anxious. The song is a rather high-pitched phrase, often sung at first light from a conspicuous high perch. It is longer than the Redstart's song, averaging 3.5–5 seconds, and comprises three clearly separate parts. It is introduced with a rattle of sweet notes followed by a pause, then a curious quiet metallic scrunching and squishing noise, likened to a handful of ball bearings being shaken together, then a final flourish of three or four clearer rising notes, such as "eee'tyu'tyu'tyu'tyu …khxkhxkhxkhx tyu-che ch'chew". On some occasions only the introductory notes are heard.

FEMALE

Redstart
Phoenicurus phoenicurus

LENGTH: 13–14.5cm

WINGSPAN: 20.5–24cm

🔊 **CALL:** "hwiid"

● **TRACK:** 2:16

IDENTIFICATION

At all ages shows a rufous-red tail and rump, with darker grey-brown central feathers. At rest it has an erect posture, and the tail is frequently shivered nervously. The male in spring is particularly striking, with a black throat and large white patch on the forehead, and a grey crown and mantle. The breast is orange-red, fading onto the belly. The female is plain, with mid-brown upperparts and head, the latter dominated by a beady eye within a pale orbital ring. The underparts are warmer and the breast is buff, tinged orange.

HABITAT

Widespread in our region, although in Britain has a markedly westerly distribution. It is a summer visitor from Africa, and favours sheltered rather open woodland of mixed and broad-leaved species (although sometimes found in pines), woodland edges, streamside trees such as pollarded willows, orchards, gardens, heaths and commons with scattered trees; the important factor is a supply of nest hollows in old trees, walls, rocks and banks. It is often encountered on autumn migration along the eastern coasts of Britain, where it can be found in scrub, hedges and open wooded areas.

CALL/SONG

The call is a simple and insistent "hwiid" or "huit", and a clicking Robin-like "tic-tic-tic" or "thic-thic-thic", typically combined to make a "hwiid-tic'tic'tic". The song is a rather high-pitched pleasant little ditty, rather melancholy in tone and regular in length, lasting just 2–2.5 seconds. It is not particularly loud, and consists of a standard introduction of five notes followed by a terminal jangle and flourish, which varies from phrase to phrase, often including mimicry; such as "eee'tyui'tyu'tyu'tyu – peee'chi'chuw 'eep" and "eee'tyui'tyu'tyu'tyu – siii si chew trrrr'si'whichoo'sii" etc. Typically sings from a high perch in a tree, the male often using the same perch throughout the breeding season.

MALE SUMMER PLUMAGE

Whinchat
Saxicola rubetra

FEMALE

LENGTH: 12–14cm

WINGSPAN: 21–24cm

CALL: "hew! tidt'idt'idt"

TRACK: 2:17

IDENTIFICATION

The male in spring is boldly marked, with blackish-brown cheeks and crown highlighted by a long, pure white supercilium, and a white bridle separating the ear coverts from the throat. The throat and breast are orangey-buff, fading to white on the belly. The tawny-brown mantle and rump are boldly streaked and spotted blackish. The tail is black with a white basal half that shows in flight as white side-flashes. The female is more demure, lacking the bold head pattern although still with an obvious pale supercilium.

HABITAT

A summer visitor, wintering south of the Sahara. It has a more northerly distribution than the Stonechat, and favours uplands and open country, often where damp, with scattered bushes, rough grassland, heaths, meadows, rough pastures, wetland margins, young conifer plantations and bracken-covered hillsides. It nests on the ground, in a grassy cup hidden in a tussock.

CALL/SONG

The commonly heard call is a short descending whistle, usually with two or three hard nasal 'tacking' notes added, such as "hew! tdt'itd', hew! tidt'idt'idt". It also gives an anxious, harsh rasping "khshrrrr" when near the nest or young. The song is a short and rapid ensemble of notes crashing together, lasting 1.5–2 seconds. It is often started with a few hesitant notes, followed by a hard churring trill which then quickly expands into a flourish of more musical but short notes, such as "ch, ch, wichu-wrrrrr ti'wichee'te'wheoo". One variant includes a short jangle, like the song of the Corn Bunting, and it often includes mimicry in the song phrase. It sings from a prominent song perch such as a bush, treetop, or tall clump of bracken, and sometimes in a short song flight when it flashes its tail pattern.

MALE

Stonechat
Saxicola torquatus

FEMALE

LENGTH: 11.5–13cm

WINGSPAN: 18–21cm

CALL: "tjak'tjak hweet"

TRACK: 2:18

CALL/SONG

This bird's name could be taken from its call, a dry 'chacking' that is supposed to sound like two pebbles knocking together. This sound is typically repeated a number of times, a "tsac tsac" or "tjak! tjak!", often combined with another call when anxious, a rather upwardly inflected "sweet" or "hweet", such as "tjak'tjak hweet" or "sweet tsac!'tsac!". The song is a short collection of rather feeble-sounding high-pitched notes, rather monotonous and reminiscent of the Dunnock's song, as in "sii'hew'ichi'hwee'tsiti'chwee'hu'whe et". It typically lasts for about 1.5 seconds and is usually delivered from the top of a bush or similar and occasionally in flight.

IDENTIFICATION

The widespread and familiar chat of open country, a small compact and dumpy species that continually flicks its wings and tail nervously when perched. The male has a wholly black head, with a prominent white half-collar extending up from the shoulder and contrasting with both the dark upperparts and the deep orangey-rufous breast and flanks. It has a white band on the inner wing coverts that is often hidden at rest, the mantle is indistinctly streaked brown and blackish, and the rump is buffy and spotted black. Females are duller and browner, with a dark-mottled throat. Birds in fresh autumn plumage look paler and browner, due to the fresh brown tips to the feathers.

HABITAT

Resident in western Europe, it favours open country with low vegetation, from uplands to plains, and is also found in coastal areas. It frequents heather, bracken, rough grassland, stony and sandy country, hillsides and cliffs, and in Britain is particularly attached to gorse thickets. It requires perches such as hedges, walls and fences to use as lookout posts, from which it can sing or scan for insect food items.

MALE

Wheatear
Oenanthe oenanthe

LENGTH: 14–16.5cm

WINGSPAN: 26–32cm

🔊 **CALL:** "heet! jk jk"

⏺ **TRACK:** 2:19

MALE

HABITAT

A summer visitor and one of our first arrivals in spring. Its habitat choices are very varied, from Arctic tundra and rocky mountain slopes to downland, heath, moorland, dunes, coastal islands, pastures, fields and meadows, sea cliffs, bogs and steppe. It is a terrestrial bird strongly tied to a habitat of short sward with bare patches where it can feed. On migration it occurs more widely, but always on short vegetation such as lawns, golf courses etc.

CALL/SONG

It shares with other chats a single whistled note and a hard chacking note, the former a high-pitched level-toned "heet!" or "hiit!", the latter a short hard "chak chak" or "jk jk", typically used together as "heet! jk jk" when excited or alarmed. The song is a brief but confident outburst of fast, rather hard and crackling notes, such as "kh. k'chee'krr'che e'nk'khr'choo'wee", often with "heet" call notes included, and also some mimicry. On average the phrase lasts for 1.2–2 seconds and is sometimes introduced with one or two short hesitant "chak" notes with a pause before the main phrase. It becomes richer and more varied when given in a short song flight, but is otherwise sung from a prominent song post such as a wall, rock or wire.

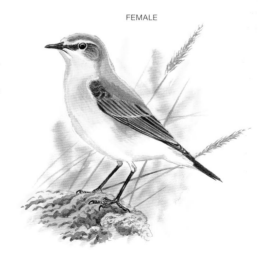

FEMALE

IDENTIFICATION

The name 'wheatear' appears to be a corruption of 'white arse', a more appropriate descriptive name as the primary field character of the bird in all plumages is a white rump and tail, the latter patterned with an inverted black T. The male in spring is blue-grey on the crown, mantle and lores, has black ear coverts and wings, and a prominent white supercilium. The underparts are white with a suffusion of orange on the throat and breast. In the female the black parts are brown, and the back is grey-brown. In autumn, males turn brown on the mantle, buffy on the underparts and they lose the solid blacks.

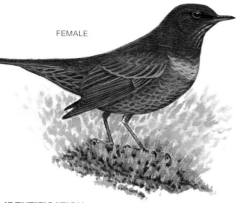

FEMALE

Ring Ouzel
Turdus torquatus

LENGTH: 23–27cm

WINGSPAN: 38–42cm

CALL: "tahk tahk tahk"

TRACK: 2:20

IDENTIFICATION

Similar in size and shape to the Blackbird, although it appears longer and slimmer with its longer wings and tail. The male in spring is unmistakable, with a broad white gorget on the breast. The plumage is charcoal-black overall, and at all ages it has pale edges to the wing feathers, giving the wings a pale appearance in flight. The female is dark brown with a duller, brown-washed scaly gorget on the breast and pale scaling on the underparts. Autumn birds are browner and much more scaly, as are immatures, which also lack any obvious breast band.

HABITAT

A summer visitor, which in Britain and northern Europe breeds in hill country, typically in broken ground with rocky outcrops. It favours open moorland and fells, bare mountainsides, boulder-strewn slopes with gullies, with only a scattering of sparse or stunted trees. Alpine populations, however, nest in open coniferous forest. On migration it can be seen in farmland, dunes, pastures, coastal scrub and in berry-bearing hedges.

CALL/SONG

The song is a far-carrying simple repetitive collection of phrases, quite rich in tone and interspersed with strangled twittering notes that often tail off. It is marked by deliberate pauses between each set of notes, sounding both languid and desolate, such as "tchue tchue tchue… tchu'ee tchu'ee tchu'ee… pl'in pl'in pl'in… trre trre trre… khshrrr… tshrrr'iii… tschrr'ir'ri'i'i… che che che…", etc. The call notes are hard 'tacking'-type sounds, quite unlike those of the Blackbird, and repeated two or three times or more, such as "tahk tahk tahk". It also has an almost clicking "trr trr trr", a rather Fieldfare-like chuckling rattle "chrk chrk chrk", and a very hard stony "trkk trkk trkk" sound with the resonant quality of a pebble bouncing on ice. Also gives a thin high squeak similar to that of the Fieldfare.

MALE

Blackbird
Turdus merula

LENGTH: 24–25cm

WINGSPAN: 34–38.5cm

🔊 **CALL:** "chink chink chink chink"

⬤ **TRACK:** 2:21

FEMALE

IDENTIFICATION

A strong-legged, sprightly, ground-feeding long-tailed bird. The male is all black, with an orange-yellow bill and eyering, the female is uniform dark brown with slightly paler central throat and faint mottling on the malar stripe and breast. Immature birds are brown like the females, with males in their first year showing a black tail and sooty plumage; fledged juveniles have rufous-tipped feathers.

HABITAT

Found in all types of forest and woodland with undergrowth, in farmland, scrub, copses, hedges, gardens and parks, as well as moorland and wetlands provided that cover and undergrowth are available; it also requires open and bare ground for feeding. Common and resident in Britain, with populations supplemented in winter by northern and eastern birds migrating to western Europe from further east.

MALE

CALL/SONG

Very vocal, with a rich repertoire of calls. One of the loudest – and therefore most familiar – is the alarm call, a loud, often hysterical, tinking and clucking such as "chink chink chink chink…" or "plih! plih! plih!", when the neighbourhood birds start 'kicking off' at dusk prior to roosting, often accelerating the calls into a manic crescendo when taking flight. This is also used in mobbing situations. Variations include a less intense, low "chuck chuck chuck". Other calls are the 'ground predator alert' call, commonly used for cats, a soft "pock" or "puhc", and frequently heard when parents have fledged young and are keeping watch for danger. It also has a thin, drawn-out and descending "sseeh", given in alarm, and a more rolling "srrri", typically used on migration. The song is rich, confidently languid and pleasing, with a series of fairly low-pitched fluty notes uttered in phrases lasting 2–4 seconds, usually tailing off into low chuckling notes and often with an equal length pause between. Each male has wide variety of song phrases, sung from a prominent perch such as a roof or treetop.

Fieldfare
Turdus pilaris

LENGTH: 22–27cm

WINGSPAN: 39–42cm

🔊 **CALL:** "schakk schakk schakk"

⏺ **TRACK:** 2:22

IDENTIFICATION

A long-tailed thrush with a black tail and a blue-grey rump, which is particularly noticeable in flight along with the white underwing coverts that flash as it flies. The head and nape are grey, with blackish lores and a yellow-based bill, and the mantle is a dull reddish-brown. The underparts are white, narrowly streaked on the throat but more heavily streaked and spotted on the breast, which is richly suffused with rusty-orange. The flanks are finely and regularly spotted.

HABITAT

Breeds across Scandinavia and central Europe eastwards, and is essentially a winter visitor to Britain, often occurring in sizeable flocks. It nests in forest and woodland, favouring alder, birch, pine and spruce, often where open, and also in montane scrub, parks, gardens, hedges and riverine belts of trees. In winter it is most commonly found in farmland with rough fields and berry-bearing hedges, but will visit parks and larger gardens.

CALL/SONG

The song is a rather strangled, high-pitched, scratchy warbling, sounding more like an undeveloped sub-song and lacking any fluty tones. Phrases can last 2–6 seconds, or be delivered as a continuous squeaky monologue for longer periods. It is more emphatic when delivered in a song flight, when the bird flies level with slow deliberate wingbeats, singing a faster warbling mixed with excited chattering. The call is a low cackling and chacking note, repeated two or four times, variable in pitch and with a loose liquid quality, as in "schakk schakk schakk" or "trrruc trrruc trrruc". Migrants calling in flight often introduce a single high squeaky note. On their breeding grounds Fieldfares give a faster and more excited chatter in alarm, akin to the call of the Mistle Thrush.

Song Thrush
Turdus philomelos

LENGTH: 20–22cm

WINGSPAN: 30–36cm

🔊 **CALL:** "ssip"

⏺ **TRACK:** 2:23

IDENTIFICATION

A compact and smallish thrush, plain brown on the upperparts and with whitish underparts that are richly suffused with yellowish-buff on the breast and flanks. It is heavily spotted with black across the breast and extending down the flanks. The cheeks often show a subtle pattern of a pale patch bordered with darker smudges, and it has a dark bar on the tips of the primary coverts. Usually seen hopping on the ground, pausing to look and listen for worms etc.

HABITAT

Resident in Britain, the population supplemented in winter by birds from northern Europe. Breeds in a wide variety of forest and woodland, in parks and well-vegetated gardens, hedges, churchyards and smaller wooded patches, requiring shade and undergrowth with adjacent open areas, particularly where damp. It also occupies sparser island habitats and moorland. In winter it makes similar habitat choices.

CALL/SONG

The loud, rich song is bold and confident, given from a tall tree or similar high position with a characteristic repetition of notes which are given three or four times and followed by a short pause before the next sequence of notes begins, such as "errp hewp hewp hewp chu chi… trrree'ch- chi trrree'ch-chi… peeoo peeoo peeoo… chuchich'ichichi… do'do'di'didee… teechoo teechoo teechoo…", etc. The song is very variable, some notes being clearly enunciated and fluty, others shrill or high-pitched, and when being sung excitedly it can sometimes completely lack any pauses. Calls include a thin sharp "ssip", often heard when flushed or from migrant birds, and a low scolding "chuck'chuck chuck" or "djuk djuk djuk", accelerated into a higher-pitched rattling chatter when alarmed.

Redwing
Turdus iliacus

LENGTH: 19–23cm

WINGSPAN: 33–34.5cm

🔊 **CALL:** "tszeeep"

⏺ **TRACK:** 2:24

IDENTIFICATION

A small thrush, boldly marked with a long whitish supercilium and whitish submoustachial stripe framing the brown ear coverts. The underparts are white with a buffish wash across the breast, a dark malar stripe and bold dark streaks and mottling on the breast and flanks. The flanks are brick-red, as are the underwing coverts. The upperparts are uniform olive-brown.

HABITAT

A common winter visitor to Britain, with odd pairs staying to breed in Scotland. Commonly found in northern Europe, breeding mainly in coniferous forests but also in mixed forest, scrub and birch. Often favours river valleys and damp areas, and will nest in parks and gardens. In winter in Britain it is found in farmland with berry-bearing hedgerows, open woodland and occasionally in parks and gardens.

CALL/SONG

The commonly heard call in Britain is uttered in flight, a thin, slightly buzzing and descending "tszeeep", often heard from migrant birds flying over at night. It also has a soft "pok" or "chup" note given by perched birds, a nasal "gak", and on the breeding grounds gives a dry scolding rattle, a hard stony "trrrr trrr ktrrrr" or "trrac trrac". Migrant flocks at rest also give a collective twittering and chuckling. The song varies much between individuals, and is a loud clear sequence of three or four repeated notes lasting 1–2 seconds, almost always followed by a strangled, hard-to-transcribe, warbling and squeaky twittering phrase that lasts two or three times as long as the clear note phrase. Variants are a rising "tlui-tlui-tlui", a descending "vee'du-vee'du-vee'du", a level-toned "tui-tui-tui-tui", a steeply ascending "kt'rt'tr'tr'tr'tr" and a cheery "ki-chirri-chirri-chirri-chirri", delivered on a level tone, all followed by the twittering "ksch't't'rr'ttschrr'tr't'tii".

Mistle Thrush
Turdus viscivorus

LENGTH: 26–29cm

WINGSPAN: 42–47.5cm

🔊 **CALL:** "tschrrrrr"

⏺ **TRACK:** 2:25

IDENTIFICATION

The largest and palest thrush in our region, with brownish-grey upperparts, long tail and upright stance. It has a pale side to the head with darker blotches on the cheek, pale lores and whitish underparts, which are well spotted with round black spots, although much sparser than in the Song Thrush. The wings have pale edges to the feathers, the rump is paler and the tail has whitish spots on the tips and pale outer feathers. The underwing is white, noticeable during its strong but languid and gently undulating flight.

HABITAT

A woodland bird, found quite widely wherever tall trees occur in conjunction with short grass, such as in pastures, fields, parks and in gardens, where it will often dominate berry-bearing bushes and defend them aggressively. Resident in Britain; northern European birds will move south and west in winter, while in the southern part of the range it is found on mountain slopes with conifers and scrub.

CALL/SONG

The song is delivered confidently from a high perch, often in the early spring before leaves appear on the trees. It is less varied and more monotonous than that of the Blackbird, consisting of loud, unhurried, clear fluty notes. The Mistle Thrush gives the impression that it has paid more attention to the musical composition, with pauses between phrases, such as "tchiou chew chu… trrruu tiou chu… tew chee-chu… chewi'oo jooii… chewi'oo jooii… tchoo'wee'di choo'ii… choo'twee'doo choo'wi… choo wee'doowee'chu…", etc. The commonly heard call is a dry ticking rattle, often given in flight and accelerating into a more scolding sound when alarmed, such as "tschrrrrr" or "tkhrrrrrrr'r'r'r'r'r'r'r". It also has a rapid "tck-tck-tck".

Cetti's Warbler
Cettia cetti

LENGTH: 13–14cm
WINGSPAN: 15–19cm
CALL: "cht! cht! cht!"
TRACK: 2:26

occur in drier reedbeds with willow and bramble scrub.

CALL/SONG

The song is a sudden explosive burst of very loud notes, typically sung once from dense cover, then not again for several minutes. The classic or most clearly structured version consists of a loud single introductory note, followed by a very short pause, then a very rapid six-note phrase repeated two or three times, such as "chett! tsitt'iwich'iwee'ju! tsitt'iwich'iwee'ju!". It is given throughout the year, sometimes by the female, and may also be used as a contact or alarm note. Other variants are commonly heard, such as "chett! chitchiwah! chitchiwah! chitchiwah!", or mixed up with call notes, as in "chip chip chitiwah chitiwah chitiwah chip" and "chit'op chit'op chit'op perchew'perchew'perchew". It has various call notes, such as "chlip chlip", a Wren-like scolding "trr'tr'trt' trt'trt'trt' trt' trt' trt' trt", or a more Blackbird-like "cht! cht! cht! cht! cht!".

IDENTIFICATION

A stocky, compact and medium-sized warbler which often carries its tail half-cocked. It is a rich red-brown on the upperparts, grey on the head sides and supercilium, with a darker line through the eye. The throat is greyish-white, the breast and belly greyish, and the undertail coverts are brown, occasionally tipped paler. The wings are short and stubby and the tail is broad. At times it is Wren-like in behaviour, and can be very skulking as it keeps to cover close to the ground.

HABITAT

A relatively recent colonist of Britain, and spreading further from its stronghold in the south-east. It is resident, favouring tangled thickets of bushes and shrubs around the margins of wetlands such as lakes, marshes, rivers, streams, canals etc, but does also

Grasshopper Warbler
Locustella naevia

LENGTH: 12.5–13.5cm
WINGSPAN: 15–19cm
CALL: "pjitt"
TRACK: 2:27

IDENTIFICATION

A small and demurely plumaged warbler, with a fine bill, short wings and fairly long graduated tail. It lacks any bold face pattern, with just a narrow pale line over the eye, and has diffuse dark streaking on the upperparts and dark-centred wing coverts and tertials. The upperparts are dull olive-brown overall, while the underparts are whitish, washed olive-buff on the breast and flanks, it is normally unstreaked below, although some may show dark flecking on the throat and upper breast. The long undertail coverts show diffuse streaking

HABITAT

A summer visitor, favouring low, tangled vegetation such as overgrown thickets, meadows, nettlebeds, grass, and the drier parts of reedbeds, particularly where there are scattered bushes, or in young trees such as conifer plantations. It is often found in damp areas or near water, marshes, lakesides and small watercourses. Often scuttles along the ground like a mouse and is very hard to spot unless singing, and so is rarely seen on migration.

CALL/SONG

The song is very distinctive, a continuous and thin insect-like trilling or 'reeling' like a free-wheeling bicycle, which can continue for many minutes and is frequently heard in the evenings or at night. The song often begins with some shorter 'practice' bursts before the main effort, and actually consists of double notes that are delivered at a rate of 24–26 per second at frequency of around 6kHz. It is usually sung from within a small bush or low in grass or reeds, where the bird can sometimes be found sitting with bill open and orange gape showing, turning its head from side to side. This action causes the sound to be 'thrown', and the volume rises and falls, depending on where the bird is facing. The call is a short sharp "pjitt" or "thsik", and short, sub-song-like ticking sounds are also given.

IDENTIFICATION

A large dark warbler with a rather long, broad, graduated tail. It is uniform dark olive greyish-brown on the upperparts, with dull and dingy underparts except for a whitish throat and centre to the belly. The throat and upper breast are streaked with diffuse mottlings making characteristic streaks, although this feature is variable. The undertail coverts are very long, olive-brown with whitish scalloping created by the pale feather tips. The head is rather plain with a faint supercilium. Similar in many respects to Savi's Warbler, although in the breeding season the River shows strong habitat differences.

HABITAT

A summer visitor, its breeding range stretches from central Europe north-eastwards across southern Finland and Russia. It is only a very rare vagrant to Britain. It is unlike its relatives in its choices of habitat, favouring dense tangled undergrowth in damp areas, moist woodland edges, bushes and tall scrub, riverine thickets, wetland margins and meadows with tall grass and herbage, and young deciduous trees such as alder, hazel, willow and birch. Rarely encountered except when singing.

River Warbler
Locustella fluviatilis

LENGTH: 14–16.5cm
WINGSPAN: 19–22cm
🔊 **CALL:** "pink"
⏺ **TRACK:** 2:28

CALL/SONG

The song is similar to those of the other two *Locustella* species, in that it is an almost mechanical, insect-like buzzing that can continue for long periods, but with a distinctly different sound. It is much slower, consisting of 8–12 'signal peaks' per second, and the sound wavers noticeably, such as "zzh'zzh'zzh'zzh' zzh'zzh'zzh'zzh'zzh'zzh'zzh'zzh'zzh'zzh", etc. It is slow enough for the individual pulses to be discernible, although the notes themselves are complex and buzzy. The song is often introduced with "prrrik" or "trrrc" notes, and when alarmed the bird gives a sharp "pink" note. It sings from quite high in a bush or small tree, and is especially vocal at night.

Savi's Warbler
Locustella luscinioides

LENGTH: 13.5–15cm

WINGSPAN: 18–21cm

CALL: "zick"

TRACK: 2:29

IDENTIFICATION

A rather plain and brown bird, superficially similar to the Reed Warbler, with which it shares the same habitat. It is larger and bulkier than that species, with long rusty-buff undertail coverts that reach almost to the tail tip, a long and broad graduated tail and a convex curve to the leading edge of the closed wing. It is uniformly warm brown on the head and upperparts, cold brownish-buff on the underparts, with a dingy wash across the breast and flanks and a whitish throat. The head is rather plain, with an indistinct short pale supercilium.

HABITAT

A summer visitor from Africa and very scarce in Britain, visiting a handful of localities in some years only. It is found almost exclusively in extensive tall *Phragmites* reedbeds, and is therefore hard to see except when singing. Typically it clambers up a tall reed stem, where it sits and sings for long periods. It is sometimes found in tall rushes, bulrush or other dense waterside vegetation, or very rarely at coastal stations while on migration.

CALL/SONG

The song is similar to that of the Grasshopper Warbler, a long continuous mechanical 'reeling', but is lower pitched (at around 4kHz) and much faster, at 48–50 double notes per second, which gives the sound a harder and more buzzing quality. Like the song of the Grasshopper Warbler, the sound has a ventriloquistic dimension as the bird turns its head from side to side. It often begins a session with a series of ticking notes, before launching into the song, which can last for many minutes. Often heard at night, at a distance the song may be confused with that of the Mole Cricket! The call is a monosyllabic "tchink" or "zick", or a more clucking "chuck", accelerating into a rattle when alarmed.

IDENTIFICATION

Most similar to the Sedge Warbler, but appearing generally paler yellowish-ochre, with a blackish crown bisected by a yellow-buff central crown stripe. The mantle shows two broad yellow-buff stripes that contrast with bold black parallel stripes, and the rump is finely streaked with black. The lores are pale, the supercilium broad and yellowish, the underparts whitish with a buff wash across the breast and fine streaks on the breast and flanks, variable in intensity. Juveniles are very bright and strongly patterned yellow and black, like a humbug sweet.

HABITAT

A scarce but regular migrant to Britain, most frequently found in autumn along the English Channel coast. It is a summer visitor to its breeding grounds in eastern Europe and Russia. It favours a very specific and fast-disappearing habitat of waterlogged *Carex* sedge meadows just 30cm high, and marshes and fens with iris beds and tussocky grass. On passage it occurs in a wider variety of wetlands, and its wintering grounds have only recently been discovered in north-western Senegal.

Aquatic Warbler
Acrocephalus paludicola

LENGTH: 11.5–13cm

WINGSPAN: 16.5–19.5cm

🔊 **CALL:** "chrrrrr"

⏺ **TRACK:** 2:30

JUVENILE

ADULT

CALL/SONG

Various calls are given, such as a low "thuk" or "chuk" contact call, a "chrrrrr" given when anxious, and a repeated short hoarse "tscht", given in alarm. The song is very simple and undeveloped when compared to Sedge Warbler, consisting of a handful of notes repeated in a lazy fashion and using the "chrrrr" call note frequently, interspersed with piping whistles, each group of notes followed by a pause, such as "tchrrrr… trrr… trrr… pee'pee'pee'pee… tchrrrrr… trrrr… trrrr… pee peee peee… krrrrriiii… heu'heu'heu'heu'heu'heu… kirrrrrr… pi'pi'pi'pip'pip-hew hew hew… tchrrrr…", etc. Typically sung in the evening, from a perch among low sedges and grass, although occasionally in a short song flight.

Sedge Warbler
Acrocephalus schoenobaenus

LENGTH: 11.5–13cm

WINGSPAN: 17–21cm

CALL: "chrrrrr"

TRACK: 2:31

HABITAT

A common summer visitor, breeding in a wide variety of wetland habitats but also away from water in drier places with lush herbage, such as in hedges, overgrown meadows, coastal scrub and cereal crops. It favours low dense vegetation, in marshy areas and reedbeds with scattered bushes, tall rushes, riverside willows, canalsides, ditches and swampy bushy areas.

CALL/SONG

It gives a grating nasal "chrrrrr" when anxious, and some scolding "tsuk" notes, which are occasionally run together into a rattle when alarmed. The song is often delivered in long sequences and is rather fast, vigorous and with abrupt changes across a wide tonal range, comprising excited churring and harsh chattering notes that vary up and down in pitch, interspersed with departures into high frequency trills and sweet whistles, and occasional mimicry of other songsters, such as "trri trri trri cheo'cheo trri trri srrreoo trri trri tue'tue'tue uh'uh'uh'i'er'i'er' cheoo chi'chi'chi' tr'tr'tr'tr peeo'chrrr'peeo'chrr chrr chrr trrrrrrrrrrrr didididididididi trrr…", etc. It is a much more energetic sound when compared to the safe pedestrian tempo of the Reed Warbler, and is frequently given in song flights.

SONGFLIGHT

IDENTIFICATION

A brown and buff bird with a boldly marked head, it has a broad buffish-white supercilium contrasting with a darker streaked crown, dark eyestripe and lores, and brown cheeks. The upperparts are brown with vague and diffuse streaking, the plain rump appearing brighter and warmer. The underparts are whitish with a buff wash on the breast and flanks. Juveniles have narrow dark streaks on the upper breast. It is often confiding, perching up on branches and reed stems.

IDENTIFICATION

A difficult bird to identify, the best pointers being song and habitat in the breeding season. It closely resembles the Reed Warbler, but has a few subtle differences. The adult is a uniform greyish-brown on the upperparts, whitish below washed olive-buff, and lacking the rusty tones of the Reed. It has a longer and more obvious supercilium which reaches to just behind the eye, a short primary projection, a long bill and flat forehead. It has a more 'pointy' appearance than the Reed, with a stouter body, a more peaked crown that makes the bill appear spikier, and the tail is often slightly cocked, giving it something of a banana shape.

HABITAT

A very scarce rarity in Britain, it is a summer visitor to Russia and southern Finland from its wintering grounds in India. It eschews very wet habitats, instead favouring bushes in open country, riverside thickets, overgrown forest clearings, scrub, edges of damp broad-leaved woodland, wooded gullies, parks and large overgrown gardens with lush herbage and tangled undergrowth. On passage it can be found in scrub and trees in both wet and dry terrain.

CALL/SONG

It gives a low churring call note "tjrrrrr", or a drier variant "tcrrrrr", on migration or when anxious, and also a dry hard "chek" or "tak", similar to the call of the Lesser Whitethroat. The song is similar to that of the Marsh Warbler, but delivered at a slower, more deliberate and measured pace with frequent short pauses, and also includes much mimicry of other species. It sings a combination of sweet and harsh notes, often with regular notes such as a low 'joor'ii', a Goldfinch-like 'djew'ii'

Blyth's Reed Warbler
Acrocephalus dumetorum

LENGTH: 12.5–14cm

WINGSPAN: 17–19cm

🔊 **CALL:** "tak"

⏺ **TRACK:** 2:32

and a characteristic "chu-ii-li" or "doo-er-dee", which rise up the scale, and a "doo-er-dee-er-doo" that ascends to the middle "dee" then down again, such as "zii'i chew zii'i chew zii'i chew didoo dee'di'di'doo pszee'i pszee' pszee'l trrrp trrrp trrrp trre trre trre doo'di! doo'di! dzhe dzhe dzhe zeeaaa chut'chut'chut jijit jijit eee-ji'ji'jo'jo eee-ji'ji'jo'jo eee-ji'ji'jo'jo ii-oo-dzhr ii-oo-dzhr ii-oo-dzhr…" etc. It sings from a song post within a bush or tree.

Marsh Warbler
Acrocephalus palustris

LENGTH: 13–15cm

WINGSPAN: 18–21cm

CALL: "tchak"

TRACK: 2:33

IDENTIFICATION

Very like the Reed Warbler, often identified by habitat and voice alone. It has a slightly shorter bill, a more rounded head shape, a bolder, pale supercilium in front of the eye and a bolder eyering, giving the face a gentler expression. The overall colouration of the upperparts is a warm grey-brown with an olive tinge, and the underparts are less buffy, more off-white with a yellowish-buff tinge. In fresh plumage it shows pale crescents on the tips of the primaries, and the legs are yellowish-pink.

HABITAT

A rare summer visitor to Britain. Occasional songsters appear in the south and east, but former breeding sites have been largely abandoned. It occurs widely across continental Europe and southern Scandinavia, right up to the Channel coast. It avoids the wetter habitat choices of some of its relatives, favouring rank growth of tall herbage, young trees, scrub and bushes, often in the zone between woodland edge and growths of reeds, or between swamp and drier vegetation.

CALL/SONG

The calls are similar to those of the Reed Warbler, such as a "dchrrr" given in alarm, a sharp loud "tchak", some quiet "tuc" notes and also a "wheet-wheet-wheet". It is a remarkable songster, giving a sweet fluid warbling chatter at a fairly fast but measured tempo with pauses in between, much of which is made up of expert mimicry, which is blended into the nasal babbling, trilling and churring, often giving characteristic harsh "zi-chay" notes and high liquid trills and tremolos, too complex and varied to attempt to transcribe here meaningfully! It often sings from a semi-exposed perch in a bush or similar, and frequently includes mimicry of Common Tern, Barn Swallow, House Martin, Blue Tit, House Sparrow and Chaffinch. It has been recorded as mimicking at least 99 European and 113 African species!

Reed Warbler
Acrocephalus scirpaceus

LENGTH: 12.5–14cm

WINGSPAN: 17–21cm

CALL: "djeh"

TRACK: 2:34

IDENTIFICATION

A slim, brown unassuming warbler with a rather streamlined shape, a long slender bill and a flat forehead. It is uniform warm brown on the upperparts, subtly warmer and brighter on the rump. It has a short and fairly indistinct pale supercilium which does not extend behind the eye, and buff underparts that are warmest on the flanks and undertail, with a whitish throat. Juveniles are brighter and richer in colour.

HABITAT

A summer visitor, breeding almost exclusively in reeds growing in water and particularly in dense and tall ones, in reedbeds, ditches, overgrown canals, lakesides, ponds, and along slow-flowing rivers, wherever reeds can be found. It often moves out of the reeds to feed in adjacent drier areas such as bushes, grass, tall herbage, overgrown meadows and crops. On passage it may be seen in hedges and scrub.

CALL/SONG

It has some short calls, such as a subdued "che" or "djeh", a short hard "chk", and a more anxious harsh grating "djerrrr!" , which may be extended into a rattle when alarmed. The song could be described as a pedestrian chuntering, a well-paced relaxed collection of pleasant churring and grating notes that bounces along, each note repeated two or more times, with occasional single high notes and twanging sounds inserted, such as "chru-chru-chru ribbit-ribbit-ribbit tssee'oo jibbit-jibbit-jibbit hwah-hwah plip-plip-plip trrru-trrru tsseeo chukchuk blrr-blrr cheh-cheh-cheh prrriiii che' che'...", etc. It can sometimes include some basic mimicry, although never as fluently as some of its relatives (notably Marsh Warbler). It may sing in a faster and more excited manner on occasion, but never with the wild and sudden changes in pitch or trilling crescendos of the Sedge Warbler. It often sings for many minutes without interruption while perched on a reed stem.

Great Reed Warbler

Acrocephalus arundinaceus

LENGTH: 16–20cm

WINGSPAN: 24–29cm

CALL: "krrrreck"

TRACK: 2:35

IDENTIFICATION

A larger version of the Reed Warbler, and roughly three times heavier! It shares similar colouration to the Reed, but is a shade greyer on the uniform brown upperparts and whitish below, washed buff on the breast, flanks and vent. The face is more boldly marked, with a stronger, pale supercilium that extends behind the eye, and a darker eyestripe. The head is proportionately larger, more peaked (the crown feathers are often raised when singing) and the bill is noticeably stouter and long. The wings show a long primary projection, and the tail is long and broad. Often visible when perched up in the reeds, looking large and thrush-like.

HABITAT

A summer migrant to our region, although it remains a scarce but annual visitor to Britain. It favours tall reeds standing in shallow water in extensive *Phragmites* reedbeds, often close to the edges or gaps by open water, but will also use smaller patches of reeds on ponds or along ditches and canals, and sometimes in tall reedmace. On passage it can occur in scrub and other marginal habitats.

CALL/SONG

Large in voice as well as in body, the song is typically delivered from high on a tall reed stem and is a very loud collection of harsh, gruff and guttural grating, croaking and creaking notes, interspersed with high falsetto ones, similar in structure to those of the Reed Warbler although lower in frequency and often audible at great range. It is often delivered in sequences of 12–15 notes or double notes, lasting 4–6 seconds, with pauses between, as in "krra-krra-krra heuw'heuw krr'akh-krr'akh-krr'akh krrugh-krrugh kriiu-kriiu-kriiu krrr'ugh-krrr'ugh pi'eee-pi'eee ijjit-ijjit-ijjit". Some guttural and croaking call notes are also given, such as a harsh "kjack" and "krrrreck", a hard rolling churring note "krrrrr", given in anxiety, and a guttural "grrrghk".

IDENTIFICATION

A large-headed warbler with a square-ended tail, it is greyish-green above and uniform primrose-yellow below. The bill is stout with a broad base and pinkish-yellow sides, and the legs are grey or blue-grey. The wingtips are quite long, and in fresh plumage it shows a pale panel on the secondaries. The lores are pale and yellowish, lacking a dark eyestripe, and it shows a short, yellowish supercilium. Immatures in autumn appear paler, greyer, and more washed out.

HABITAT

A scarce but regular migrant on the south and east coasts of Britain, breeding in central and northern Europe. It is a woodland bird, favouring sunny and fairly moist forest edge, open deciduous woods with large trees and bushy undergrowth, parks, gardens, tall hedgerows and other similar patches of trees and bushes. Migrants can appear in coastal scrub and trees.

CALL/SONG

The song is a vigorous and rhythmic collection of rich, harsh and musical sounds, much mimicry

Icterine Warbler
Hippolais icterina

LENGTH: 12–13.5cm
WINGSPAN: 20.5–24cm
CALL: "vvht-vihht-vheed"
TRACK: 2:36

and some weird shrill nasal buzzes that are the best indicator of the species, all delivered rapidly and fluently. It is most similar to the song of the Marsh Warbler, but is more manic, higher pitched, and generally delivered in longer verses without pauses, comprising notes that are repeated more times, such as "ffuht-ffuht-jiiooo ffuht-ffuht-jiiooo ffuht-ffuht-jiiooo trrrt-trrrt-trrrt vvht-vihht-vheed vvht-vihht-vheed chedit-chedit-chedit ving-ving-hrrrrrieh ving-ving-hrrrrrieh tzizidi'di'doo tzizidi'di'doo vidu-vidu veet zu-zu-zu-zu…", etc.

A distinctive three-note call is given during the breeding season and is often integrated into the song, a nasal ascending "vvht-vihht-vheed". It also has some basic "tek" notes, given in anxiety, and a low "djeh" note, sometimes repeated in a series. Another occasional call is an ascending "hwuerrp", a little like the call of the Willow Warbler.

Blackcap
Sylvia atricapilla

LENGTH: 13.5–15cm

WINGSPAN: 20–23cm

CALL: "teck"

TRACK: 2:37

MALE

IDENTIFICATION

One of the most common and familiar warblers of our region. Unmistakable, and as its name suggests, the male has a striking glossy black cap. The cap -– which is rusty-brown in the female and immature birds – extends down to the eye, which is rather bold and beady in an otherwise plain face. The plumage overall is a rather drab ash-grey, browner in the female, and confusable with the Garden Warbler if the head is not seen. It may at times be quite skulking, but is fairly robust and often draws attention as it moves about in bushes.

FEMALE

HABITAT:

Primarily a summer visitor, arriving from Africa at the beginning of April. In southern Britain it is sometimes recorded in the winter months, often in gardens, either overwintering locally or moving in from the continent. In the breeding season it favours shady woodland with rich undergrowth, in mixed or deciduous forest, thickets, parks, overgrown gardens, hedges and dense bushy areas, and is very arboreal, singing from taller bushes and trees.

CALL/SONG:

The call is a rather clear and loud clicking "teck", repeated several times when anxious. It also has a low churring "dzrrrr" and a bleating "schweehh" call when alarmed or distressed. It is quite vocal, and has a loud and distinctive cheery song consisting of rich warbling that breaks into a louder, clearer and rather strident fluty song phrase. The initial warbling may cause confusion with the song of the Garden Warbler, but the Blackcap should burst forth into the loud terminal flourish part of the song, whereas the Garden Warbler maintains the same level of intensity throughout. The loud part of the song is usually 2–4 seconds long, but the initial warbling can carry on for much longer.

IDENTIFICATION

A demure and unassuming bird, lacking any major plumage features. It is rather plump and stocky, with a rounded head, plain mouse-brown upperparts, and whitish underparts washed browner on the flanks. The tail is plain and lacks white outer feathers. The dark staring eye is obvious, with pale crescents above and below, and is set in a gentle-looking face. The bill is fairly stout and pale grey on the lower mandible, and the stout legs are light grey.

HABITAT

A summer visitor, breeding in mixed and deciduous open woodland with clearings and rich undergrowth, in parks, large gardens, streamside woods, thickets and heaths. It requires taller trees mixed with shrubbery, and so has much habitat overlap with the Blackcap, but it generally favours more shrubby areas. It is rather shy and skulking, and sensitive to disturbance.

CALL/SONG

The song is a very pleasant, confident and sweet baritone warbling, sustained for 3–8 seconds and rising and falling throughout the song phrase.

Garden Warbler
Sylvia borin

LENGTH: 13–14.5cm

WINGSPAN: 20–24.5cm

CALL: "djeck djeck djeck"

TRACK: 2:38

It is similar to that of the Blackcap and often confused with it, but is quicker, more subdued, has a mellower sound and is often sung in longer phrases and without the sudden changes in pitch towards the end. It descends into lower frequency notes more often than the Blackcap, and was once described as "having taken singing lessons from a brook passing under a small bridge"! The call is a rather nasal chacking sound, often repeated in a series of calls, particularly when anxious, such as "djeck djeck djeck…". It also has a low grating "chrrrr" and a soft ascending "duij", given in alarm.

Barred Warbler
Sylvia nisoria

ADULT

LENGTH: 15.5–17cm
WINGSPAN: 323–27cm
🔊 **CALL:** "khr'r'r'r'r'r'r..."
⬤ **TRACK:** 2:39

IDENTIFICATION

A large and heavy warbler, with a long white-tipped tail. The upperparts are lead-grey in the adult male, the wing feathers have bold white tips to the coverts and tertials, and the iris is yellow, giving it a mad staring expression. The underparts are whitish, variably barred with dark scallops from chin to undertail, strongest in the male, while the female is much more sparsely barred. The female is generally duller, browner and has a duller yellow eye; immatures are grey-brown with pale edges to the wing feathers, and faint scallops on the vent and rump.

HABITAT

A scarce but regular autumn migrant to Britain, usually appearing along the east coast after

IMMATURE

easterly winds. It breeds from central Europe eastwards and favours open country with tall bushes and scattered trees, bushy woodland clearings and edges, shelter belts, tall hedgerows, riverine thickets, large gardens and scrubby hillsides. Often nests in very close association with Red-backed Shrike. On passage it frequents coastal scrub.

CALL/SONG

The most distinctive call is a hard, rattling, rather Magpie-like chatter, "khr'r'r'r'r'r'r...", lasting about a second with a rate of about 24 notes per second, sometimes tailing off towards the end. It also gives a Blackcap-like "tak", a short nasal "czow", and a repeated "cha-cha-cha". The song is rather similar to that of Garden Warbler, a vigorous throaty warbling with a rich thrush-like quality. It is rather higher-pitched and brighter-sounding, is paced a little more slowly and delivered in shorter complete phrases lasting 2–5 seconds, with pauses in between that are usually longer than the actual song phrase. It often includes some harsher sounds and the hard rattling call, and it occasionally uses mimicry, particularly of Red-backed Shrike. The song is given from a bush or in a well-developed song flight, ascending with deep slow wingbeats, and parachuting down on spread wings while rocking from side to side.

IDENTIFICATION

A smallish and compact warbler with dull grey-brown upperparts, dark grey ear coverts that contrast with a grey head, and a shortish grey-brown tail with white outer tail feathers. The wing is plain and without any rufous or pale panels. The underparts are dull whitish, washed browner on the sides. The bill is fairly short, grey with a paler base, and the legs are dark grey. A little more secretive than the Common Whitethroat, the best indicator is its voice.

HABITAT

A summer visitor, favouring taller vegetation than the Common Whitethroat and found mainly in bushy areas between woodland and open country, such as in mature farmland hedgerows, heath-land, plantations, well-grown gardens, parks and cemeteries, woodland edge and clearings, scrub and thickets.

CALL/SONG

The call is a hard and dry, tongue-clicking "tekk" or "thekk", often repeated freely. It also has a hoarse, grating churr, and an alarmed rattle similar to that of the Wren. The song is a distinctive hard wooden rattling, reminiscent of

Lesser Whitethroat
Sylvia curruca

LENGTH: 11.5–13.5cm
WINGSPAN: 16.5–20.5cm
CALL: "tekk"
TRACK: 2:40

part of the song of the Chaffinch, and is made up of 6–12 double notes at a rate of roughly 10 per second, a "djeh'djeh'djeh'djeh'djeh'djeh". This is typically preceded by a weak and subdued warbling of varying length, longer variants sounding similar to the warbling of the Blackcap or Common Whitethroat. It starts quietly and builds up in volume to the louder rattle part, and is often audible only at close range. It can sometimes deliver these two parts of the song separately. There seems to be quite a variation in songs regionally, birds in Europe often sounding rather different from those in Britain.

Common Whitethroat
Sylvia communis

LENGTH: 13–15cm

WINGSPAN: 18.5–23cm

🔊 **CALL:** "dverhr dverhr dverhr"

⏺ **TRACK:** 2:41

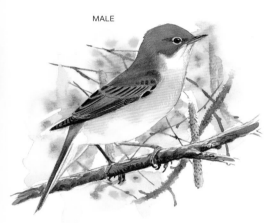

MALE

bushes, bramble thickets, shrubby margins of wetlands, open woodland clearings and forest edge, from sunny lowland areas to upland hillsides. Often confiding and curious, posing on the tops of bushes.

CALL/SONG

Quite vocal, with a range of call notes, such as a nervous, nasal "dverhr dverhr dverhr" and a low "dzhuurrr", a lively "whit-whit-whit" which often precedes song, and a sharp, often repeated "tak". The song is a brisk and lively warble, quite shrill and scratchy and delivered from a raised perch, or a little longer, richer and more fluid when given in a jerky little song flight. In its simplest version it is just 1–1.5 seconds long, with 6–12 note components, such as an easy-to-remember "witchetty-witchetty-witchetty-witch!" or more accurately as "weech'u-cheh'weh-i'chu-chi'chiih!", often slightly descending through the sequence and ascending sometimes on the final two or three notes. Longer and more complex versions can last up to 10 seconds or more, and sound more warbling and similar to other *Sylvia* species.

IDENTIFICATION

A sturdy and large-headed warbler with a fairly long white-sided tail. The male has a greyish head, a white orbital ring and a grey-brown back, and in all plumages shows broad bright rufous margins to the secondaries, tertials and wing coverts. The underparts are whitish, with pure white on the throat contrasting with a pink flush on the breast. The female is browner, washed buff on the breast, with a brown head, pale orbital eyering and pale brown eye.

HABITAT

A summer visitor, favouring scrubby places in a wide range of habitats. It can be found in farmland with hedges, tall herbage, crops, low

DISPLAY FLIGHT

IDENTIFICATION

A perky, short-winged little bird with a long narrow tail, often held cocked or jerking up and down as it flies from thicket to thicket. The male is subtly hued, with vinous-red underparts, spotted white in lines on the throat. The head, back and tail are slate-grey, with a red orbital eyering and reddish-brown eye. The spiky little bill is yellowish at the base, and the legs are yellow-brown. The female is duller, brown-tinged on the back and greyish-pink below.

HABITAT

A resident species, found mainly in southern and eastern counties of Britain, in western Europe and around the western Mediterranean basin. In Britain it favours sandy heaths with heather, bracken and stands of gorse, but otherwise is found in open bushy habitats, scrub, in *maquis* and *garrigue*, and also in open pine or oak woodland with low scrub; it has an affinity for coastal areas. Sensitive to cold weather, it spreads its range in mild winters.

CALL/SONG

The song is a very fast burst of scratchy warbling, not unlike the song of the Common Whitethroat but being sung at double speed. It undulates quickly in tone, including both high-frequency notes

Dartford Warbler
Sylvia undata

LENGTH: 13–14cm

WINGSPAN: 13–18.5cm

CALL: "djjaehhr"

TRACK: 2:42

and some hard 'pebbly' rattling notes. The song phrases last for 1.5–6 seconds, songsters often alternating with different length phrases. The song is delivered either in a song flight or from the top of a bush such as gorse, and although sounding fairly weak it can be quite far-carrying across quiet heaths. The call note is a harsh "djjaehhr", similar to Common Whitethroat but more buzzing and nasal. It also gives a quieter version of that call, and a short hard "tuk", which may be extended into a rattling "trr'r'r'r'r'r" in alarm.

MALE

Greenish Warbler

Phylloscopus trochiloides

LENGTH: 9.5–10.5cm

WINGSPAN: 15–21cm

CALL: "tizh'oo!"

TRACK: 2:43

IDENTIFICATION

A small, restless warbler with a rather large rounded head. It is greyish-green above, with a short, narrow, whitish wingbar formed by pale tips to the greater coverts. The underparts are whitish, the legs are grey-brown and the bill has a pinkish-orange lower mandible which makes it appear stouter. The head is strongly marked, with a long, whitish supercilium reaching the nape at the rear and extending over the bill and on to the forehead, highlighted by a prominent dark eyestripe and a pale cheek below.

HABITAT

A scarce but annual visitor to the east coast of Britain, usually as a spring overshoot or an autumn migrant. It breeds from the eastern Baltic eastwards and favours open mixed or broad-leaved woodland with tall trees and rich undergrowth, parks, large gardens, riverine woods and thickets. Migrants appear in coastal scrub and bushy areas, particularly where taller trees are found. It winters in India.

CALL/SONG

The song is a rapid, jerky shuttling burst of notes that sound as if they overlap with each other, delivered more or less on a level tone, such as "tseuu-tseuu-tseuu tsi'wee schi'schi'schi tsit'si-chew-si si-chew-si si-chew-si" or "tsii tsii tsii tsittisee tsitti-see'tsee'tsee'tsee-tsechu-si". Marginally slower at the start, it then accelerates in the middle with a slight flourish at the end. It can include a rattle of more quickly repeated notes, and typically lasts for 2–4 seconds. It is often likened to the song of the White Wagtail, as is the common call note, which is a slightly descending, disyllabic, rather quick "tizh'oo!" or "tiss'yip". It also gives a milder version of this call, a flatter "swee-er", "swss-eh" or "ts'sieh". Sings from the crown of a tall tree.

IDENTIFICATION

An attractive warbler, with a bright lemon-yellow throat, cheek and upper breast, sharply demarcated from a silky-white belly and vent. It has a broad lemon-yellow supercilium and a rich moss-green eyestripe and upperparts. The wings are long, mostly occluding the tail, with wing coverts and remiges brightly fringed with greenish-yellow. The white undertail coverts are very long and almost reach the tail tip.

HABITAT

A summer visitor, with a marked westerly distribution in Britain. It is a forest bird, found in shady, open, mixed and deciduous woodland, frequently in hilly country, with mature trees and little or no undergrowth. In Britain it is often found in sessile oakwoods, with mature beechwoods also favoured both here and in other parts of Europe. Infrequently recorded on passage.

Wood Warbler
Phylloscopus sibilatrix

LENGTH: 11–12.5cm

WINGSPAN: 19.5–24cm

🔊 **CALL:** "tyuu"

⏺ **TRACK:** 2:44

CALL/SONG

There are two very different types of song, both used freely and often together. The most frequently heard is a beautiful descending and accelerating crescendo of notes, typically lasting 3.5 seconds but occasionally longer when the introduction is prolonged. It starts hesitantly with a few notes that quicken and get louder, then dropping into a liquid rolling trill, such as "tit-tit-tit it'tit'it'it'it'it'it'it trrrrr'r'r'r'r'r'r'r'r", the trill lasting 1.3–1.5 seconds and consisting of about 14–16 notes per second. The second song type, which often accompanies the first, is a simple series of 5–6 longer piping notes, lasting about 2 seconds, such as "peww-peww-peww-peww-peww…", occasionally with a quiet "tsit" on the end. The call is a monosyllabic, flat, piping "tyuu", not unlike the note used in the second song type. It can also give a shrill, penetrating "see-see-see" when excited, and a soft "wit'wit'wit'wit".

Chiffchaff
Phylloscopus collybita

LENGTH: 10–12cm

WINGSPAN: 15–21cm

CALL: "h'weet"

TRACK: 2:45

IDENTIFICATION

A demure little warbler with a distinctive song, confiding and active and frequently flicking its wings and dipping its tail. Most similar to the Willow Warbler, it can be separated by its dark brown or blackish legs. The overall colouration is more olive-brown than the Willow Warbler, with less yellow tones. The underparts are off-white, with a variable amount of yellow-buff washing on the throat and breast, and the face is less strongly marked, with a more indistinct supercilium and darker cheeks that highlight the whitish eyering which is bisected by a dark eyestripe. It is also dumpier and shorter-winged.

HABITAT

A common summer visitor and one of the earliest arrivals in spring, with the first songsters heard in Britain in early March. It favours rather tall trees, and can be found in open mixed and deciduous woodland with tall trees and shrubs, in large gardens, parks, churchyards, tall hedgerows, tall scrub and plantations. Many overwinter in milder parts of southern Britain, appearing in sheltered gardens etc.

CALL/SONG

The call is a simpler, more monosyllabic and higher-pitched version of the call of the Willow Warbler, a slightly upslurred and emphatic "huitt", "pwee!" or "h'weet". When anxious it will give a flatter "peep", and juveniles give a similar call. The eponymous song is a rather slow and measured, monotonous clear two-note repetition, the first note higher than the second, as in "tsilf-tsalf tsilf-tsalf tsilf-tsalf…", often ending on a lower note. It occasionally elaborates on this simple rhythm, with variations such as a three-note "chiff-chiff'chaff, chiff-chiff-chaff chiff-chiff-chaff…". Between bouts of song it often gives a "trrrr… trrrr…" sound, audible only at fairly close range. Often sings from high in a tall tree.

JUVENILE AUTUMN
PLUMAGE

Willow Warbler
Phylloscopus trochilus

LENGTH: 11–12.5cm

WINGSPAN: 16.5–22cm

CALL: "hoo-eet"

TRACK: 2:46

IDENTIFICATION

A small, slim warbler, restless and active. Most similar to the Chiffchaff, but at all ages can be told by its pinkish-brown legs. It is greyish-green with a hint of brown on the upperparts, the underparts are whitish with a pale yellow wash on the throat and breast. The face is well marked, with a long, pale yellow supercilium and a well-defined dark eyestripe. The wings show quite a long primary projection, giving it a slightly elongated shape. Immatures in autumn are suffused with a brighter yellow on the whole of the underparts and face.

HABITAT

A common summer visitor, found in a wide variety of bushy habitats. It can be found in open woodland, both deciduous and coniferous, birch forest, willow scrub, heaths, commons, plantations, parks, large gardens, indeed virtually anywhere with shrubs and small trees. Its range extends right up to the higher latitudes and beyond the Arctic Circle.

CALL/SONG

The call is a rather soft, plaintive, enquiring, disyllabic and upslurred "hoo-eet", the second syllable higher than the first. It can also give a more monotone "hwuu" version of the call when anxious, and a repeated nasal scolding "chwherr" when alarmed near the nest, not unlike a *Sylvia* warbler. The song is a pleasing cadence of simple whistles descending through the scales, such as "svi'svi'svi'svi tue-tue-tue-tuee hweh-hweh-hweeo-hweo-hweo hi'hi-hiwe'oo". The initial 3–4 notes are slightly faster, sharper and higher, followed by 8–10 notes which are given quite strongly and descend the scale in steps. The final notes sound weaker and more stifled, tailing off at the end (although this is variable). The song generally lasts for 2–3 seconds or in longer phrases of up to 4.5 seconds.

ADULT SPRING PLUMAGE

Goldcrest
Regulus regulus

LENGTH: 8.5–9.5cm

WINGSPAN: 13.5–15.5cm

🔊 **CALL:** "sszi-sszi-sszi-sszi"

⏺ **TRACK:** 2:47

IDENTIFICATION

Our tiniest bird, weighing as little as 5g! It is dumpy and rotund, with a large head, a thin blackish bill and a beady black pale-ringed eye, set in an otherwise plain face. It is pale green on the upperparts with a bold wing pattern of a broad whitish bar on the tips of the greater coverts and primary coverts, contrasting with a black bar on the base of the secondaries. The crown is yellow in the centre, mixed with flame-orange in the male, and bordered on each side by black lines.

HABITAT

It is resident in our region, with northern breeders migrating south in winter and supplementing local populations. In the breeding season it favours mixed and coniferous woodland, often keeping high in the branches. At other times it ranges more widely, and can be found in deciduous woodland and bushy areas, parks and gardens, particularly where conifers are present. It often joins feeding flocks of tits, and in autumn immigrants arrive in variable numbers, when they can be found in coastal scrub before they disperse inland.

CALL/SONG

The calls and song are very high-pitched, between 7–8kHz, and sadly for older birders they are one of the first common bird sounds lost when hearing begins to deteriorate. The common call is a thin, 3–4-note "sszi-sszi-sszi-sszi", often used as a contact call, and also a rather more shrill and stronger-sounding "zzit-zzit-zzit", also given singly and occasionally sounding a little rough and hoarse. It also gives random little high-pitched "zze" sounds when feeding. The song is a rapid shuttling high-pitched sequence, the main phrase repeated with a cyclical quality and finished off with a variable lower-pitched trilling flourish, such as "ti'wii'titoo-wii'titoo-wii'titoo-wii'titoo zee'ti't'trrrrreo".

MALE

IDENTIFICATION

A similar size to the Goldcrest, but a shade more robust. It is greener on the upperparts, with a bold head pattern of a black-bordered yellow-orange crownstripe (brightest in the male), a broad white supercilium, a blackish line through the eye and a small whitish patch below the eye on a grey cheek. It has an orange bronze collar patch on the side of the neck, and the wing is similarly patterned to the Goldcrest.

HABITAT

An uncommon but regular visitor to Britain, with a small localized breeding population in the south and south-east of England. Breeds across Europe in mixed and deciduous woodland, also in parks, gardens and small wooded patches, usually with good under-growth. It is less tied to conifers than Goldcrest, although birds breeding in Britain tend to be in spruce or similar species.

CALL/SONG

The song is sung by the male, and is a rapid repetition of a single high-pitched note, accelerating and rising in pitch, and becoming louder towards the end of the phrase, which is roughly 2 seconds in length, as in "sssi-zsi-zsi-zsi-zsi'zs'zs'zs'zs'zs'zssi". The song phrase begins with some very thin and high notes, the final one sounding slightly longer. It lacks the cyclical rhythm and terminal flourish present in the song of the Goldcrest, and sounds fuller and less thin, even though it is of a similar frequency. The call note is a rising "zzi-ziii'zizizi", with a quieter introductory note, a short

Firecrest
Regulus ignicapillus

LENGTH: 9–10cm

WINGSPAN: 13–16cm

CALL: "zzi-ziii'zizizi"

TRACK: 2:48

pause, then 3–4 notes led by a slightly longer first note, with a fuller and coarser quality than that of the Goldcrest. It also gives a more peeping series of notes, which are more spaced out and typically repeated up to 12 times, such as "pzeep! zeep! zeep! zeep! zeep!".

MALE

Spotted Flycatcher
Muscicapa striata

LENGTH: 13.5–15cm

WINGSPAN: 23–25.5cm

CALL: "zee'thk"

TRACK: 2:49

IDENTIFICATION

A medium-small, long-winged bird with a rounded head, lacking any obvious plumage features. It is grey-brown on the head and upperparts, faintly streaked and spotted darker on the forecrown, the face is plain with a beady black eye and a thin, broad-based black bill. The underparts are whitish, with indistinct mottled streaking on the throat sides and breast. It perches upright on short black legs, making quick sallies after insects from an exposed perch, often returning to the same branch.

HABITAT

A summer visitor, widespread in Britain but declining, with nest predation by Grey Squirrels possibly a contributing factor. It is a bird of the forest edge, favouring tall deciduous trees that offer flycatching perches and open surrounding airspace such as clearings and glades. It can be found often in man-made habitats such as parks, large gardens, avenues of tall trees, orchards and churchyards. Also sometimes found in pine and larch.

CALL/SONG

The song is a very simple, primitive and quiet series of single high-pitched squeaks and strangled sounds, delivered at a rate of one note per 0.7–1.5 seconds with regular pauses in between, such as "u'ii… tzii… tzi'i… pzzt… pzzt… tzhrr… tzhrr… tz'i… u'ii… u'ii… tzu… tzu… u'ii… u'ii…" etc. There is no formation of phrases as with other flycatchers. The call is also rather unobtrusive, a short shrill "zee", not unlike the calls of the Robin or Hawfinch. The alarm call, often given near the nest, is a combination of this call and a couple of hard tacking notes, such as "zee'thk" or "zee'thk'thk". It also makes some loud bill-snapping sounds, often rapid and sounding rattle-like.

ADULT
MALE

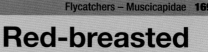

Red-breasted Flycatcher
Ficedula parva

LENGTH: 11–12cm

WINGSPAN: 18.5–21cm

🔊 **CALL:** "trr'r'r'r'rt!"

⏺ **TRACK:** 2:50

IDENTIFICATION

A small flycatcher with a long tail which is frequently flicked upwards, revealing extensive wheatear-like white tail-sides that are obvious in flight. The remainder of the tail and the upper-tail coverts are jet black. The mantle, nape and wings are brown, and the underparts are buffish-white. The male has a grey head and an orange-red throat and upper breast, although the extent is variable with age. Females and immatures are more buffy on the throat and breast, and the head is uniform with the brown back.

HABITAT

A scarce but annual visitor to Britain, mainly in autumn along eastern coasts. It is a summer visitor to eastern Europe from its winter quarters in southern Asia, and in the breeding season favours deciduous woodland, preferably mature and lush with streams or standing water and thick undergrowth; it also occurs in mixed forest, orchards and, in the north of its range, spruce forest. Migrants can be found in coastal scrub and trees.

CALL/SONG

The song is a delightful sequence of simple, repeated liquid notes, delivered confidently and sweetly. A repeated introductory note is followed by a repeated couplet of notes, see-sawing in pitch, the lower note repeated singly at the end. The end notes vary, sometimes being delivered on a level tone or, at other times, descending, such as "tsii'tsii'tsii'tsii tsee-tsoo tsee-tsoo tsee-tsoo soo'soo'soo'soo". It often precedes the song phrase with some very high-pitched and quiet "tsi" notes. The song phrase lasts for 2.5–3.5 seconds, and occasionally up to 5 seconds if makes more repetitions. The commonly heard call from migrants is a buzzing rattle, similar to the Wren's call, a five- or six-note "trr'r'r'r'rt", which can be mimicked by sucking on the corner of one's mouth. On the breeding grounds it gives other calls, such as a disyllabic plaintive "wee'lu", a dry clicking "teck" and a sharp little "zit".

FEMALE

Collared Flycatcher
Ficedula albicollis

LENGTH: 12–13.5cm

WING SPAN: 22.5–24.5cm

CALL: "eee'p"

TRACK: 2:51

FEMALE

IDENTIFICATION

Very similar to the Pied Flycatcher, but the male has a very obvious broad white collar isolating the black cap. The forehead has a bold white patch and the wings show more white than the Pied, with a large white patch on the base of the primaries. It also has a white patch on the rump and an all black tail. The females require care to separate them from Pied, but show a larger white patch on the primary bases and greyer, paler upperparts with a hint of a white rump patch.

MALE

HABITAT

A very rare visitor to Britain from further east, where it is a summer visitor to central and eastern Europe and Russia. It is a woodland bird, favouring deciduous forest and particularly oak, and often staying high in the crown of the tree. It can also be found in mixed woodland, parks, orchards and large gardens, with open areas such as clearings and glades.

CALL/SONG

The commonly uttered call is quite unlike that of the Pied Flycatcher, a high, slightly descending "szeer" or "eee'p", used both as an alarm and an advertising note. It also gives a quieter "tec" note and a soft "tsrr". The song is a simple and tuneful sequence of high-pitched, clearly defined notes. Delivered languidly and in a drawling fashion, with some notes sounding strained or harsh, it is frequently introduced by the thin high call note, which can be repeated during the phrase along with quieter "tec" notes, such as "srriii – sii – srrriii, szzi-szoo-sziii sooo", "siiii… zzii szeerr'iir tx szeer ii'cheo'ii'zrrrr hiiii" or "szeeer, zii'szeeer' szi'szeer'szii". Often given in a rather short sequence of 6–8 notes lasting 2–3 seconds, it can however feature longer and more excited sequences of up to six seconds that include melodious sequences reminiscent of the Robin's song.

JUVENILE
AUTUMN PLUMAGE

Pied Flycatcher
Ficedula hypoleuca

LENGTH: 12–13.5cm

WING SPAN: 21.5–24cm

🔊 **CALL:** "bidt!"

● **TRACK:** 2:52

IDENTIFICATION

Strongly sexually dimorphic. The male in spring is black-and-white, with a black back and head and black tail with white on the basal half of the outer feathers; the wings can appear duller and less black, but there is a large white patch on the base of the secondaries and half of the tertials. The underparts are white, and there is a small white patch over the bill. Females and immatures are tawny grey-brown above, darker on the wings and tail, with a white patch on the tertials and a white band on the tips of the greater coverts.

HABITAT

A summer visitor, with a marked westerly distribution in Britain, where it is particularly attracted to insect-rich sessile oakwoods in hilly country. Elsewhere in its range it can be found in mixed or deciduous forest with glades and clearings, the availability of nest holes being an important factor. It is also found in avenues, orchards, parks, and sometimes in large gardens. Adapts well where nest boxes are provided. It can also be found more widely on passage.

CALL/SONG

The calls are an insistent "bidt!", frequently repeated, a loud, penetrating, Chaffinch-like "whit" and a short "ttuc", which is sometimes given together with the previous call to make "whit-ttuc". In alarm it will give a Chiffchaff-like "wheet". The advertising song of the male is a simple but confident phrase of 7–12 notes, typically lasting 1.5–3 seconds, such as "tsi'chu tsi'chu tsi'chu tsi'tsi'tsi'che", the repeated introductory notes always constant, the later ones variable from one song phrase to the next, and often delivered in a little flourish. Reminiscent of the Redstart's song, it is slower and more evenly paced. It also gives a less well-structured, more strangled and excited variant when it has attracted a female to a potential nest.

ADULT MALE SPRING PLUMAGE

Bearded Tit
Panurus biarmicus

LENGTH: 14–15.5cm

WING SPAN: 16–18cm

CALL: "djjjuu"

TRACK: 2:53

MALE

IDENTIFICATION

A striking and attractive little bird with a long tapering tail. The head is large and rounded, with a small stubby orange-yellow bill and a yellow eye. The rump, tail and back are uniform tawny-russet with short wings brightly patterned with rufous-orange, black and white. The underparts are whitish with rufous-tinged flanks and black undertail coverts. The male has a blue-grey head and long black drooping 'moustaches' extending downwards from the lores and framing a white throat. The head of the female is uniform with the back; juveniles have a black panel on the back and black on the tail sides.

HABITAT

A resident in Britain, although mostly found in the south and south-east. It is widespread across Europe, but restricted by habitat requirements into well-separated blocks. Strongly tied to large *Phragmites* reedbeds in freshwater marshes, it occasionally uses other adjacent vegetation. It is sensitive to cold weather, with birds dispersing in winter when they may occur in isolated small patches of reeds and reedy ditches. The species occasionally undergoes population irruptions. Up to four broods are raised when conditions are right.

CALL/SONG

The commonly heard call as birds buzz about in the reeds is a nasal twanging "djjjuu", "tjjii!" and "tching", often repeated in chorus by small flocks and family parties. It has other often-used conversational calls, such as a hard "plic" or "thrrc", a low descending "dzhiir" and a rising finch-like "dweeh". The song is unobtrusive and easily overlooked, consisting of three or four of these call notes run together, such as "tching-djick-dweeh".

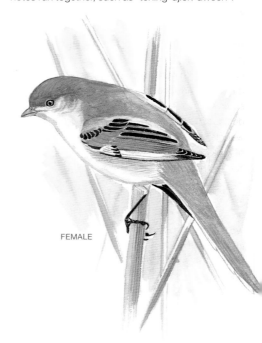

FEMALE

Long-tailed Tit
Aegithalos caudatus

IDENTIFICATION

A cute little bird, with a small body and very long tail. It is round-headed with a tiny black bill, and is often seen moving in restless flocks with a weak bouncing flight, playing follow-my-leader between gaps in the trees and along hedgerows. The head and underparts are whitish, with a broad black band that runs from in front of the eye along the side of the crown to the nape, and faint black streaks on the cheek. The upperparts are black, with a large panel of dirty pink on the scapulars. The tail is black with white on the outer feathers, and the short stubby wings have broad white edges on the tertials and secondaries. Northern populations of the nominate race have a completely snowy-white head.

HABITAT

A resident bird, common and widespread in Britain, with northern populations occasionally undergoing irruptions southwards. It favours deciduous and mixed woodland, with plenty of thick undergrowth such as hazel and willow. It is also found in scrub and bushy areas outside of woodland, such as in gardens, parks, hedges in farmland and other marginal habitats with secondary growth.

LENGTH: 13–15cm (inc. tail of 7–9cm)
WING SPAN: 16–19cm
CALL: "tss'ss'ss'ss'ssi'ssi'ssi'ssi"
TRACK: 2:54

CALL/SONG

A noisy and vocal bird, frequently heard uttering a thin and weak-sounding "ssi'ssi'ssi'ssi" when in flight or as a contact note. This call is easy to mimic and will often bring birds close when copied. Another commonly heard call is a dry and slurred "trrrr", and a short little conversational "pt" note. It also gives a harder, scolding "tsrr'r'r'r'r" when excited or alarmed, and an agitated and alert-sounding "tsrrr-tsrrr", a little like a Yellow Wagtail song note. The song is infrequently heard, and is a rather random and hurried collection of short dry chipping notes, interspersed with nasal twittering, bubbling sounds and a few short melodious whistles.

Blue Tit
Cyanistes caeruleus

JUVENILLE

LENGTH: 10.5–12cm

WING SPAN: 17.5–20cm

🔊 **CALL:** "chwrrr'r'r'r'r"

⏺ **TRACK:** 2:55

IDENTIFICATION

A familiar garden bird to many, it is very small and lightweight, with primrose-yellow underparts. The rounded head is patterned with broad white cheeks, and has a white forehead and white extending in a ring round to the nape, isolating a rounded crown patch of blue. A blackish bridle through the eye separates cheek from crown, with a darker blue collar-ring below the cheek, broadest at the rear and joining a blackish-blue chin and throat at the front. The mantle is green, and the wings and tail are blue with white tertial tips and a white wingbar on the tips of the greater coverts. Females are duller than males.

ADULT

HABITAT

A common resident, favouring deciduous or mixed woodland and forest, parks, gardens, orchards, hedges and scrub, and indeed any bushy areas with scattered trees, wherever it can find a ready food supply and holes in which to nest. It readily occupies nest boxes, and is a familiar visitor to garden bird feeders. It is single brooded, with an average of 10–12 eggs per brood. Outside the breeding season it readily joins mixed flocks that roam widely.

CALL/SONG

A commonly used call is a churring note that starts low and rises in a short rolling trill, and is delivered in various permutations, such as "chwrrr'r'r'r'r'r", "chwrr'hi'ih'ih" or "twr'r'r'i'i'i'i'i", or commencing with high notes before dropping sharply, such as "tsii'tsii'tsii-chwrr'r'r'r'r". It uses a more scolding "trrrrr-bii'beep!" and a drawn-out "seeer" in response to aerial predators, a conversational high-pitched "tsee" when in a group, and a repeated drier note "di'di'di'di". Song variants include a repeated high-pitched, clear silvery "bii'bi-sisisi-srr'r'r'r'r'r'r'r, bii'bi-sisisi-srr'r'r'r'r'r'r'r, bii'bi-sisisi-srr'r'r'r'r'r'r'r" or a high, cyclical and buzzing "tsee-zzi'zi, tzii'zi'zee- tzii'zi'zee- tzii'zi'zee-tzii'zi'zee".

IDENTIFICATION

The largest tit in the region, it is a bulky bird with striking plumage. The underparts are bright yellow, bisected by a bold black stripe from throat to vent. The head and throat are glossy black with a large white cheek patch that is fully enclosed. The mantle is green, and the wings are slaty-blue with a broad white wingbar on the tips of the greater coverts. The tail is quite long, grey-blue and with white outer feathers. Females are slightly less bright than males and have a narrower belly-stripe.

HABITAT

A familiar bird throughout our region, it favours similar habitats to the Blue Tit and is found in deciduous and mixed woodland (sometimes purely coniferous), hedges, thickets, parks, churchyards, gardens and virtually any area with scattered trees, shrubs and bushes. Primarily a lowland bird, it can occur up to the tree line in mountainous areas. Adapts well to the presence of humans, and is a regular visitor to bird feeders.

CALL/SONG

Highly vocal, with many different calls, which often have a clear, ringing bell-like quality. Variants include a "psi! ping ping", a Chaffinch-like "pink-pink" and a "tii-twerr, tii-twerr". It commonly utters a low purring or scolding and slightly rising "tchr'r'r'r'r", which can be combined with higher-pitched calls as in "tii'tii'wrrrrr". The song is also highly variable, but is typically a repeated series of two or three loud, clear and ringing notes,

Great Tit
Parus major

LENGTH: 13.5–15cm

WING SPAN: 22.5–25.5cm

CALL: "psi! ping ping"

TRACK: 2:56

repeated in a 'see-sawing' style between three and ten times, although often just for four or five. Just some of the many possible examples are listed here: "dti'too dti'too dti'too dti'too dti'too", "pu'tingk pu'tingk pu'tingk pu'tingk", "chi'wer chi'wer chi'wer chi'wer chi'wer", "ba'ba'ding-ba'ba'ding-ba'ba'ding-ba'ba'ding" and the classic "tea'cher tea'cher tea'cher tea'cher".

Crested Tit
Lophophanes cristatus

LENGTH: 10.5–12cm

WING SPAN: 17–20cm

CALL: "chr'r'r'r'r'r"

TRACK: 2:57

IDENTIFICATION

A delightful little tit that is immediately recognizable by its distinctive pointed triangular crest, which is whitish-grey and speckled and scalloped with blackish markings. The head is whitish, neatly patterned with a narrow black line through the eye which curves down at the rear, forming a border around the ear coverts. It has an extensive black throat, the lower edge of which is joined to a black collar extending round to the nape. The upperparts are brown and the underparts are whitish-buff, washed warmer buff on the flanks. The sexes are similar.

HABITAT

Highly sedentary, it occurs widely across Europe yet in Britain is represented only by a relict population in the pine forests of central–northern Scotland. Typically preferring coniferous forest, and often in moss and lichen-rich spruce, it can also be found occasionally in mixed forest, and in Iberia is found in deciduous woods. The nest hole is excavated by the female, although the species will use existing holes and nest boxes.

CALL/SONG

The commonly heard call, used for advertising and contact, is a cheery, low, almost purring "chr'r'r'r'r'r" or "br'r'r'r'r'r", on an even scale or descending in tone slightly. It is quite vocal and frequently uses other short calls, such as high-pitched "see" and "zit" sounds, often running them together and sounding not unlike the calls of a Goldcrest or Firecrest, or combining them with the purring call, such as "see-si-sit, si-see-sit chr'r'r'r'r". The song is a poorly developed, rising and falling combination of purring call notes preceded by rather hoarse high-pitched notes, as in "iir'szi'zzi-churr'r'r'r'r, iir'szi'zzi-churr'r'r'r'r, iir'szi'zzi-churr'r'r'r'r".

CONTINENTAL
RACE

Coal Tit
Periparus ater

LENGTH: 10–11.5cm

WING SPAN: 17–21cm

🔊 **CALL:** "tyu'ii"

● **TRACK:** 2:58

IDENTIFICATION

A small short-tailed tit with a small fine bill. It has a big, boldly marked head, with a black cap that extends on to the nape, framing an oblong white nape-patch. The cheeks are white and it has a large amount of black on the throat, which spreads onto the shoulder where it breaks up into black flecking. The underparts are whitish-buff, more strongly coloured on the flanks. It has white spots on the tips of the greater and median coverts, forming a double wingbar. Various races occur within our region; British birds have an olive-grey mantle and wings, which are blue-grey on birds from continental Europe.

HABITAT

Resident, although in some years northern populations may head southwards in large numbers. It is a bird of conifer forest, and found at a wide range of altitudes. It has a preference for spruce, and also occurs widely in mixed forest, although in some parts of its range it lives in purely deciduous woods. It is common in parks and large gardens, almost always where some conifers are present. It ranges more widely in winter, joining mixed flocks and often visiting feeders in gardens.

CALL/SONG

The song is a rapid, rather high-pitched repetition of a clear double note, reminiscent of the Great Tit's song but delivered at a brisker pace and sounding sweeter and 'tighter', as in "pew-ti-tew ti-tew ti-tew ti-tew ti-tew-pi", "tii'cher tii'cher tii'cher tii'cher tii'cher" or "ti'chew ti'chew ti'chew ti'chew ti'chew", or a more trisyllabic "too'i'tee too'i'tee too'i'tee too'i'tee". Individual songsters can give a wide variety of versions, all sung on the same basic theme but differing in rhythm, pace and emphasis. It also has many different calls; a frequently heard one is a twanging "tyu'ii" or "ti'duu'ii", or a monosyllabic "tuuy". It also has high-pitched conversational calls such as a sharp "psitt, psitt" and a shivering Goldcrest-like "tss'ss'ss'ss'ii".

BRITISH RACE

Willow Tit
Poecile montanus

LENGTH: 12–13cm

WING SPAN: 17–20.5cm

CALL: "zzi'zi djaeeer djaeer djaeer djaeer"

TRACK: 2:59

IDENTIFICATION

Very similar to the Marsh Tit, with which it shares a black cap, white cheek and brown upperparts. It is big-headed, more so than the Marsh, and has a matt black cap and a more extensive black bib, which tends to be more triangular in shape. It shows a pale panel on the wing of pale-edged secondaries, tertials and greater coverts, a feature lacking in the Marsh. The underparts are buffish-white, with warm buff on the flanks.

HABITAT

A resident across the region, but in serious decline in many parts of Britain. It can be found in deciduous and mixed woodland, with a preference for damp or marshy areas with willow, alder, elder and birch, hedgerows, copses, and scrub in overgrown marshes, all with dead or rotting wood in which it excavates its own nest hole. In the north of its range it favours coniferous forest.

CALL/SONG

The call is the best way to tell it from the similar Marsh Tit, and is usually a sequence of two different notes. The first is a high, short "zzi", repeated just once or twice, and the second is a hoarse, nasal drawn-out note, "zzi'zi djaeeer djaeer djaeer". Often just the "djaeer" notes are given, and this is used as a contact call or given more excitedly in alarm. It also gives some short "chup" or "chit" notes, and some short typically tit-like high-pitched "sit" calls. The main song type is similar to the second song type of the Wood Warbler, a series of 3–5 loud, downwardly-inflected piping whistles such as "tiou'tiou'tiou'tiou'tiou". Another song, although rarely heard, comprises a collection of sweet, rather strangled and subdued warbling phrases, plus a Greenfinch-like rattle.

Marsh Tit
Poecile palustris

LENGTH: 11.5–13cm

WING SPAN: 18–19.5cm

🔊 **CALL:** "pssi'chew!"

⏺ **TRACK:** 2:60

IDENTIFICATION

A compact, large-headed and dumpy-bodied tit, most likely to be confused with the Willow Tit, to which it is very similar. It has a glossy black cap, which extends to the nape in a narrow line and borders a large whitish cheek. It has a small black bill and a small black 'bib' or chin and upper throat, typically much smaller than on the Willow Tit. The upperparts are uniform mouse-brown, without the Willow's pale panel on the wing. The tail is brown and the underparts are whitish, washed buff on the flanks. The sexes are similar.

HABITAT

A widespread resident across much of England, Wales and Continental Europe, found in deciduous and mixed woodland and with a preference for oak and beech. It prefers moist habitats, and can also be found in alder carr and in riverine trees and shrubs at the margins of wetland, ideally with some dead or decaying trees, as it requires ready-made holes for nesting. It is also found in parks and large gardens where suitable broad-leaved vegetation occurs, and will often visit feeders.

CALL/SONG

The diagnostic call is a quick, explosive "pssi' chew!" or "ssi'ssi'chew", often followed by, and combined with, a scolding nasal "jhe'jhe'jhe'jhe" to make "pssi'chew! jhe'jhe'jhe'jhe", or a softer, more chattering and more Blue Tit-like "eh'eh'eh'eh". It also uses a monosyllabic "sip" and a high-pitched "tsip'sip" note in territorial disputes. The song is highly variable between individuals, and is a loud and clear ringing series of 5–7 notes delivered on an even scale. Versions include "tiiup tiiup tiiup tiiup tiiup", "tue'tue'tue'tue'tue", "tseer'tserr'tseer'tseer'tseer" or a more disyllabic "p'chirh p'chirh p'chirh p'chirh p'chirh p'chirh".

Nuthatch
Sitta europaea

LENGTH: 12–14.5cm

WING SPAN: 22.5–27cm

🔊 **CALL:** "twehp'twehp"

⏺ **TRACK:** 2:61

IDENTIFICATION

A stocky, short-tailed and 'spear-headed' bird,
usually seen climbing on tree trunks and branches
and often coming downwards, headfirst. The
bill is long and deep like a small chisel, and the
upperparts are plain blue-grey with a strong black
line through the eye from bill to nape. The throat
is whitish and the remainder of the underparts are
rufous-buff, darker and more intensely coloured on
the flanks, with a rich red-brown vent that is boldly
spotted with white. Females are less intensely
coloured below. Birds of the nominate Scandinavian
race are white on the belly.

HABITAT

A woodland bird found in deciduous and mixed
forest, favouring mature trees and particularly very
old gnarled and decaying ones offering nooks and
crannies for feeding and cavities for nesting. It is also
found in parks and large gardens, mature hedgerows
and smaller wooded areas, as long as the trees are
not too widely spaced. In the far north of its range it
will nest in pure coniferous forest. It uses an existing
hole for nesting, often plastering the entrance with
mud to customize the diameter of the hole.

CALL/SONG

Very vocal, with a wide variety of rather loud
and far-carrying vocalizations that function
as territorial, advertising and contact calls.
Commonly heard is an excited single or slightly
disyllabic "tyupp", "tu'iip" or "twehp", frequently
repeated and often in rapid couplets such as
"twehp'twehp, twehp'twehp, twehp'twehp".
It also gives a flatter, quick "chud'ud'ud" and
a longer "chtd'chtd'chtd'chtd'chtd'chtd" or
"thk'thk'thk'thk'thk". It gives a conversational
"sit" contact note when feeding generally, and a
shivering, silvery "fsr'r'r'r'r'r'r". The song is variable,
usually a loud clear piping whistle, repeated either
slowly as "viou' viou' viou' viou' viou'…" or "pwee'
pwee' pwee' pwee' pwee…", or rapidly as a liquid
trilling "pi'pi'pi'pi'pi'…" or "pr'r'r'r'r'r'r…", as well as
a nasal "ve've've've've've've".

Eurasian Treecreeper
Certhia familiaris

LENGTH: 12.5–14cm

WING SPAN: 17.5–21cm

🔊 **CALL:** "zssii"

⏺ **TRACK:** 2:62

IDENTIFICATION

A slight bird with a long and slender shape, a thin decurved bill and a long, stiff and 'spiky' tail. It creeps up tree trunks like a mouse, often starting at the base and then climbing up before dropping down to the base of an adjoining tree and starting again. It is essentially bark-coloured above, with a complex pattern of brown finely marked with whitish spots and streaks. It is white below, faintly tinged with brown on the rear flanks and vent, and has a white supercilium that is strongest behind the eye.

HABITAT

A resident and arboreal bird, found in deciduous, mixed and coniferous forest. In Britain it favours broadleaved woodland, often where quite dense, but commonly in small marginal patches of trees in farmland, hedges, parks, large gardens and in riverine strips of alder and other species. It requires bark with crevices for feeding, with decaying wood and loose and flaky bark needed for nesting and roosting. Where its range overlaps with the Short-toed Treecreeper, it is generally found in more montane and coniferous areas.

CALL/SONG

The song is a very high-pitched, regularly structured little ditty lasting 2–2.5 seconds, starting with high flat notes and then accelerating and descending in tone before a flourish at the end. The penultimate note is the lowest of the sequence and the final note is rather higher, such as "tseee, tsee'tsee tsi'sisisisi sisoo'wit". Variations occur, and where both treecreeper species occur together, this one may mimic the other! The calls are also very high pitched, as high as a Goldcrest at 8.5kHz, as in the short and often repeated contact call "zssii" or "tiih", sometimes given with a dipping inflexion, such as "tsu'ui", as well as a harsher, slightly buzzing "zsih'h'h'h" and a more trilling, high and flat "tsirrrr".

Short-toed Treecreeper
Certhia brachydactyla

LENGTH: 12–13.5cm

WING SPAN: 17–20.5cm

🔊 **CALL:** "tenk!"

⏺ **TRACK:** 2:63

IDENTIFICATION

Almost identical to the Eurasian Treecreeper, its distinctive call being the best guide to identification. It generally has a longer bill, browner rear flanks, and – of course – a shorter hindclaw! Subtle differences in the complex patterns on the closed wing can also assist identification, but to study this feature in close detail ideally requires photographic evidence.

HABITAT

A very rare visitor to Britain, with just 22 records since 1969, mostly from south-east England. It is found just across the Channel, however, and widely through continental Europe. It favours similar habitat to Eurasian Treecreeper, preferring lowlands, although it does go higher in the southern part of its range and has a preference for oak or pine in some areas.

CALL/SONG

The song is a jerkily rhythmed, halting collection of harsher and lower-pitched notes when compared to the song of the Eurasian Treecreeper, and is significantly shorter, lasting for 1–1.5 seconds. It comprises six notes on average, each quite widely varied in tone, such as "teh–too'seh'sissoo'wii'sehr". In some areas it reduces this phrase to just three or four notes. It also gives call and song variations, such as a rather rasping "tseh, tszu'tzeh tzerr, tszu'tzeh tzerr" and a bright "tuh! tu'teet!". The main call is quite different and is a sure way to tell Short-toed and Eurasian apart. Short-toed gives a short, shrill and penetrating "tenk!" or "tehh!", very similar to the calls of Coal Tit or Dunnock. Another call is a high, slightly rolling "tserrrrh", similar to that of the Eurasian, but lower pitched and rougher sounding. In flight it gives a short "zit" or "sit" flight call, similar to that of the Eurasian.

Penduline Tit
Remiz pendulinus

LENGTH: 10–11.5cm

WING SPAN: 16–17.5cm

🔊 **CALL:** "tsseeeo"

⏺ **TRACK:** 2:64

HABITAT

A rare but annual and increasingly regular visitor to Britain, it breeds from central Europe eastwards, where it is a summer visitor, and in southern Europe, where it is resident. It is usually found along the margins of swamps, lakes and rivers in scrubby deciduous trees and bushes, or in reedbeds with bushy clumps and edges. It constructs a pouch-shaped nest with an entrance tunnel, hanging in the thin outer branches of a small tree, often over water or sometimes within a reedbed.

CALL/SONG

The call is a rather high-pitched (about 6kHz) and plaintive single descending note "tsseeeo", lasting an average of 0.6 seconds, quite far-carrying and with a penetrating quality. It is similar to the call of the Reed Bunting but longer, stronger and more downward-inflected. It can give various versions of this call in different contexts, often using a shorter "tssu", and in alarm a sharper, even-pitched, trilling "srrri" or "sreee". It also has a buzzing note, "tzzz". The full song is a collection of trills and whistles interspersed with call notes, very like the songs of the Greenfinch or even Canary, delivered at a measured pace and fairly slowly, with pauses between short phrases, as in "pyuu…tsi pyuu… tzzssrrrrrrrrr… tzzssrrrrrrrrr… yup'piy'ioou… trr'r'r'r'r… ichivichivichivi…pyuu… tsi pyuu… tzzssrrrrrrrrr…" etc.

IDENTIFICATION

A very small and rather delicate tit-like bird, with a sharp little bill. It has a pale greyish-white head dominated by a long black 'bank robber' mask that meets over the bill, boldest in the male but narrower in the female. It has a white throat and pinky-buff underparts, and the male has reddish-brown blotching on the breast. The mantle and wing coverts are chestnut and contrast strongly with the pale head, although this feature is duller and browner on the female.

Golden Oriole
Oriolus oriolus

LENGTH: 22–25cm

WING SPAN: 44–47cm

🔊 **CALL:** "hwi'lli'oo'hweoo"

⏺ **TRACK:** 2:65

FEMALE

IDENTIFICATION

The male is a striking thrush-sized bird, with a bright yellow body contrasting with black wings, tail and lores. It has yellow corners to the tail and a small yellow patch at the base of the primaries, and the bill is red. The female is rather more demure, but still quite bright with yellow-green upperparts and wing coverts, blackish-grey wings and tail. The underparts are whitish, with long prominent streaks and a variable amount of yellow wash down the flanks and onto the vent. Despite the bright colouration it can easily disappear in a sunlit tree.

HABITAT

A summer visitor found right across continental Europe. It is a mainly scarce migrant to Britain, although small breeding colonies persist in the south-east of England, where they nest in commercial poplar plantations. Their generally favoured habitat is open deciduous woodland, particularly with mature trees, and they can be found in parks, large gardens, avenues, riverine woodland and shelter belts. They can be rather elusive, however, staying high in the trees or within the crown, and are often only seen when flying between wooded patches.

CALL/SONG

Quite vocal. The commonly heard call note is a rather unlovely harsh squawk, quite high pitched and nasal, such as "arr'aa'arrhk" or a more insistent and emphatic "hrrrahhhk!". The 'o-ri-ole' song is a sweeter and more beautiful sound, and gives the bird its name in several languages. It is sung by both sexes during the breeding season, but more quietly and less fluently by the female. It is made up of loud fluty, mellow but full-voiced yodelling whistles, and typically consists of three or four notes that sound as if they overlap, with characteristic jumps in pitch, such as "hwi'loo'hweeo", "hwi'lli'oo'hweoo", " idlii'hweeeoo", a descending "hweedli'hwoh" and a shorter "hii'hweeoo".

MALE

MALE

Red-backed Shrike
Lanius collurio

LENGTH: 16–18cm

WING SPAN: 24–27cm

CALL: "kvaer"

TRACK: 2:66

IDENTIFICATION

The male has a pale grey crown and nape, and a black mask that meets over a black bill. The mantle and wing coverts are chestnut-red, the rump is pale grey and contrasts with the black tail, which has large white blocks on the basal half of the outer tail feathers, reminiscent of the tail pattern of the Wheatear. The throat is white, while the underparts are whitish and flushed pink. The female is browner, with a grey-brown head and a brown mask behind the eye, darker upperparts and whitish-buff underparts with fine vermiculations. Juveniles are similar to the female and have fresh pale edges to the wing feathers, a darker brown crown, and clearer vermiculations and dark scallops on the underparts.

CALL/SONG

The male sings a subdued, sub-song-like, scratchy twittering warble, often including much mimicry of small-bird calls. It can sustain this song for 10 minutes at a time, and uses it to advertise to the female. It will give a more excited version of the song when the female arrives on territory, but both these song variants are given only for a short period and are actually rarely heard. It has a range of call notes, such as a nasal chirp "kscha" or "kvaer", used by the male as a territorial call. The commonest alarm call is a hard "chack" or "tsheck", often repeated rapidly and accompanied by vigorous tail movements. It also gives a bleating, repeated "ivvik".

HABITAT

Formerly a widespread and common breeding bird in Britain, but now scarce, breeding only occasionally and with as few as 220 migrants recorded nationwide in any one year. It is widespread across Europe as a summer visitor, favouring warm and sunny open country with scattered trees, woodland edges, clearings, heaths, pastures, hedges and bushy thickets, particularly thorny scrub.

FEMALE

Great Grey Shrike
Lanius excubitor

LENGTH: 22–26cm
WING SPAN: 30–35cm
🔊 **CALL:** "trr'r'r'rih"
⏺ **TRACK:** 2:67

IDENTIFICATION

A large, pale shrike with a big head and long tail, which is often twitched from side to side. The crown, mantle and rump are clean grey, the tail is black with white sides. It has a bold black mask stretching from the top of the bill across the face to the rear of the cheek, highlighted by a white supercilium. The wings are rather short and black, with a bold white patch on the inner primaries and white tips to the tertials. The underparts are white. Usually seen perched on top of a prominent lookout post, scanning for prey, and it will occasionally hover.

HABITAT

A scarce passage migrant and winter visitor to Britain, with an average of 60 widely scattered birds wintering annually. It is a summer visitor to Scandinavia and also breeds across continental Europe, where it is partially sedentary. A bird of open country, more so than other shrikes, it favours open spaces with a scattering of bushes and trees, yet in winter can adapt to almost treeless environments so long as raised perches are available. It breeds in partly wooded tundra, birch forest, bogs, marshes, heaths and parkland, and wintering birds in Britain are often found in woodland clearings and on heaths with gorse and bushes.

CALL/SONG

The main song is a rather simple repetition of a clipped, almost chirruping double note, often followed by a hoarse, rasping, but fairly soft trill, such as "tlip tlip…hwrrrrr… tlip tlip…hwrrrrr… tlip tlip…hwrrrrr…", frequently varied and including other higher-pitched sounds. It also gives a quiet twittering scratchy song, interspersed with harsh and raucous sounds, mimicry of other birds and finch-like twanging notes, which may be appended to the main song. It has a range of call notes, a commonly heard one being a drawn-out trilling "trr'r'r'rih" or "shr'r'r'ee", plus a harsh "khwaerrr", a raucous nasal "hwearrr", and a nasal "shack" that may be repeated in a Magpie-like chatter.

IDENTIFICATION

A fairly large and colourful bird, with a longish tail, rounded head and short bill. The body, head and wing coverts are a pinkish-brown, with a white rump, throat and vent. The tail is black, which contrasts strongly with the rump, and the flight feathers are blackish with a white patch on the secondaries that is visible at rest. On the 'shoulder' or primary coverts and inner greater coverts, it has a distinctive bright blue panel vermiculated with black. The eye is pale, the forecrown is streaked black and it has an oblong black moustachial patch.

Jay
Garrulus glandarius

LENGTH: 32–35cm
WING SPAN: 52–58cm
CALL: "skaaaaaak!"
TRACK: 2:68

HABITAT

Common throughout our region and favouring both deciduous and coniferous forests, with a special affinity for oak. It can also be found in parks, large gardens, hedgerows and scattered smaller wooded areas. It is mostly resident, but northern birds often move south, and in autumn birds can be seen more widely. They collect and store acorns as winter food caches, and in autumn can often be seen in flight transporting acorns to their hiding places.

CALL/SONG

The commonly heard vocalization is the harsh and raucous call, a rather hoarse upward-inflected "skaaaaaak!" or "schaaaaach", often repeated twice or more. It is used as an alarm or warning, such as when mobbing an owl, or as an advertising call. It has a range of other calls, less frequently heard, such as an almost perfect copy of the Buzzard's call, such as "pee'yah", as well as some conversational and rather gruff "eerhhh" calls, a soft rising "eerrrrr'eh", and other softer mewing notes. It also has a song, often only audible at close range and which is a fairly sweet subdued warbling and twittering, like a sub-song and often including mimicry. It is usually sung by the male in late winter and early spring.

Magpie
Pica pica

LENGTH: 40–51cm (inc. tail of 20–30cm)
WING SPAN: 52–60cm
🔊 **CALL:** "jakh'akh'akh'akh'akh'akh"
⬤ **TRACK:** 2:69

IDENTIFICATION

A familiar bird to many, with a distinctively pied plumage and a long green-glossed tail that exceeds the length of the body and is longer in the male. The head, breast, vent and upperparts are black, the belly white, and it has a long white stripe along the scapulars. The wings are black with a blue gloss and a large white panel across the whole of the primaries. The metallic sheen on the wings and tail varies between green, blue and purple, depending on the angle of the light. The flight is rather flappy, fluttering and direct.

HABITAT

A widespread and common resident, found in a wide range of habitats and even in urban areas. It generally favours lightly wooded open country, with adequate open ground and short grass for feeding, and can be found in open deciduous and coniferous woodland, farmland with hedges and often close to man in villages, parks and gardens. It builds a ragged domed stick nest, and feeds on insects and worms; when it has young it will plunder the nests of other birds.

CALL/SONG

It has a range of calls, all rather harsh and unmusical, with the familiar 'rattle' call the most frequently heard. It is a "cha" or "jakh" note, rapidly repeated to make a staccato chattering, as in "jakh'akh'akh'akh'akh'akh", and is typically given in alarm or anxiety, such as when mobbing predators. Another commonly heard call is a two-note "ch'chack", "akh'jack" or "schrach-ak", and a single, more drawn-out "shree'akh", which are both used in a conversational context and often heard when a group of birds are together. It has other, less well-defined, harsh notes and also a rarely heard song, used in courtship and comprising a subdued chuntering and twittering, interspersed with some sweet notes.

IDENTIFICATION

A Jay-sized bird, with the short tail, long bill and big head giving it a front-heavy appearance in flight. The crown is unspotted and dark brown, the wings are blackish, and much of the remainder of the body feathering is dark chocolate-brown patterned with white spots. The vent is pure white, contrasting with the black tail, which has a broad white terminal band, widest at the corners, and provides a bold field character when in flight. The wings are broad and rounded, and the flight is direct but with rather weak-looking and hesitant wingbeats.

HABITAT

A very rare visitor to Britain, with just one or two recorded every few years, although it can undergo irruptions from Siberia during pine cone famine, such as in 1968 when 324 turned up in Britain. Otherwise it is resident in southern Scandinavia, central and eastern Europe. It favours coniferous forests of spruce and arolla pine, but also occurs in stands of hazel. Like the Jay, it stores food for winter in the ground. As a vagrant in Britain it can occur in any habitat, including gardens.

CALL/SONG

Silent during the winter, it becomes vocal in spring during courtship and again in summer when the young have fledged. The commonly heard call is a mechanical-sounding, loud and drawn-out, emphatic rasping "kraaaahhhhrrrr!", longer and higher-pitched than the "caw" of a crow, but otherwise is unlike any other bird's call. This is usually repeated a few times, more so when birds are agitated. It can also give some quiet conversational Jackdaw-like calls, and has a seldom-heard song, a subdued and quiet sub-song-like twittering sound, very varied and ranging between babbling, piping, whistling, gurgling and mewing, and sometimes including mimicry.

Nutcracker
Nucifraga caryocatactes

LENGTH: 32–35cm

WING SPAN: 52–58cm

CALL: "kraaaahhhhrrrr!"

TRACK: 2:70

Chough
Pyrrhocorax pyrrhocorax

LENGTH: 37–41cm

WING SPAN: 73–90cm

🔊 **CALL:** "chiaow"

⏺ **TRACK:** 2:71

IDENTIFICATION

A rather elegant corvid, with a uniform glossy black plumage. It has a fairly long, slender and gently decurved red bill, and longish red legs. In flight it reveals broad wings with blunt wingtips, the primary feathers showing as clearly defined deep 'fingers', and is highly acrobatic and very much at home in the air, soaring on flat wings, tumbling around on the updraughts or making steep dives on folded wings. The wings cover the tail at rest. Juveniles are identifiable by their dull yellow bill.

HABITAT

A bird with a wide distribution across the Palaearctic, often breeding in high mountainous areas but also occurring along the Atlantic coasts of Scotland, Wales, Ireland and Brittany, and at lower elevations generally in Spain and other parts of the Mediterranean. In recent years it has recolonized Cornwall after an absence of 50 years, thanks to careful habitat management. Its favoured habitat is rocky coasts and sea cliffs, with sea caves and deep clefts required for nesting, and it will also use quarries. For feeding it needs a short sward, which can be provided by grazing animals keeping cliff-top vegetation to a minimum and thereby allowing Choughs access to invertebrate prey in the soil. Birds will also forage more widely, in stubble and ploughed fields.

CALL/SONG

The familiar call is a bright, downward-inflected and rather explosive "chiaow" or "piao", also given as a more subdued "chiaah" or "kyaah" and often accompanied by simultaneous wing- and tail-flicking when calling from the ground. The call is frequently given in flight, when it may serve as an advertising call. Other variants are given, and there is also a rarely heard and subdued twittering song, in the manner of several other corvid species. The author speculates that if the name of this species is meant to be onomatopoeic, as claimed, then it should be pronounced 'Chow' as opposed to 'Chuff'!

BRITISH RACE

Jackdaw
Corvus monedula

LENGTH: 30–34cm

WING SPAN: 67–74cm

🔊 **CALL:** "tjakk!"

⏺ **TRACK:** 2:72

IDENTIFICATION

A gregarious and small blackish corvid, with a rather short and slender bill. At range it can appear all dark, but with a reasonable view it shows a pale eye and a grey nape and sides to the head, which contrast with the charcoal-grey upperparts and black face, crown and throat. The underparts are dark grey, as is the remainder of the plumage. The eastern race *soemmerringii* shows a silver collar at the lower edge of the neck side. A very sociable bird, it is frequently seen in tight flocks in farmland, where it often mixes with Rooks, or in couples, being attentive to each other and strengthening their lifelong pair bond.

HABITAT

Resident throughout our region, although northern birds can wander southwards. Often found close to humans, using chimneys and other cavities in buildings for nesting, it otherwise occurs in many types of open habitat with scattered trees. It often favours deciduous woodland, where old hollow or mature trees with cavities are preferred, such as in old parkland or large gardens, and also occurs in farmland with mature hedgerows and locally in mountainous or cliff habitats and quarries.

CALL/SONG

A vocal bird, so much so that it is named after its commonly heard call, a rather high, bright and pleasing "tjakk!", "khakk" or "kyak", often repeated in a series or given in chorus by a flock, when it can sound like "k'chak k'chik k'chakk" or an even faster 'yickering' sound when gathering to roost. It gives this or similar calls at varying volumes and intensities, such as the quieter and more conversational 'chakking' given by pairs sitting together or when adults announce their return to the nest. It gives more of a crow-like "caw" in alarm, a harsh drawn-out "jaairrr" or "kyarrrr". It also has a song, a quiet medley of call notes run together.

SOEMMERRINGII
EASTERN RACE

Rook
Corvus frugilegus

LENGTH: 41–49cm

WING SPAN: 81–99cm

CALL: "graaah"

TRACK: 2:73

ROOKERY

IDENTIFICATION

An all black corvid with a purple metallic sheen to its plumage. The main difference from its close relatives is its grey bill, with greyish-white skin extending around the bill base and up to the eye, and the lack of the nostril feathering so prominent on both the Carrion Crow and Raven. As a consequence the bill appears more pointed and dagger-like. The head is more domed with a peaked crown, and when walking the bird often appears fuller bellied. Juveniles are very similar to Carrion Crow juveniles, lacking the whitish face of an adult Rook and having black feathering over the nostrils until their first spring.

HABITAT

Common, widespread and resident across the region, with birds in northern parts of the range moving south- and westwards in winter. Essentially a lowland bird, it favours agricultural areas and can be found in flocks feeding in pastures and on ploughed fields. Areas with tall trees are required for its nesting colonies (rookeries), which are most commonly located in isolated stands of trees and copses in farmland and in adjacent villages.

CALL/SONG

Calls include a simple "caw", similar to that of the Carrion Crow but less rolling and more grinding in quality, a harsher, hoarse and nasal "graaah" or "geeeah", and a multi-syllable "gra'gra' grrahh". This call is lower in pitch than the Carrion Crow's and delivered in an even flat tone; however, the call can be varied somewhat and there is also a higher-pitched 'hiccup' sound, such as "khuow". Females also give a longer, higher-pitched call, "kraaa-a". As so often in flocks, the calls sound repeated and even overlapping, and when at a rookery can provide a near-deafening cacophony of sound at close range. The male gives a 'song' in courtship, a medley of various call notes and said to resemble the Starling's song.

IDENTIFICATION

All black, with a slight metallic sheen. Similar to the Raven, it can be told by its smaller size, rounded tail, shorter bill, shorter wings and weaker flight, plus vocal differences. It is almost impossible to separate from a juvenile Rook, however, but shows a blunter, thicker bill. Generally less gregarious than the Rook, it is a solitary nester but can form flocks, particularly after breeding. The Hooded Crow *Corvus cornix,* often treated as a race of this species, is pale dirty grey on the body, with a black hood and breast.

HABITAT

Common across Britain, western and central Europe, it is found in a wide variety of habitats and favours open country with scattered trees, woodland, farmland with hedgerows and parks. It frequently penetrates into urban areas, its only real requirement being trees in which to nest. In Britain it is often found foraging in tidal habitats, such as estuaries, saltmarshes and coastal areas. The Hooded Crow replaces the Carrion in Scotland, Ireland, Scandinavia and eastern Europe.

CALL/SONG

Quite vocal, the commonly heard call throughout the year being a repeated, slightly nasal "kraaaah" or a softer "oarrgh", which dip in pitch at the end of the note, with a slightly rolling and liquid tone at times and often repeated in a sequence of two to six notes. It can sound of varying pitch, and is sometimes delivered more urgently on a level tone, such as "kraaaa! kraaah!"

Carrion Crow
Corvus corone

LENGTH: 44–51cm

WING SPAN: 93–104cm

🔊 **CALL:** "kraaaa"

⏺ **TRACK:** 2:74

or "kruaah-kruaah". The female sometimes gives a more mechanical-sounding "krrgh krrgh krrgh", reminiscent of a Raven's call but usually accompanied by the main call to avert any confusion. Hoarse and strangled-sounding variants may also be heard, and a rarely heard song of subdued variable notes is also given. The calls of the Hooded Crow are very similar.

Raven
Corvus corax

LENGTH: 54–67cm

WING SPAN: 120–150cm

 CALL: "krahhk krahhk"

TRACK: 2:75

IDENTIFICATION

Our largest passerine, and comparable to the size of a Buzzard, which is noticeable when both species are in the air together. Black all over with a bluish-lilac sheen, it has a very deep, heavy bill with a strongly arched culmen and often shows ragged throat feathering. The tail is long and wedge-shaped, and the wings are long and appear rather pointed at times, with a long 'hand' and distinct 'fingers' formed by the long primaries. The neck is fairly long and protrudes noticeably in flight, when the bill is often held open.

HABITAT

A very widespread species. In our region it is found in Iceland, Ireland, Scandinavia, central and eastern Europe, and the less densely populated regions of western and northern Britain; it also occurs in southern France, Iberia and throughout the Mediterranean. It favours a wide range of habitats, but is particularly partial to wild and undisturbed places offering secure or inaccessible nest sites, such as on sea cliffs, in mountainous areas and uplands, sparse woodlands, low intensity farmland (particularly in hilly country) or any other wilderness-type habitats. It has very large territories and will travel long distances when foraging.

CALL/SONG

Quite vocal, the commonly heard call being distinctly different from other corvids – a deep, gruff, rolling, grunting sound such as "krruuk-krruuk", "krahhk krahhk", "grrahnk" or even "korrp", the latter being the bird's name in Swedish. It can give a variety of calls, some sounding more strangled or conversational, as well as a repeated shorter version of the main call, as in "ghok'ghok'ghok" and "krahk'krack'krack". It also gives a honking, higher-pitched "hrrak" or "prahhk". In spring it has a subdued and rather primitive little 'song', comprising various creaking croaks and soft calls.

WINTER
PLUMAGE

Starling
Sturnus vulgaris

LENGTH: 19–22cm

WING SPAN: 37–42cm

CALL: "tchaaeerr"

TRACK: 2:76

IDENTIFICATION

A stocky black bird, with a metallic green and violet sheen to the plumage, a short tail and pointed triangular wings. In winter it is profusely spotted with buffish-white spots and has a dark bill. In summer it loses most of this spotting and appears wholly glossy black. The bill also turns yellow, with a blue-grey base on the male and a yellowish-white base on the female. Juveniles are grey-brown with a pale throat, and gradually acquire white-spotted black feathers during their first winter.

HABITAT

Resident in western Europe, with large influxes in winter of birds from further north and east. It is common and found in many habitats, particularly in urban areas, occurring in woodland, farmland, parks and gardens as well as in almost any open country, including along seashores and on saltmarshes. Although requiring holes for nesting, outside the breeding season it disperses widely and can sometimes form massive flocks, particularly at roost sites.

CALL/SONG

Very vocal, with a rich repertoire of song and mimicry. Commonly heard calls include a rasping, descending "tchaaeerr", often given when taking flight. Other calls include a sharp and repeated "kyik" or "kyett", given in alarm when an aerial predator is about, and often a good indication of a Sparrowhawk in the area. The song is a rambling continuous collection of rather strangled and subdued sounds, throaty warblings and musical whistles, many of them high pitched, including much mimicry and unusual noises such as a rising "schweee'errrr", and a descending "wheeeeeoooooooo" 'bomb-drop' whistle, plus clicking, gurgling and croaking noises, and scrunching sounds like a handful of ball-bearings being rubbed together. It is famous for mimicking mechanical sounds such as telephones and car alarms!

SUMMER PLUMAGE

House Sparrow
Passer domesticus

LENGTH: 14–16cm

WING SPAN: 21–25.5cm

CALL: "cheeup"

TRACK: 2:77

FEMALE

MALE

IDENTIFICATION

A stout, large-headed and thick-billed bird. The male has a grey crown, with a chestnut brown nape and head sides between crown and cheek, pale grey cheeks and greyish underparts. It has black lores, chin and throat, and a black upper breast that flares out into a broader patch. The mantle is brown and boldly streaked black, with a grey rump in summer; in winter it is duller and browner overall, with a reduced amount of black on the underparts. The female is more demure, grey-brown all over, heavily streaked on the mantle and with a buff supercilium.

HABITAT

Commonly found wherever there is human habitation, although in urban Britain there has been a marked decline in some areas in recent years. It ranges from city centres to small villages and particularly favours farms and farmland, where it can be found feeding, especially in grain crops and typically where there are hedgerows and other cover to retreat to. It avoids both wide open plains and densely vegetated or forested areas, and nests in crevices, holes and under loose roof tiles in buildings or, more traditionally, in a domed nest made of grass in a bush or a hole in a sandbank.

CALL/SONG

A rather uncomplicated set of vocalizations that sound bright and 'chirpy'. Frequently heard is the 'song' of the male, given when advertising to the female from close to the nest and comprising a series of chirps and cheeps that vary slightly in pitch, such as "cheerp cheerp chilp chahp chaairp chearp…" or a more liquid "tchlrrp schleeip schlep tchleeip schleeip schlrrp…" etc. Other calls include a more clipped and drier "cheeup" or "chuurp", often repeated and given excitedly by a group, plus a disyllabic and conversational "che'chep". It calls in flight with a single "cherp" note or a disyllabic "churrip", and in anxiety or excitement gives a harder and more rattling "chrr'rr'rr'rr'rr".

IDENTIFICATION

In contrast to the House Sparrow, the sexes have similar plumage. It is slightly smaller and more compact than the House Sparrow, and generally brighter, with a red-brown crown and white cheeks that are punctuated with a prominent black cheek spot. The white extends around the neck in an almost complete collar, and it has black lores and a black chin and centre to the throat. The mantle is rufous streaked with black, the rump is brown and the underparts are pale buffy-brown and unmarked.

HABITAT

A widespread resident in our region, although subject to population fluctuations, and has dramatically decreased in Britain in recent years. In Europe it is less frequent than the House Sparrow near human habitation (although across much of Asia it is the common sparrow in towns and cities), and can usually be found in farmland areas with tall hedge-rows, woodland edges and scattered trees, parkland, and other open habitats with occasional trees. It nests in a tree hole or in cavities in buildings.

CALL/SONG

The calls and 'song' are similar to those of the House Sparrow, with a repeated cheeping and chirping, but the note has a brisker and drier quality to it and is slightly higher pitched. The song is a simple "tcheep tchirp tcheep tchirp tcheep tchirp...", varying between just one

Tree Sparrow
Passer montanus

LENGTH: 12.5–14cm

WING SPAN: 20–22cm

CALL: "tcheep tchirp tcheep tchirp"

TRACK: 2:78

repeated note and alternating between two notes at slightly different pitches. It also has a sweeter and thinner, rather swallowed and ascending "tssu'eet", and in flight has a distinctive hard and dry "chek", repeated as "chekk-et'et'ett" and which becomes a rolling chatter when given by a flock.

Chaffinch
Fringilla coelebs

LENGTH: 14–16cm

WING SPAN: 24.5–28.5cm

CALL: "pink pink"

TRACK: 2:79

FEMALE

IDENTIFICATION

A compact, rather long-tailed and sparrow-sized bird. The male in summer is ruddy-pink from the throat and cheeks to the belly, with a blue-grey crown, nape and shoulder, a brown back and black wings boldly marked with double white wingbars. In all plumages the species shows white or pale wingbars, white sides to the tail and a grey-green rump. In winter the colours of the male are subdued and duller, and the female is much more of a monochrome sepia overall, with dull buffish-white underparts, a pale head and face, with a darker grey-brown crown and nape.

MALE

HABITAT

Widespread across the region and one of the commonest British birds, resident but with numbers augmented in winter by migrants from northern Europe. It can be found in a variety of wooded habitats, both coniferous and deciduous, plus parks, orchards, gardens, and farmland with hedgerows. In winter it disperses into arable fields and open areas adjacent to woodland.

CALL/SONG

A familiar sound of spring, the song is a loud, vigorous and slightly accelerating series of sweet but hard notes, descending in four tonal steps and ending in a trisyllabic flourish; in some areas a high 'kik' is added at the end. It can sound almost rattle-like, and is usually unvarying in delivery, as in "chich-ich-ich-ich-ich-ich churr'rr'rr'rr'rr' cho'cho'cho'cho'cho chippit' churri'weeoo". It typically lasts 2.5–3 seconds, but variations are not uncommon and it may sing with varying and out-of-sequence pitches. It has a wide repertoire of calls, a familiar one being a sharp repeated "pink" or "fink", as well as a rather soft "hyupp" given in flight, an upward-inflected clear "hweet", and a short buzzing even-toned "hwwrrr" or "zhwrrr" note, reminiscent of the Brambling's song.

FEMALE
WINTER
PLUMAGE

Brambling
Fringilla montifringilla

LENGTH: 14–16cm

WING SPAN: 25–26cm

CALL: "dweee'ap"

TRACK: 2:80

IDENTIFICATION

The male in summer is a gorgeous bird, with a glossy blue-black head and mantle offset by a tangerine-orange breast and shoulder. In all plumages the wing is strongly patterned, black and orangey-buff or black with white bars in the summer male, plus a whitish belly neatly spotted with dark on the flanks, a forked blackish tail and a long white central stripe on the rump. In winter the bill is yellowish with a dusky tip, with the black head and mantle of the male frosted with pale and brownish fringes; the female has a paler, greyer head with some blackish markings on the crown and a double dark line on the nape, plus an orange band across the upper breast from shoulder to shoulder.

HABITAT

A Scandinavian breeder which winters throughout western Europe including Britain, with numbers fluctuating from year to year depending on food availability. In winter it is strongly tied to open woodland and woodland edge, churchyards, large parks and occasionally gardens, particularly where beech mast has fallen, as well as in farmland and fields with hedgerows and scattered trees. It breeds in northern birch forests and in open mixed and coniferous woods, often in upland areas.

CALL/SONG

The commonly heard call is a twangy, slightly explosive and sharply ascending nasal "dweee'ap", "chwa'ingt" or "thwaai'ip", given both in flight and when perched. It also has a crossbill-like "chup chup" or "chyk chyk" given in flight, harder, deeper and more nasal than that of the Chaffinch. The song is a simple monosyllabic note, a fairly low and drawn-out nasal buzz or wheeze, such as "nwhhaaeerrrr"or "zhwheeeehhh", lasting about 0.6–0.8 seconds and repeated persistently and monotonously, at regular intervals several seconds apart. It may also add a liquid buzzy note, shorter and lower than the song buzz, and a quicker higher-pitched version with a sparrow-like quality, given more excitedly. The anxiety note is a repeated short, high-pitched and penetrating "tzilt" or "zrriillt".

MALE SUMMER
PLUMAGE

Serin
Serinus serinus

LENGTH: 11–12cm

WING SPAN: 20–23cm

🔊 **CALL:** "tzr'r'r'r'r'l"

⬤ **TRACK:** 2:81

IDENTIFICATION

A small and compact finch, with a large head and tiny stubby bill. Often seen in flight, when it shows its yellow rump and dark cleft tail; it also has double yellowish wingbars. The male is bright lemon-yellow on the throat, breast, neck, eyebrow and forehead, with a white belly and heavily dark-streaked flanks. The crown, cheek and dark-streaked mantle are green. The female is duller green, washed yellow-green on the breast and head, and overall appears less bright or contrasting.

HABITAT

A rare but regular overshooting visitor to Britain, particularly on the south coast. It breeds commonly across Europe and is resident in Iberia and in western Europe. It favours sunny woodland edge, clearings, and scattered clumps of trees, and occurs commonly in orchards, cemeteries, parks and gardens, particularly where there are conifers (in which it prefers to nest).

CALL/SONG

It gives a short silvery, slightly descending rippling trill, such as "tzr'r'r'r'r'l", used as a contact call and frequently given by flying birds, plus a high, Dunnock-like "szit", repeated several times, and also a hard and rising forced "tuu'tweet", or a level "thweet" or "tsooeet", given in anxiety. The song is a high-pitched (7kHz), slightly undulating and continual jingling twitter, interspersed with the slower trilling call and delivered at an incredibly fast rate. It has the quality of glass fragments being ground together, with individual notes barely discernible and laid over a background of high electronic-like 'mush'. Notable for being sung throughout the year, the song is often delivered in a Greenfinch-like song-flight of slow flapping on stiff wings.

MALE

Greenfinch
Carduelis chloris

LENGTH: 14–16cm

WING SPAN: 24.5–27.5cm

🔊 **CALL:** "ju'wee"

⏺ **TRACK:** 2:82

IDENTIFICATION

A big-headed, plump and compact finch, readily recognized by the bright yellow wing panel formed by the yellow edges to the primaries, and with a deep, thick whitish or pale pink bill. It also has blocks of yellow on the sides of the basal half of the tail. The male is light green all over, yellower on the breast and greyer on the upperparts, with a grey panel on the wing and grey head sides. The female is duller, brownish-green, faintly streaked on the mantle.

HABITAT

A common resident in our region, with some immigration in winter by northern birds. A bird of the woodland edge, it favours taller trees in clearings, scrub, hedgerows and parks, and is a familiar visitor to gardens. It can also be found on arable fields and other open habitats, often feeding on the ground.

CALL/SONG

A vocal bird with a range of bright and bouncy calls. Typically heard are monosyllabic 'chips' and nasal sounds, such as an upward-inflected "ju'wee", or higher-pitched "chwai'ii" or "pwai'ii" notes, which may act as alarm or anxiety calls. It also gives a single or repeated "chud", "jup" or "ju'jup", often in flight, and which can be extended into a slow trilling "chid'id'id'id'id'id" or "jup'up'up'up'up", as well as a faster, more silvery trilling "tchrr'r'r'r'r'r'r'r".

It has two song types; the first is a frequently heard, very nasal, drawn-out and downward-inflected "djeeeeeuuuooo", lasting 1–1.6 seconds, with regular longer pauses between. A flatter or slightly upward-inflected version of this is also given, as in "jweeeiiie". The more complex song incorporates many of these calls, including the "djeeuuuoo" sound, and alternates between Canary-like trills and other more slowly delivered notes, such as "djuw djuw djuw, jup jup jup, chi'di'di'di'di'dit, ju'wee, chud'chd'chd, chid'id'id'id'id'id, ju'wee, djui djui djui djui, tilng tilng tilng tilng, tiisssrrrrrr, djeeeeeuuuooo…", etc. It is often given in a bat-like display flight.

FEMALE

Goldfinch
Carduelis carduelis

LENGTH: 12–13.5cm

WING SPAN: 21–25.5cm

🔊 **CALL:** "twiddit'widdit"

⏺ **TRACK:** 2:83

IDENTIFICATION

One of our most attractive birds, with both sexes similar. The head is white with a large red patch from the forehead around the face to the chin, and with a black crown and nape that curls downwards and forwards to the shoulder. The wings are black, with a broad golden-yellow stripe across the flight feathers and greater coverts, and large white spots on the tips of the flight feathers, which are visible at rest. The underparts are white with buffy-brown flanks and an incomplete breast band. The mantle is brown, the rump is white, and the tail is black with white spots.

HABITAT

Resident across most of Britain and continental Europe, with more easterly and northern populations moving south in winter. It favours deciduous and mixed woodland edge, farmland hedgerows, orchards, parks, gardens and overgrown waste ground, frequently close to human habitation. Outside the breeding season it relies on a supply of seeds from weedy fields and grassy areas, where it can often be seen feeding in flocks, and it will also gather food in pines and alders.

CALL/SONG

A vocal bird with a variety of calls. The typical contact call is a cheery and variable "twiddit'widdit", also given in single "twtt" components or extended into "di'wit'iwit'iwidli'wit", when it sounds more like a segment of song. It also gives a slightly mewing and nasal "tch'weeoo", "theoo'wt" and "diu'lii", and a harsh buzzing "jhr'r'r'r'r'r" or "jjh'jjh'jjh'jit". The song, given either from a perch or in flight, is a bright, fast, tinkling, rattling and trilling affair with a bell-like quality, such as "twiddli'widdli'twidi'trrrwiddit-ti'r'r'r'r'r'r'r'r-jjeeoow", sometimes given in a continuous sequence or in well-marked phrases of 2–3 seconds interspersed with pauses. Although quite complex and often variable, it is usually recognizable by the inclusion of call notes.

Siskin
Carduelis spinus

MALE

LENGTH: 11–12.5cm

WING SPAN: 20–23cm

🔊 **CALL:** "b'diow"

⏺ **TRACK:** 2:84

IDENTIFICATION

A small and rather delicate finch, with a rather pointed bill and at all ages showing yellow bases to the outer tail feathers. The male has a black crown, lores and chin, with a lemony greenish-yellow face, eyebrows, breast and rump. The mantle is green with narrow black streaks and the wings are black with boldly contrasting yellow wingbars on the greater coverts and shoulder. The belly is white, with black streaking on the flanks. Females are duller green, lacking the stronger yellow tones, and are dull green on the head, greenish-white on the rump and white below with finely streaked flanks. Juveniles are paler and very streaky.

HABITAT

A resident over much of central and eastern Europe and southern Scandinavia, and which in Britain is most concentrated in the north and west, occurring more locally elsewhere. Numbers are boosted in winter by immigrants from the north and east, and it can often be found in large flocks at this time, frequently mixed with Goldfinches and Lesser Redpolls. In winter it is commonly found in birch and alder along watercourses, as well as in parks and gardens, where it will come to feeders. In the breeding season it favours mixed and coniferous forest, with a special preference for spruce.

CALL/SONG

Typical call notes heard from flying birds include a downward-inflected and disyllabic "b'diow" and an upward-inflected "dju'lii", "b'deee" or "diu'lee", both given equally often. It also utters a simple "tchiou", and commonly gives a chittering dry trill "cht't't't't't't", given conversationally when feeding with other birds or flying together. The song is a rapid undulating collection of trilling, twittering and repeated call notes, sometimes including a strangled and drawn-out high nasal wheeze "jhwrrrrrr" near the end of the sequence, such as "dwee'dwee'dwee chich'ich'ich'ich, tsirri tsirri pi'tiou pi'tiou pi'tiou cht't't't't't't ch'wee ch'wee jhwrrrrrr djiew djiew…", etc.

FEMALE

Linnet
Carduelis cannabina

LENGTH: 12.5–14cm

WING SPAN: 21–25.5cm

🔊 **CALL:** "chd'it chd'it"

⏺ **TRACK:** 2:85

MALE
SUMMER
PLUMAGE

IDENTIFICATION

A small and slim finch with a longish cleft tail with whitish edges to the feathers and whitish edges to the primaries, showing both at rest and in flight. The male is rather colourful with a grey head and nape and a red patch on the forehead, and a large crimson breast patch which varies in intensity with wear. The throat is whitish, mottled and streaked grey, the belly is white, and both sexes show a brown mantle. Females are rather dull, with a buff streaky breast and a grey-brown head, which is paler on the cheek and above and below the eye.

HABITAT

A widespread resident in much of Europe, but only a summer visitor to Scandinavia. In the breeding season it can be found in farmland, scrub, hedgerows, thickets, industrial wastelands and parks with rank weedy growths, and particularly on heaths where it shows a special preference for gorse. Outside the breeding season it ranges more widely on to open fields, saltmarshes and dune slacks, and is frequently seen on open rough ground with a plentiful supply of seed-bearing plants.

CALL/SONG

The call, often given in flight and especially on take-off, is a rapid, staccato but bright "chud'ut'ut" or a "chd'it chd'it". It also gives a nasal twanging "chi'ou", as well as other nasal monosyllabic sounds which sound more like short segments of song. The advertising song of the male is a varied ensemble of twittering, trills and nasal fluty sounds, run together in a rambling and often rather low-key sequence, sometimes just with short segments repeated idly. In full voice, however, it can give a continuous collection of notes that span a wide frequency range, such as "chippeti-chippeti jiou chp't-chp't-chp't pt'idoo dzhrrrr seee'oo chiwee chu'chu'chu' trr'r'r'r'r'r chi'oo" and "chi' whii'whii pt'pee'tiou ch'ch'ch'wheeea bt'bt'bt'piouu", "chrr'r'r'r'chee'chee'chee' ch'wrrrr tu'wee tu'wu ti'wheeeoo".

FEMALE

MALE SUMMER PLUMAGE

Twite
Carduelis flavirostris

LENGTH: 12.5–14cm

WING SPAN: 22–24cm

🔊 **CALL:** "chweek"

⏺ **TRACK:** 2:86

IDENTIFICATION

A rather demure, streaky little finch with a longish cleft tail and a yellow bill in winter. Similar to a female or immature Linnet, it appears darker and has strong tawny-buff tones, particularly on the face and the unmarked throat, and also on the flanks and breast, which contrast with the white belly. It is boldly streaked dark on the mantle, and the flanks are heavily streaked from the shoulders, sometimes extending across the centre of the breast. It also has an obvious buff wingbar on the tips of the greater coverts. The male has a pink rump, most obvious in spring, and at all ages shows whitish edges to the tail and flight feathers, much like a Linnet.

HABITAT

A partial migrant, breeding in upland areas of northern and western Britain and in Norway, wintering along North Sea coasts, in central and eastern Europe and southern Scandinavia. In the breeding season it favours upland grassy fells and treeless heather moors, hill farms, upland pastures, bare coastal heaths and barren mountain slopes at higher altitudes in Norway. In winter it disperses to coastal areas, saltmarshes, dunes and slacks, where it feeds on *Salicornia* sp. and asters; it will also visit pastures and bare weedy fields.

CALL/SONG

It has a Linnet-like twittering bouncy flight call, as in "tchp'up'up" or "chut chululutt", plus a monosyllabic "yett", but the call that gives the bird its name is a harsh, bleating and upward-inflected "chweek" or "chwai'it", often audible from some distance. Winter flocks can frequently be heard making a nasal jangling twitter of many call notes run together. The song is quite similar to that of the Linnet but is less musical and more metallic, with wheezy drawn-out nasal notes mixed with buzzing trills, rattles and nasal twanging. It is delivered in short sequences interspersed with pauses, such as "dzhur'iwhee dzheh'wheee'er dzheh'wrrrrrrrr…", etc.

MALE WINTER PLUMAGE

Lesser Redpoll
Carduelis cabaret

LENGTH: 11.5–14cm
WING SPAN: 20–22.5cm
🔊 **CALL:** "che'che'che'che"
● **TRACK:** 2:87

IDENTIFICATION

A small, rather dark little finch, with a short, stubby yellowish bill. It has a small red patch on the forehead, and black on the lores and chin. The upperparts are brown, streaked dark brown on the crown, nape and mantle. The underparts are buffish, whiter on the belly, with brown streaks on the shoulder and down the flanks, plus dark streaks on the white under-tail coverts. The male has a variable amount of pinky-red on the throat, breast and rump, brightest in spring, when the female can also show a rosy hue on the breast. The wing is dark, with a buffy wingbar formed by paler tips to the greater coverts, and uniform in general colour with the remainder of the bird. The similar Mealy Redpoll *Carduelis flammea* is paler and greyer, lacking the buffy tones, and has a white wingbar.

HABITAT

A resident in Britain, southern Scandinavia and central Europe, which disperses and gathers in flocks in winter. It can be found in mixed and coniferous woodlands, with a special preference for the latter, as well as in birch, alder, willow, scrubby areas and hedgerows. In winter it can often been found feeding in alders and birches along watercourses. The Mealy Redpoll is a winter visitor to Britain in small numbers from Scandinavia.

CALL/SONG

The typical call, often heard in flight, is a dry, rattling "che'che'che'che". It also gives a higher and sweeter, more slowly repeated "chie'chie'chie". It also has a typical *Carduelis* call, a nasal rising "chwaiii" or "djuu'wi", and a longer, rolling buzzing note "dzhiiiiiiirrrrrr", given either singly or included in the more developed song. The song, delivered in roving flights as well as from a perch, is a rather unhurried, staccato and unmusical collection of call notes, as in "chi'chi' chi tzrrrrrrrrr chi'chi' dweeeeiiii tway'tway'tway' dweeeiii che'che'che dzhiiiirr che'che'che' di'di' di tway'tway'tway' dzhiiirrr che'che'che'…", etc.

MALE

Common Crossbill
Loxia curvirostra

LENGTH: 15–17cm

WING SPAN: 27–30.5cm

CALL: "chlip chlip chlip"

TRACK: 2:88

IDENTIFICATION

A stocky finch comparable to a Greenfinch in build, with a thick neck and largish head. The bill has elongated tips to the mandibles, which cross over – an adaptation for prising seeds out of conifer cones. The tail is rather short and deeply cleft, visible in the undulating flight. Males are red all over, except for dark brown wings and tail and a pale vent. Females are grey-green, diffusely streaked on the mantle and yellower on the rump. Young birds are grey-brown and streaked all over. This species closely resembles both the Scottish and Parrot Crossbills, so attention must be paid to the voice and also to the bill, which in the Common Crossbill is longer than it is deep, with a gently curved culmen.

HABITAT

Resident and widespread, although rather localized and highly irruptive, travelling long distances when new food sources are required. It is found exclusively in conifers, and has a preference for spruce. In Britain it is found in scattered pockets of suitable habitat, such as upland areas of Scotland and Wales and conifer-forested parts of England.

CALL/SONG

Often vocal. The calls can be divided into flight and excitement calls: the 'flight' call (not necessarily given in flight, however!) is a fairly loud and explosive repeated "glipp glipp…" or "chlip chlip chlip"; the 'excitement' call is

a deeper, highly infectious call, repeated excitedly, and can be described as "chuop, choup…" or "chuk, chuk…". It also gives a downward-inflected "tchi'choo tchi'choo" call. The song is a fairly slow collection of call notes, whistles and nasal trills, interspersed with some higher "chiree chiree" sounds, such as "chiree chiree chiree chup-chup-chup chue cheu cheu dzhirrroo dzhirrroo chip chip chiree chiree tup tup tup…", etc. Recent studies have shown that there are as many as seven different 'cryptic' forms of Common Crossbill occurring in north-western Europe, all with subtly different calls.

FEMALE

Scottish Crossbill
Loxia scotica

LENGTH: 15.5–17cm

WING SPAN: 27.5–31.5cm

CALL: "chlupp chlupp.."

TRACK: 2:89

FEMALE

IDENTIFICATION

Plumages are similar to those of the Common and Parrot Crossbills, red in the male and greenish in the female. This species differs in voice, and also in biometrics and structure, being intermediate between the other two. It shares a preference for pine trees with the Parrot Crossbill, and has a similar bill, but without the pronounced 'S'-shaped curve on the lower mandible. The bill appears blunter and more massive than the Common's and is nearly as deep as it is long, with a stronger curve to the culmen and with the base of the culmen relatively less curved. It is broader headed than the Common, and larger and bulkier overall. Particular care must be exercised when assigning identity to crossbills within the breeding range of this species, as not only Parrot Crossbill can occur but at least three 'cryptic' forms of Common Crossbill have been recorded!

HABITAT

Restricted to tracts of mature Scots pine in the Scottish Highlands, particularly Strathspey and Deeside. It is dispersive, but difficulties in identification mean that it is under-recorded and overlooked outside its core breeding area.

CALL/SONG

The calls, like the bird itself, are intermediate between those of the Common and Parrot Crossbills. The flight call is a simple "chp chp chp", more similar to the Parrot Crossbill in its plainness but slightly higher pitched, and also without the 'clip' quality of the Common. The diagnostic call is the excitement call, a deep "chlupp chlupp", like two notes, one on top of the other. The song follows a similar pattern, perhaps with shorter and less complex phrases, and with longer pauses between segments, as in "dzhip dzhip dzhip p'chuwi p'chuwi… tchptchp.. pt'jhirri jhirri tchrrr tchrrrr".

MALE

IDENTIFICATION

The plumage is similar to that of the Common Crossbill, being red in the male and green in the female, but this is the largest of the crossbills, with a bigger head and a thicker, more bull-necked profile than the others. Apart from the subtle differences in the voice, close study of the bill should indicate this species. It is large and heavy, as deep as it is long, and with a deep lower mandible that has a deeply curving lower edge forming an 'S' shape, a strongly arched culmen and shorter extended tips to the bill. This gives it a front-heavy appearance, enhanced by a flatter forehead, and it is a larger and bulkier bird overall.

HABITAT

Resident but dispersive and occasionally irruptive, although less frequently than Common Crossbill. It breeds in Scandinavia and eastwards, and is a scarce visitor to much of Britain, although it has recently been detected as being present and occasionally breeding in the Scottish Highlands. It favours coniferous forest, particularly of Scots Pine, and during irruptions may also occur in spruces. Irruptive birds may stay to breed in the areas that they reach.

CALL/SONG

Quite vocal, the calls and song being very similar to those of the Common Crossbill but discernible by

Parrot Crossbill
Loxia pytyopsittacus

LENGTH: 16–18cm

WING SPAN: 30.5–33cm

CALL: "djup djup.."

TRACK: 2:90

FEMALE

a practised ear. The flight calls are deeper, harder and less ringing, without the 'clip' quality that Common Crossbill has, as in "chop chop chop" or "djup djup". The excitement calls are similarly rather deep, but softer and rather percussive, sounding more conversational, such as "chhp chhp chhp". The song is rather better defined and, although in a similar pattern to Common Crossbill, sounds more emphatic – with loud, harsh, slightly upward-inflected metallic trills, and sometimes more fluty whistles reminiscent of a Tree Pipit, such as "dzhrrr'eh dzhrrr'eh dzhrrr'eh chp'chp'chp' tsiri tsiri i'chup i'chup zhr'p zhr'p izhp'izhp bt'bt'bt…", etc.

MALE

Common Rosefinch
Carpodacus erythrinus

LENGTH: 13.5–15cm

WING SPAN: 24–26.5cm

🔊 **CALL:** "chuu'ih"

⏺ **TRACK:** 2:91

FEMALE

IDENTIFICATION

Often unobtrusive except when singing, this is a thick-headed, swollen-billed bird with a longish cleft tail. The male is strongly coloured, with red on the head, throat and breast, as well as on the rump. The belly is white with a fainter red wash on the flanks, and the mantle and wings are brown with pink-tinged wingbars. The females are demure and nondescript, grey-brown all over and paler on the underparts, which are streaked. The black eye is beady, the mantle is streaked and the wings show pale wingbars formed by pale tips to the wing coverts. Juveniles are similar but somewhat more olive-toned, with bolder wingbars.

HABITAT

A scarce but annual visitor to Britain, most frequent in autumn (such as on the Isles of Scilly) and in years of spring influxes it may stay to breed in very small numbers. It is a summer visitor to Scandinavia and eastern Europe, wintering in southern Asia. It favours deciduous or mixed woodland clearings, forest edge, bushy thickets, damp meadows, willow scrub along watercourses and large parks.

CALL/SONG

The call is a very 'finchy' and upward-inflected "chuu'ih" or "shwe'eek", reminiscent of one of the calls of the Greenfinch and given at rest or in flight. It also can make a slightly falling "vee-oh" or more urgent-sounding "du'eei", given in anxiety. The song is a simple and pleasant cheery whistle of three to six syllables, sometimes described as 'pleased to meet you!' and frequently heard on the breeding grounds. It rises and falls in pitch and lasts about a second in length, such as "ii'vhid ii'veiow", "seee to'whee'chew" or "chewee'wee'chu", commonly with individual or regional variations. When in courtship excitement the male may add some energetic twittering notes between phrases.

MALE

MALE

Bullfinch
Pyrrhula pyrrhula

LENGTH: 15.5–17.5cm

WING SPAN: 22–29cm

◀)) **CALL:** "peuw"

● **TRACK:** 2:92

IDENTIFICATION

An attractive bird with a plump and rounded body, a large head and a short, thick black bill. It has a black cap that extends on to the face and around the bill, and the upperparts are grey (tinged browner in the female), with a black tail contrasting with a white rump and black wings with a broad whitish wingbar on the tips of the greater coverts. The male has soft pinky-red underparts from cheek to belly, which on the female are greyish-buff. The nominate race or Northern Bullfinch, which occasionally occurs within Britain as a winter visitor, is larger and the underparts of the male are a paler rosy-pink.

FEMALE

HABITAT

A secretive bird that favours deciduous and mixed woodland with dense undergrowth, as well as coniferous forest in the north of its range. It can be found in woodland edge, clearings, tall scrub, hedgerows, parks, large gardens, churchyards and seasonally in orchards. Although resident in Britain, it has undergone a sharp decline in recent decades.

CALL/SONG

The commonly heard call is a piping single note, used as a contact call and often the first indication of the presence of this species. It is a pleasant soft "peuw" or "heouw", slightly descending at the end, and is quite far-carrying and repeated

at regular intervals. The Northern Bullfinch has a different 'trumpeting' call, a higher-pitched and even-toned "heeh" or "pihh", as well as a quiet "tip" note. The song, usually given by the male, is rarely heard, no doubt partly due to its being rather quiet and often audible only from close range. It is a rambling twittering without clear phrases, including typical call notes and some very nasal and deep double notes similar to the call, as well as long purring wheezes and higher-pitched long piping notes, such as "hong-hong tu'tu'tu'didi'peew heeuuuw pwrrrrrrr heeeeee hong-hong tu'di'tu'di'tuu hwrrrrrr…".

Hawfinch
Coccothraustes coccothraustes

LENGTH: 16.5–18cm

WING SPAN: 29–33cm

CALL: "zzic"

TRACK: 2:93

MALE
SUMMER
PLUMAGE

IDENTIFICATION

A starling-sized finch with a massive bill, capable of cracking any nuts or fruit stones it comes across! It has a distinctive outline, with a short tail and a large head and bill, and is often seen in a bounding flight, when it displays a broad white band on the tail tips and a bold white band on the primaries. The overall colouration is buff and brown, with an orangey-buff head, a black line from eye to bill and a broad black chin framing the swollen bill, which is grey in summer and yellow-brown in winter. It has a grey shawl around the nape, the mantle is dark chestnut-brown, and the rump is orange-brown. The underparts are pinkish-brown, with a white vent. The closed wing shows a large white patch on the greater coverts and blackish flight feathers.

HABITAT

Resident and widespread across the region, although rather localized in Britain and often overlooked due to its shy nature. It favours mixed and deciduous woodland, with a particular affinity for mature oaks and hornbeams, spending much of its time in the very top branches of tall trees. It also frequents other large deciduous species, and can be found in riverine belts of trees, avenues, churchyards, parks and large gardens, particularly in winter when it spreads more widely and immigrant birds may arrive in Britain from the continent.

CALL/SONG

It has a rather limited vocabulary, but the most frequently heard call is a sharp metallic "zzic" or "pix", not dissimilar to the 'tic' call of the Robin and given from a perch or often when in flight. Another, more discreet, call is an inconspicuous high "zree" or "zseeh", harder to hear in a woodland noisy with birdsong. The song is simple and primitive, a rather quiet series of alternating "zzic" and "sii" notes given slowly and methodically. It also has a rarely heard, low and quiet whistling "deek-deek tur-wee-wee" or "teek-wa'ree-ree-ree", with a strained quality and often with a liquid and musical end to the phrase that suggests a Goldfinch.

GROUP
FEEDING

JUVENILE AUTUMN PLUMAGE

Lapland Bunting
Calcarius lapponicus

LENGTH: 14–15.5cm

WING SPAN: 25.5–28cm

🔊 **CALL:** "ticky-tik-tik chu"

⬤ **TRACK:** 2:94

IDENTIFICATION

The male in summer is very striking, with a black crown, face, throat and upper breast, a 'snake' of white curling from supercilium to shoulder, and a bright chestnut nape-patch. The female in summer has reduced amounts of black, a whitish throat and submoustachial stripes and a chestnut nape. The upperparts are brown, boldly streaked in black. In winter adults show a rich buffy-brown head with a black outline to the cheek, a pale median crown-stripe, a bold chestnut panel on the greater coverts and tertials, and two white wingbars. They are variably marked with dark on the breast, and streaked on the flanks. Juveniles are generally more streaky below.

HABITAT

A scarce migrant and winter visitor to Britain, typically found along North Sea coasts. It breeds in northern Scandinavia and across Arctic Russia, mostly wintering on cultivated steppe in southern Russia. In the breeding season it favours upland willow scrub, boggy areas with dwarf birch and willow, tundra, bare mountainsides and moorland. In Britain it is usually found in coastal areas on grassy meadows, saltmarshes and ploughed fields.

CALL/SONG

Some calls given by migrants are fairly similar to those of the Snow Bunting, such as a dry rattling "pr'r'r'r'rt" or "ticky-tik-tik", harder and drier than the call of that species and often coupled with a short, clear whistled "chu". It can also give a hoarse "chup". On the breeding grounds it gives a disyllabic, piping "ti'leuu" in alarm, or a more clipped and metallic "teeu" or "teelu". The song is a bright and cheery jangling musical sequence, rather undulating and unhurried in delivery, such as "djui'ji ju'iwee ti'uwee ki'wee'djurrr u'wii djurrr iwo'jii u'wii chiwee tirrichrrr". It typically lasts for 3–5 seconds and is given either from a prominent perch or in a pipit-like song flight, where it glides down in a slow spiral on outstretched wings.

MALE SUMMER PLUMAGE

Snow Bunting
Plectrophenax nivalis

LENGTH: 15.5–18cm

WING SPAN: 32–38cm

🔊 **CALL:** "prrirrirririt"

⏺ **TRACK:** 2:95

MALE SUMMER PLUMAGE

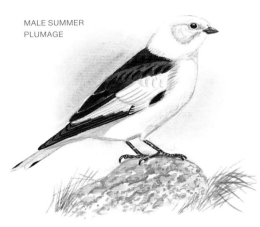

IDENTIFICATION

Males in summer are black-and-white, with black back, wingtips, central tail feathers and bill, the remainder of the plumage being white. In winter they show a buffy-brown back patterned with black, rich warm buff on the shoulder, cheek and crown, and a yellow bill. Females in summer are similar to males but with grey-brown on the head and grey-brown mixed with black on the mantle, with just the inner half of the wing showing white. In autumn and winter they show much more brown on the upperparts. A flock in flight has a twinkling visual quality, like dancing snowflakes.

HABITAT

A breeder of the high Arctic, with as many as 100 pairs nesting in Britain on the highest Scottish mountains. It is also a regular winter visitor to Britain, particularly along the east coast. In the breeding season they favour barren mountaintops, rocky crags, open treeless moors and sea cliffs, and in some localities (e.g. Iceland) will nest down to sea level on coastal pastures with rocky areas or even around human habitation. In winter they can be found on grassy dunes, shingle beaches and saltmarshes, as well as on stubble fields, coastal pasture and moorland.

CALL/SONG

It has a distinctive dry, rippling call, a short, rather musical, "prrirrirririt" or "ter'r'r'r'rit", typically given in flight and frequently the first indication of birds flying overhead. It also gives a single clear ringing "chew" or "piiou", given either with the previous call or uttered singly, particularly by lone flying birds. Birds in busy feeding flocks also give a hoarse buzzing "brrzsch". The song is a rather bright and cheery fluty whistling phrase, such as "che' ju'ji j'wow tsu'cheo djuh dzheee", rising at the end or with repeated four- or five-note sections such as "u'chi djuh-dji-dje'wow, 'chi djuh-dji-dje'wow, 'chi djuh-dji-dje'wow", although much regional variation occurs. It sings from a prominent perch, such as a boulder or building, or in a short song flight in which it ascends then glides down on trembling, outstretched wings.

WINTER PLUMAGE

MALE
SINGING

Yellowhammer
Emberiza citrinella

LENGTH: 15.5–17cm

WING SPAN: 23–29.5cm

CALL: "djih"

TRACK: 2:96

IDENTIFICATION

The male is bright yellow on the head and underparts, with a few dark markings on the head, a rusty-brown wash on the breast and streaks down the flanks. The upperparts are rich brown streaked with black, and in all plumages it shows a rich red-brown rump and uppertail, and white outer feathers on a longish tail. In winter the male is duller, with less yellow on the head and streakier overall. The female is washed with a paler yellow on the head and underparts, and is more streaky, with a darker crown and cheeks.

HABITAT

A common resident across much of Europe, with some northern birds moving south in winter. It is typically found in farmland with edgerows, woodland edge, open bushy country, heaths, wooded pastures and shrubby hillsides. In winter it can often be found in flocks in stubble fields and other open areas.

CALL/SONG

The typical contact call note is a dry and rather harsh, slightly downward-inflected "djou", or a similar even-toned "djih". It also gives some dry clicking notes, often in flight or when disturbed, such as "tit'tit'tit tic'atic", sometimes

accelerated into a trilling sound, and a more liquid "trrp-trrp" when flying together in a flock. The alarm note is a thin "see". The song is familiar to many, and in Britain is traditionally rendered as 'a-little-bit-of-bread-and-no-cheese'. It is a simple rattling repetition of a single note, repeated 10–15 times, accelerating and rising slightly in both pitch and volume before being finished off with a higher drawn-out terminal note, such as "dji'dji'dj i'dji'dji'dji'dji'dji'dji-shjeeee". The song phrase lasts for 1.8–2.5 seconds and is often followed by a high descending "tseeoo". Variations occur, and songsters may regularly omit the terminal "shjeeee" note.

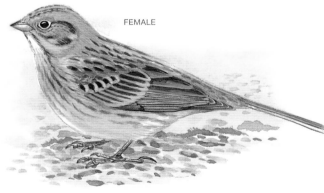

FEMALE

Cirl Bunting
Emberiza cirlus

LENGTH: 15–16.5cm

WING SPAN: 22–25.5cm

🔊 **CALL:** "tsii"

● **TRACK:** 2:97

HABITAT

Essentially a bird of the Mediterranean, it is found across France and has a localized population restricted to south-west Britain, to where it has retreated in recent decades from elsewhere in England and Wales. It favours sunny slopes and rolling country, avoiding open plains and preferring woodland edge, thickets and bushy areas, orchards, vineyards and large gardens. In Britain it is found in farmland with small fields and lots of bushy hedgerows with some tall trees.

CALL/SONG

The main call type is a very thin and high, slightly downward-inflected "tsii" or "seep", and it also has a more sparrow-like and chirpy "tsuu" or "cheuu". The song is a rather long rattle of notes, not dissimilar to the song rattle of the Lesser Whitethroat, slightly ascending in pitch and increasing in volume over the course of the sequence, such as "chi'di'di'di'di'di'di'di'di'di". It typically lasts about 1.5 seconds, at a rate of 11 notes per second, but some individuals may sing at a much faster rate or give a shorter, harder and more half-hearted version, which may often be sung alternately with the typical sequence.

MALE SINGING

IDENTIFICATION

A colourful bunting, although rather subtle and can easily blend into its surroundings. The male has a black throat extending back to the neck sides, a black bridle through the eye and primrose-yellow underparts, supercilium and long cheek-stripe. It has a grey-green breast band that extends into a narrow collar, rusty-brown patches at the breast sides and dark streaks on the flanks. The upperparts are brown with black streaks, and the rump is olive-grey in all plumages. The female is more demure and streaky, with fairly bold pale yellow and dark striped sides to the head, and yellow-tinged underparts that are streaked from breast to flanks.

FEMALE

IDENTIFICATION

In all plumages shows a prominent yellowish eye-ring, a dark malar stripe on a pale yellow background, a grey-brown mantle with prominent dark streaking, and a grey-brown rump. The underparts are variably tinged rusty-buff, palest in a juvenile but quite orangey-brown in the male. The male has a clean grey-green head and a pale yellow throat and moustachial stripe, duller in the female, which also has some fine streaking and spotting on the upper breast, malar stripe and crown. Juveniles are more streaky, with a grey-brown head.

HABITAT

A scarce migrant to Britain, with a few in spring along the east coasts or in autumn in the south-west. It is a summer visitor to eastern Europe and Scandinavia, and also occurs quite widely in the Mediterranean basin. It favours sunny aspects, such as trees along woodland edges and clearings, farmland with hedgerows, scattered copses, vineyards, orchards and parks, and in the southern part of its range can be found on bare rocky mountain slopes with bushy thickets. It feeds on the ground, and migrants can often be found in stubble fields.

Ortolan Bunting
Emberiza hortulana

LENGTH: 15–16.5cm

WING SPAN: 23–29cm

CALL: "chleuu"

TRACK: 2:98

FEMALE

MALE
SINGING

CALL/SONG

The typical call is a sharp metallic, disyllabic and sparrow-like chirpy "chleuu" or a shorter, flatter "chleeip", and also a piping "chu". Autumn migrants typically give a flat and clipped "plic" or "plett" when flushed. The song is a rather slow and mournful ditty with a ringing quality, a simple collection of notes lasting 1.3–1.6 seconds, recalling the Yellowhammer's song and with a change in note near the end, such as "swea-swea-swea-swea-swea druu druu druu". More often in the southern part of their range, the final part is truncated to a single note, as in "siu-siu-siu-siu-siu-siu hweurr".

Reed Bunting
Emberiza schoeniclus

LENGTH: 13.5–15.5cm

WING SPAN: 21–28cm

CALL: "tseeou"

TRACK: 2:99a

MALE
SINGING

IDENTIFICATION

The male has a black throat outlined by white submoustachial stripes, and a black head with a complete white collar. The solid blacks are acquired by losing the paler feather tips through wear; in fresh plumage in autumn the head is browner and the throat is scaled white. The female has brown upperparts streaked and patterned with black, while the underparts are buffish-white streaked black, densest on the breast, with a dark malar stripe highlighted by a pale submoustachial stripe. The head has dull brown cheeks, and a pale supercilium and eye-ring. Both sexes have bold white outer tail feathers at all ages.

HABITAT

A common resident in our region, with numbers in winter augmented by migrants from further north and east. It favours damp areas with scrub, bushes and tall herbage, typically occurring in reedbeds, marshes, lake margins, bogs, marshy tundra, wet meadows and saltmarshes, as well as in drier non-marshy areas and not infrequently in crops such as barley and rape. Outside the breeding season it ranges more generally, moving onto farmland and grassland and occasionally appearing in gardens.

FEMALE

CALL/SONG

The commonly heard call is a downward-inflected, rather penetrating "tseeou" or "zseeo", given as a contact call and also used as an anxiety call. It also has a nasal rasping "djuh", often given by autumn migrants, and a "tzi'tzi", given on the breeding grounds and similar to the Meadow Pipit alarm note. Two variants of song are used by the male, with considerable individual variation. Unpaired males sing a faster, bright and chirpy series of simple rather metallic notes, with 10–12 notes in a sequence lasting 1.5–2 seconds, such as "tjew, tjew, tjew tsitsi'zeuw chichi'zree'e'e" or "dze tchew'tchew dze'chichi zweee". Once paired, they sing a slower, halting and barely musical version, with longer pauses (0.5–1 second) between notes, such as "dzi… dziwi'… tzhur'r'r… tzhur'r'r… zeeuup" or "tju… tju… dzing… dzing… ji'ji'ji zwee".

IDENTIFICATION

An unspectacular sparrow-like bird, but conspicuous in its behaviour and often seen singing from wires and posts. The plumage is uniform and subtle, lacking outstanding features, and the sexes are similar. The crown and mantle are uniform brown with blackish-brown streaks, the rump is plainer and the wing feathers are dark-brown edged with pale buff. The tail is uniformly dark brown, lacking white in the outer tail feathers – unlike any of its close relatives. The underparts are buffish-white, the breast and flanks are clearly streaked blackish-brown, with the denser blacker streaks on the upper breast sometimes forming a 'V'-shaped gorget, joined by dark malar stripes that enclose a whitish-buff throat. Its bill is horn-coloured with a dark culmen, and looks large and bulky with a pronounced jagged outline to cutting edges. In flight the legs are frequently dangled.

HABITAT

Resident across much of the region, although in rapid decline across north-western Europe, and absent from Scandinavia. It favours lowland

Corn Bunting
Emberiza calandra

LENGTH: 16–19cm

WING SPAN: 26–32cm

🔊 **CALL:** "plic"

⏺ **TRACK:** 2:99b

or rolling open country, and is typically found in farmland and arable country, pastures, grasslands and rough open areas, generally away from woodland and tall hedgerows and with a liking for coastal areas. Males are polygamous.

CALL/SONG

The song is frequently likened to the jangling of a bunch of keys, and is delivered by the male in spring and summer from a prominent perch such as a wire or post, and quite often from the top of a tall plant among the crops and grasslands that it favours. The song phrase accelerates and rises in pitch, beginning slowly and then quickly accelerating to a discordant crash of notes, typically of 1.5–2 seconds in length, as in "chut chit'it'it'tr'r'r'r'r' schri'i'i'i'i'i'eeee". The call notes are an abrupt yet soft "quit", "plic" or "bt", often delivered in flight and occasionally run together as "plic'plc 'plc'plc", and also a sharp "tsritt" or "chip".

MALE SINGING

Index

Recording Credits

Dave Farrow

(1:7) Teal
(1:17) Pheasant (14–41)
(1:31) Kestrel (24–41)
(1:34) Water Rail (27–42)
(1:35) Spotted Crake
(1:40) Oystercatcher
(1:42) Stone Curlew
(1:43) Little Ringed Plover (21–42)
(1:44) Ringed Plover (28–41)
(1:54) Curlew
(1:56) Redshank (21–42)
(1:58) Green Sandpiper (22–42)
(1:60) Common Sandpiper (29–42)
(1:62) Arctic Skua
(1:63) Black-headed Gull (11–41)
(1:64) Common Gull
(1:65) Lesser Black-backed Gull
  (*L. fuscus fuscus*) (28–40)
(1:65) Lesser Black-backed Gull
  (*L. fuscus graellsi*) (40–45)
(1:66) Herring Gull (22–43)
(1:69) Little Tern
(1:70) Sandwich Tern
(1:71) Common Tern (15–42)
(1:75) Woodpigeon
(1:85) Nightjar
(1:92) Green Woodpecker
(1:95) Woodlark (0–29)
(1:96) Skylark
(1:99a) Swallow
(1:99b) House Martin
(2:1) Tree Pipit (0–33)
(2:2) Meadow Pipit
(2:3) Rock Pipit (28–42)
(2:4) Yellow Wagtail (31–42)
(2:5) Grey Wagtail (38–42)
(2:6) White Wagtail (27–42)
(2:9) Wren
(2:10) Dunnock (38–44)
(2:11) Robin
(2:13) Nightingale
(2:17) Whinchat
(2:14) Bluethroat (0–34)

(2:18) Stonechat
(2:21) Blackbird
(2:24) Redwing (0–31)
(2:25) Mistle Thrush
(2:26) Cetti's Warbler
(2:27) Grasshopper Warbler (0–18)
(2:29) Savi's Warbler (22–30)
(2:30) Aquatic Warbler
(2:31) Sedge Warbler (0–37)
(2:32) Blyth's Reed Warbler
(2:34) Reed Warbler (0–38)
(2:36) Icterine Warbler (0–34)
(2:37) Blackcap
(2:38) Garden Warbler (0–38)
(2:39) Barred Warbler
(2:40) Lesser Whitethroat (0–19)
(2:41) Common Whitethroat
(2:42) Dartford Warbler
(2:43) Greenish Warbler (0–31)
(2:44) Wood Warbler (0–29)
(2:45) Chiffchaff
(2:46) Willow Warbler
(2:47) Goldcrest (0–35)
(2:51) Collared Flycatcher
(2:54) Long-tailed Tit
(2:55) Blue Tit
(2:56) Great Tit
(2:58) Coal Tit
(2:61) Nuthatch (0–13)
(2:62) Eurasian Treecreeper (21-30)
(2:63) Short-toed Treecreeper
(2:64) Penduline Tit (31–41)
(2:71) Chough (29–40)
(2:73) Rook
(2:74) Carrion Crow
(2:76) Starling
(2:77) House Sparrow
(2:79) Chaffinch
(2:81) Serin (0–29)
(2:82) Greenfinch
(2:83) Goldfinch
(2:85) Linnet (0–37)
(2:87) Lesser Redpoll (12–42)
(2:88) Common Crossbill (32–46)
(2:89) Scottish Crossbill (34–45)

(2:91) Common Rosefinch (0-32)
(2:92) Bullfinch (0–29)
(2:95) Snow Bunting (33–45)
(2:96) Yellowhammer
(2:99a) Reed Bunting (0–35)
(2:99b) Corn Bunting

Hannu Jannes

(1:2) Whooper Swan
(1:4) Greylag Goose
(1:8) Mallard
(1:10) Red Grouse
(1:12) Black Grouse
(1:13) Capercaillie
(1:17) Pheasant (0–14)
(1:19) Little Grebe
(1:20) Great Crested Grebe
(1:23) Bittern
(1:24) Grey Heron
(1:28) Sparrowhawk
(1:36) Corncrake
(1:38) Coot
(1:39) Crane
(1:41) Avocet
(1:46) Grey Plover
(1:50) Woodcock
(1:56) Redshank (0–21)
(1:63) Black-headed Gull (0–11)
(1:66) Herring Gull (0–23)
(1:68) Kittiwake
(1:74) Stock Dove
(1:80) Eagle Owl
(1:82) Tawny Owl (0–26)
(1:83) Long-eared Owl
(1:87) Kingfisher
(1:90) Black Woodpecker
(1:91) Grey-headed Woodpecker
(1:93) Great Spotted Woodpecker
(1:94) Lesser Spotted Woodpecker
(2:1) Tree Pipit (33–42)
(2:4) Yellow Wagtail (0–31)
(2:5) Grey Wagtail (0–29)
(2:6) White Wagtail (0–27)

(2:7) Waxwing
(2:10) Dunnock (0–38)
(2:12) Thrush Nightingale
(2:14) Bluethroat (34–46)
(2:15) Black Redstart
(2:16) Redstart
(2:22) Fieldfare
(2:23) Song Thrush
(2:29) Savi's Warbler (0–22)
(2:31) Sedge Warbler (37–44)
(2:38) Garden Warbler (38–43)
(2:40) Lesser Whitethroat (36–43)
(2:43) Greenish Warbler (31–42)
(2:47) Goldcrest (35–44)
(2:49) Spotted Flycatcher
(2:50) Red-breasted Flycatcher
(2:52) Pied Flycatcher
(2:53) Bearded Tit
(2:59) Willow Tit
(2:62) Eurasian Treecreeper
 (0-21; 30-43)
(2:64) Penduline Tit (0–31)
(2:69) Magpie
(2:71) Chough (0-29)
(2:72) Jackdaw
(2:75) Raven
(2:78) Tree Sparrow
(2:80) Brambling
(2:84) Siskin
(2:85) Linnet (37-45)
(2:91) Common Rosefinch (32-42)
(2:92) Bullfinch (29–42)
(2:97) Cirl Bunting.
(2:99a) Reed Bunting (35–45)

Jan-Erik Bruun

(1:1) Bewick's Swan
(1:3) Pink-footed Goose
(1:5) Brent Goose
(1:6) Wigeon
(1:9) Eider
(1:11) Ptarmigan
(1:15) Grey Partridge

(1:16) Quail
(1:25) Black Kite
(1:27) Marsh Harrier
(1:29) Buzzard
(1:30) Osprey
(1:31) Kestrel (0–24)
(1:32) Hobby
(1:33) Peregrine
(1:34) Water Rail (0–27)
(1:37) Moorhen
(1:43) Little Ringed Plover (0–21)
(1:44) Ringed Plover (0–28)
(1:45) Golden Plover
(1:47) Lapwing
(1:48) Dunlin
(1:49) Snipe
(1:51) Black-tailed Godwit
(1:52) Bar-tailed Godwit
(1:53) Whimbrel
(1:55) Spotted Redshank
(1:57) Greenshank
(1:58) Green Sandpiper (0–22)
(1:59) Wood Sandpiper
(1:60) Common Sandpiper (0–29)
(1:61) Turnstone
(1:65) Lesser Black backed Gull
 (*L. fuscus fuscus*) (0–28)
(1:67) Great Black-backed Gull
(1:71) Common Tern (0–15)
(1:72) Arctic Tern
(1:76) Collared Dove
(1:77) Turtle Dove
(1:78) Cuckoo
(1:82) Tawny Owl (26–45)
(1:84) Tengmalm's Owl
(1:88) Hoopoe
(1:89) Wryneck
(1:95) Woodlark (32–43)
(1:97) Shore Lark
(1:98) Sand Martin
(2:3) Rock Pipit (0–28)
(2:8) Dipper
(2:19) Wheatear
(2:20) Ring Ouzel
(2:24) Redwing (31–45)

(2:27) Grasshopper Warbler (18–34)
(2:28) River Warbler
(2:33) Marsh Warbler
(2:34) Reed Warbler (38–45)
(2:35) Great Reed Warbler
(2:36) Icterine Warbler (34–46)
(2:44) Wood Warbler (29–42)
(2:57) Crested Tit
(2:60) Marsh Tit
(2:61) Nuthatch (13–42)
(2:65) Golden Oriole
(2:66) Red-backed Shrike
(2:67) Great Grey Shrike
(2:68) Jay
(2:70) Nutcracker
(2:81) Serin (29–41)
(2:86) Twite
(2:87) Lesser Redpoll (0–12)
(2:88) Common Crossbill (0–32)
(2:90) Parrot Crossbill (0–24)
(2:93) Hawfinch
(2:94) Lapland Bunting
(2:95) Snow Bunting (0–33)
(2:98) Ortolan Bunting

**Jean C. Roché
& Jérôme Chevereau**

(1:14) Red-legged Partridge
(1:18) Great Northern Diver
(1:21) Manx Shearwater
(1:22) Storm Petrel
(1:26) Red Kite
(1:73) Puffin
(1:79) Barn Owl
(1:81) Little Owl
(2:48) Firecrest
(2:89) Scottish Crossbill (0–34)
(2:90) Parrot Crossbill (24–44)

Artwork Credits

Brin Edwards

Aquatic Warbler pp13; 149
Arctic Skua p81
Arctic Tern p91
Barred Warbler p158
Bearded Tit p172
Bewick's Swan p20
Bittern p42
Black Redstart p134
Black Woodpecker p109
Blackbird p140
Blackcap Front Cover/
    Left; p156
Black-headed Gull p82
Blue Tit p174
Bluethroat p133
Blyth's Reed Warbler p151
Brambling p199
Brent Goose p24
Bullfinch p211
Carrion Crow p193
Cetti's Warbler p145
Chaffinch CD2/Main;
    pp1; 198
Chiffchaff p164
Chough p190
Cirl Bunting p216
Coal Tit p177
Collared Dove p95
Collared Flycatcher p170
Common Crossbill p207
Common Gull 83
Common Rosefinch p210
Common Tern p90
Common Whitethroat p160
Corn Bunting p219
Crested Tit p176
Cuckoo p97
Dartford Warbler p161
Dipper p127
Dunnock p129
Eider p28
Eurasian Treecreeper p181
Fieldfare p141

Firecrest p167
Garden Warbler pp4; 157
Goldcrest pp7; p166
Golden Oriole p184
Goldfinch p202
Grasshopper Warbler
    p146
Great Black-backed
    Gull p86
Great Crested Grebe p39
Great Grey Shrike p186
Great Northern Diver p37
Great Reed Warbler p154
Great Spotted Woodpecker
    Front Cover/Right;
    p112
Great Tit p175
Green Woodpecker pp5;
    111
Greenfinch p201
Greenish Warbler p162
Grey Heron p43
Grey Wagtail pp11; p124
Grey-headed Woodpecker
    p110
Greylag Goose CD1/
    Main; p23
Hawfinch p212
Herring Gull p85
Hoopoe p107
House Martin p119
House Sparrow p196
Icterine Warbler p155
Jackdaw p191
Jay pp6; 13; 187
Kingfisher Back Cover/
    Bottom; p106
Kittiwake p87
Lapland Bunting p213
Lesser Black-backed
    Gull p84
Lesser Redpoll p206
Lesser Spotted Woodpecker
    p113

Lesser Whitethroat p159
Linnet p204
Little Grebe p38
Little Tern p88
Long-tailed Tit pp2; 173
Magpie p188
Mallard p27
Manx Shearwater p40
Marsh Tit p179
Marsh Warbler p152
Meadow Pipit p121
Mistle Thrush p144
Nightingale p132
Nightjar p104
Nutcracker p189
Nuthatch p180
Ortolan Bunting p217
Parrot Crossbill p209
Penduline Tit p183
Pied Flycatcher p171
Pied/White Wagtail p125
Pink-footed Goose p22
Puffin p92
Raven CD2/Background;
    p194
Red-backed Shrike p185
Red-breasted Flycatcher
    p169
Redstart p135
Redwing p143
Reed Bunting p218
Reed Warbler p153
Ring Ouzel p139
River Warbler p147
Robin Cover/Spine; p130
Rock Pipit p122
Rook p192
Sand Martin p117
Sandwich Tern p89
Savi's Warbler p148
Scottish Crossbill p208
Sedge Warbler p150
Serin p200
Shore Lark p116

Short-toed Treecreeper
    p182
Siskin p203
Skylark p115
Snipe p68
Snow Bunting p214
Song Thrush p142
Spotted Flycatcher p168
Starling p195
Stock Dove p93
Stonechat p137
Storm Petrel p41
Swallow p118
Swift p105
Teal p26
Thrush Nightingale p131
Tree Pipit p120
Tree Sparrow p197
Turtle Dove p96
Twite p205
Waxwing Back Cover/
    Top; p126
Wheatear p138
Whinchat p136
Whooper Swan p21
Wigeon p25
Willow Tit p178
Willow Warbler p165
Wood Warbler p163
Woodlark p114
Woodpigeon p94
Wren p128
Wryneck p108
Yellow Wagtail p123
Yellowhammer p215

Mike Langman

Red Grouse p29
Ptarmigan p30
Black Grouse p31
Capercaillie p32
Red-legged Partridge p33
Grey Partridge p34
Quail p35

Pheasant p36
Black Kite p44
Red Kite p45
Marsh Harrier p46
Sparrowhawk p47
Buzzard p48
Osprey p49
Kestrel pp3; 50
Hobby p51
Peregrine p52
Water Rail p53
Spotted Crake p54
Corncrake p55
Moorhen p56
Coot p57
Crane CD1/Background;
    p58
Oystercatcher p59
Avocet p60
Stone Curlew p61
Little Ringed Plover p62
Ringed Plover p63
Golden Plover p64
Grey Plover p65
Lapwing p66
Dunlin p67
Woodcock p69
Black-tailed Godwit p70
Bar-tailed Godwit p71
Whimbrel p72
Curlew p73
Spotted Redshank p74
Redshank p75
Greenshank p76
Green Sandpiper p77
Wood Sandpiper p78
Common Sandpiper p79
Turnstone p80
Barn Owl p98
Eagle Owl p99
Little Owl pp8; 100
Tawny Owl p101
Long-eared Owl p102
Tengmalm's Owl p103